[redacted]

[redacted]

THE CIVILIZATION OF THE AMERICAN INDIAN SERIES

(*Complete list on pages 266–69*)

The Mixtec Kings and Their People

THE MIXTEC KINGS AND THEIR PEOPLE

BY RONALD SPORES

UNIVERSITY OF OKLAHOMA PRESS
NORMAN

Library of Congress Catalog Card Number: 66–22717

 Composed and printed at Norman, Oklahoma, U.S.A., by the University of Oklahoma Press. First edition.

For F. V. S. and M. S.

PREFACE

THIS VOLUME deals with the culture history of the Mixtec people of northwestern Oaxaca, Mexico. Attention is focused upon developments in the sixteenth century, and the raw data are derived mainly from documentation emanating from the complex administrative and judicial machinery maintained by Spain in her Mexican colony. These varied source materials, now found in the archives of Mexico and Spain and in published form, deal with many aspects of Spanish and Indian life during the Colonial and pre-Colonial phases of the sixteenth century and provide a wealth of cultural data that can be utilized by the modern anthropologist and historian.

Traditionally, anthropologists have concentrated their efforts on living groups or the material remains of extinct societies. Historians, on the other hand, have devoted themselves to the "great traditions" of East and West and have shown little inclination to examine the lesser traditions that have been of interest to the anthropologist. Much important historical material, then, has been relegated to a "no man's land" lying somewhere between anthropology and history. Recently, however, anthropologists have come to appreciate the value of the historical document as an ethnographic resource, and the historian has become involved in the study of the "little tradition" societies. As old biases have withered, the study of culture history has begun to be enriched by the contributions of both historians and anthropologists.

So far as research on the native cultures of the New World is concerned, the best demonstration of the value of historical sources comes from scholars who have dealt with the abundantly documented areas of

Mexico, Guatemala, Central America, and northwestern and western South America. The importance of early Spanish colonial documents in the study of native American cultural traditions has been established through the pioneering efforts of France V. Scholes and Ralph L. Roys in Yucatán, Suzanne W. Miles in highland Guatemala, Barbro Dahlgren in western Oaxaca, Charles Gibson in Tlaxcala and the Valley of Mexico, A. L. Kroeber in Colombia, John H. Rowe, George Kubler, and Sally F. Moore in Peru, and Louis C. Faron in Chile.

Following the precedent established by these predecessors, I have used the historical document as the nucleus of this work. However, in order to augment and elucidate this resource, I have relied on recent ethnographic and archaeological data, both gathered in the field during 1963 and found in published sources.

Documentary sources which have appeared in published form are contained in the great collections entitled *Papeles de Nueva España* and *Epistolario de Nueva España*, both edited by Paso y Troncoso, the *Colección de Documentos Inéditos . . .*, the *Recopilación de las leyes . . .*, the *Libro de las Tasaciones*, and in other similar, but more limited, collections. Published chronicles include those of Burgoa, Bernal Díaz, Cortés, Durán, Torquemada, Clavijero, Herrera, Veytia, López de Gómara, the *Códice Ramírez*, the *Anales and Códice of Tlatelolco, Códice Chimalpopoca*, and many other sources listed in the bibliography. Unpublished materials have come mainly from the Archivo General de la Nación, México, and the Archivo de Indias, Sevilla.

The Mixtec codices of the pre-Colonial Period are considered to some extent in the present volume, but a detailed analysis is not made. Miss Mary Elizabeth Smith of Yale University is currently engaged in an extensive study of the cultural content of the Mixtec pictographic materials, and Alfonso Caso continues his monumental researches on the same subject. In anticipation of the appearance of these studies, I have directed my efforts toward written sources but with reference, when necessary to proper elucidation, to the work and analyses of pictographic materials by these and other workers.

The material in this book falls rather logically into two sections. The first four chapters are devoted to consideration of Mixtec history and culture from pre-Conquest times to the end of the sixteenth century. Chapter

1 contains a broad outline of sixteenth-century Mixtec culture. Chapter 2 deals with the cultural history of the Mixteca Alta as revealed by an interpretation of the meager archaeological record, and Chapter 3 is a brief but more specific account of later Mixtec history as derived from documentary sources. In Chapter 4 an attempt has been made to reconstruct the Mixtec community and to describe some of its more notable features as revealed by archaeology, documents, and observations of modern patterns of settlement.

Chapters 5 through 8, which comprise the second broad division, consider patterns of native government and examine the role and function of the hereditary native rulers who dominated the political and social life of the Mixteca Alta in the sixteenth century. This discussion is prefaced in Chapter 5 by a general review of native rule and government in central Mexico. Rules of succession specifically for the Mixteca Alta constitute the subject matter of Chapter 6. Chapter 7 proceeds to a discussion of the content, composition, and development of the kingdom-*cacicazgo* of Yanhuitlan from A.D. 1500 to A.D. 1600. Chapter 8 deals with the changing role of the ruler-cacique in sixteenth-century Mixtec society, reviews the achievements of Mixtec culture, and presents general conclusions.

I wish to make appropriate acknowledgments to many individuals who have provided assistance and guidance in my studies of Mixtec culture and in the preparation of this book. Professor France V. Scholes, University of New Mexico, has provided many source materials and has guided me through the complexities of sixteenth-century Spanish documentation and archival research. Professor Scholes has, in fact, been the directing force behind my labors and has been a constant source of inspiration.

Professors Gordon Willey, Stephen Williams, and A. Richard Diebold of Harvard University, Miss Tatiana Proskouriakoff of the Peabody Museum, and Professor Woodrow Borah of the University of California read earlier versions of the manuscript and offered many useful criticisms and suggestions. Assistance and encouragement have also come from Professors Evon Z. Vogt and J. O. Brew of Harvard University, Professors John Paddock and Richard Greenleaf of the University of the Americas, Professor Dave Warren of Oklahoma State

University, Miss Mary Elizabeth Smith of Yale University, and Mrs. Marianne Spores. Mr. Robert Gilbert assisted in the preparation of maps and illustrations, and Mr. Robert Ferguson and Mr. Howard Cooper prepared photographic materials for publication. Mrs. Ruth Maxwell typed the final draft.

Professors Ignacio Bernal and Wigberto Jiménez Moreno of the Instituto Nacional de Antropología e Historia and Dr. Gonzalo Aguirre Beltrán and Dr. Caso of the Instituto Nacional Indigenista (I.N.I.) very kindly furnished permission to utilize the resources of their institutions and provided permits to enter the Mixteca Alta of Oaxaca for research purposes. Professor Hernández of the Tlaxiaco installation of I.N.I. offered valuable advice on research procedure and provided the important letters of introduction which allowed free movement in the Mixteca.

Sr. J. Ignacio Rubio Mañé, director of the Archivo General de la Nación, Mexico City, and other members of his staff courteously provided unlimited access to the resources of that great collection and facilitated my research in countless ways. Sr. José de la Peña y Cámara, director of the Archivo General de Indias, Sevilla, kindly gave permission for the photographic reproduction of documents housed in that archive.

The native informants of Tlaxiaco, San Juan Ñumi, Huamelulpan, Yolomecatl, Teposcolula, Tejupan, Yanhuitlán, Chachoapan, Yucuita, Soyaltepec, Nochixtlán, Jaltepec, and Tilantongo contributed in a very substantial way to this volume. They were, if at times overly hospitable, always helpful and interested in my work.

Finally, I wish to acknowledge the very generous support of the National Institutes of Health and the United States Department of Education in providing funds for the completion of several phases of my research. The contribution of these institutions to the growth of anthropological knowledge has been, and continues to be, very great.

RONALD SPORES

July, 1966
Nashville, Tennessee

A GUIDE TO FOOTNOTES

AGI:	Archivo General de Indias. Sevilla.
AGN:	Archivo General de la Nación. México.
AMN:	*Anales del Museo Nacional de Arqueología, Historia, y Etnografía.*
BEO:	*Boletín de estudios oaxaqueños.*
DII:	*Colección de documentos inéditos, relativos al descubrimiento, conquista y organización de las antiguas posesiones españolas de América y Oceanía.* 42 vols. Madrid, 1864–84.
ENE:	Paso y Troncoso, Francisco del, ed. *Epistolario de Nueva España.* 16 vols. México, 1932–42.
IJAL:	*International Journal of American Linguistics.*
INAH:	Instituto Nacional de Antropología e Historia.
IPP:	*Instituto Panamericana de Geografía e Historia Publicación.*
JM and MH:	Jiménez Moreno, Wigberto, and Salvador Mateos Higuera, *Códice de Yanhuitlán.* México, 1940.
Oviedo:	Oviedo y Valdés, G. F. de. *Historia general y natural de las Indias.* 4 vols. Madrid, 1851–55.
PNE:	Paso y Troncoso, Francisco del, ed. *Papeles de Nueva España.* Vols. 1, 3–7. Madrid, 1905–1906.
Recopilación:	*Recopilación de leyes de los reynos de las Indias.* 3 vols. Madrid, 1943.
RMEA:	*Revista mexicana de estudios antropológicos.*
RMEH:	*Revista mexicana de estudios históricos.*

CONTENTS

ILLUSTRATIONS

Figures

Maps

The Mixtec Kings and Their People

1.

The Principal Features of Mixtec Culture on the Eve of the Spanish Conquest

THE SIXTEENTH-CENTURY Mixtec lived during a time of change and transition when the cultures of Hispanic America, autonomous for the first two decades of the period, underwent redirection from the traditional way of life to one that was heavily influenced by Spanish culture. Much has been written about the events of the Spanish Conquest of Mexico and its aftermath, and such important cultures as the Aztec and Yucatec Maya are familiar to most students of American culture history. It is significant, however, that relatively little is known of the non-Aztec and non-Mayan peoples of Mexico either before or after the arrival of the Spaniards. The Zapotecs, Mixtecs, Mixes, Mazatecs, Huaves, Chinantecs, Tlapanecs, Totonacs, Tarascans, Otomis, and Huastecs, to name but a few, were groups of considerable size and importance that have received only passing attention from historians and anthropologists. Gross misconceptions have resulted from attempts to project Aztec or Maya patterns onto other cultures. To say that Aztec or Maya patterns are entirely typical of all Mexican peoples at the time of the Conquest is wholly inaccurate.

Only through detailed studies can the true nature and diversity of the cultures of proto-historic and early historic Mexico be fully appreciated. Thus, in this volume, Mixtec culture will be examined in detail and some of its more significant and pivotal institutions will be analyzed.

In order to understand the function and development of Mixtec social and political institutions during the sixteenth century, it is essential to have a rather detailed knowledge of the culture as it existed at the time of the Spanish Conquest. Such a reconstruction can be made on the basis of manuscript records in Mexican and Spanish archives, various published writings of the sixteenth and seventeenth centuries,[1] and the modern investigations of Gay, Martínez Gracida, Caso, Bernal, Guzmán, Jiménez Moreno, Paddock, Acosta, and Dahlgren.[2]

Regional Subdivisions

On the eve of the Spanish Conquest, Mixtec culture had spread over most of western Oaxaca from the valley of Oaxaca, the valley of Miahuatlán, and the Almoloyas-Sosola region on the east to beyond the Guerrero border on the west, the Pacific Ocean on the south, and to beyond the Puebla border on the north. The area of Mixtec culture has customarily been divided into three subregions, the Mixteca Baja in western and northwestern Oaxaca, the Mixteca Alta bordering the first-mentioned area to the east and south, and the Mixteca de la Costa comprising the southwestern coastal lowland of Oaxaca. While all three areas come under discussion in the present work, the focus of attention is directed most specifically to the Mixteca Alta. The three main provinces, which could also be called the Western, Eastern, and Southern Mixteca, are for the present mainly geographical. It is anticipated that future study will also show them to vary appreciably in culture. A recent realignment of the Mixtec zone by Cook and Borah utilizes both cultural-historical and geographical criteria.[3] De la Peña compares the geographical divisions of the Mixteca, their modern economies, and demography.[4]

[1] The most important of the sixteenth- and seventeenth-century writings are: the *relaciones* of 1579–80 published in PNE, IV; the Alvarado dictionary of the Mixtec language, Wigberto Jiménez Moreno, *Vocabulario en lengua Mixteca por Fray Francisco de Alvarado*; the Reyes grammar of Mixtec, Fray Antonio de las Reyes, *Arte en lengua Mixteca*; the chronicle of Fray Francisco de Burgoa, *Geográfica descripción*; the work of Antonio Herrera y Tordesillas, *Historia general de los hechos de los castellanos in las Islas y Tierra firme del Mar Océano* (cited hereafter as Herrera, *Historia*).

[2] Barbro Dahlgren, in *La Mixteca: su cultura e historia prehispánicas* (cited hereafter as Dahlgren, *La Mixteca*), has presented a comprehensive description of pre-Hispanic–Mixtec culture; the present chapter derives much from Miss Dahlgren's prior efforts and seeks to offer supplementary data and further interpretations.

[3] Sherburne F. Cook and Woodrow Borah, "Quelle fut la stratification sociale au Centre du Mexique durant la première moitié de XVIe siècle?" *Annales Economies Societés Civilisations*, Vol. II (1963), 226–58.

[4] Moises T. de la Peña, "*Problemas sociales y económicos de las Mixtecas*," *Memorias del Instituto Nacional Indigenista*, Vol. II, No. 1 (1950).

Location of the Mixteca and the Mixteca Alta in Middle America

Cook presents a brief study of the geography of parts of the Mixteca Alta and Baja with particular emphasis on soil erosion, its causes and consequences.[5]

Economy and Subsistence

Intensive agriculture practiced in generally temperate intermontane valleys and on the humid coastal plain furnished the economic base of Mixtec culture. Hunting and gathering of wild plants were important subsidiary components in the Mixtec subsistence quest. While the Mesoamerican agricultural and dietary complex of maize, beans, chili, squash, and gourds was raised and consumed throughout the zone, the lowland areas specialized in the production of cotton and cacao which were not suited to cultivation in an upland environment. The multipurpose maguey was an upland cultigen poorly adapted to the humid environment of the lower elevations. Geographical diversity between the highland and lowland provinces must have induced considerable variation in the inventories of wild and domesticated fruits and plants.

[5] Sherburne F. Cook, "Dwelling construction in the Mixteca," *México Antiguo*, Vol. IV (1939), 375–86.

Animal domestication was limited to the edible dog and the turkey. The dye-producing cochineal insect (*Dactylopius coccus* or *Coccus cacti*) was raised in the Mixtec highlands and was an important item in native industry and trade. The plumage of lowland wild fowl was prized throughout Mesoamerica, but there is no indication of any domestication of parrots and other tropical birds. The frequency with which such birds are kept as pets in lowland Oaxaca today and are offered for sale in the public markets throughout the Mixteca hints of possible domestication. Fish, which is sold in the modern markets of Nochixtlán and Tlaxiaco in dried form, was an important economic item for the lowland people, particularly along the coast. Salt, although available in the highlands, was abundant along the coast and must have been an important item in the internal trade of the Mixteca. Precious metal and stone were mined in both the highlands and the lowlands.

Regional diversity encouraged brisk interregional commerce, and the periodic market was as notable and long-standing a feature of ancient Mixtec life as it is of the modern scene. Cotton, clothing, cacao, tropical fruit, fish, salt, and probably precious feathers moving from the coast and humid lowlands into the high valleys of the Mixteca Alta were exchangeable there for maguey fiber and beverage, maize, beans and chili, the precious metals and stone, the valuable dye-producing cochineal insect to be used in the manufacture of cotton cloth and clothing in the lowlands, and perhaps the manufactured paper and ceramics of the Mixteca Alta and northern Mixteca Baja. This regional interstimulation, although affected by vastly improved forms of transportation and communication, is readily ascertainable to the present day in the great markets of Tlaxiaco, Nochixtlán, Pinotepa, Tututepec, and Oaxaca.

The principal elements of the Mixtec diet corresponded to the typical Mesoamerican dietary complex of maize, beans, chili, salt, and squash. Maize was normally ground with metate and mano and made into a variety of gruels, a pastelike mixture called "masa," tortillas, and tamales. Limewater was an important additive in the preparation of many maize dishes. The 1580 *Relaciones*[6] and Herrera[7] indicate that the native diet was supplemented to considerable degree by wild berries, fruits, herbs,

[6] PNE, IV.

[7] Herrera, *Historia*, déc. 3, lib. 3, cap. 12.

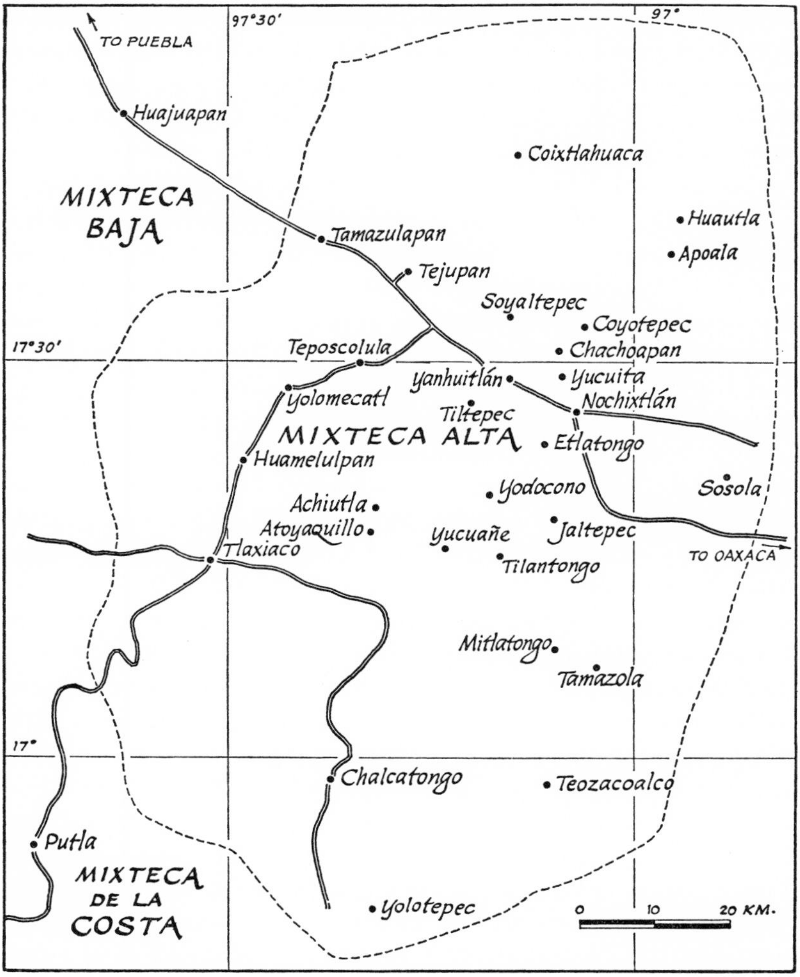

Present-day Communities of the Mixteca Alta

roots, leaves, nuts, and various plants collected from the countryside. In addition, the meat of rodents, snakes, lizards, and other small animals was consumed. The more important domesticated or game animals such as the turkey, edible dog, deer, and wild fowl were reserved for the nobility and the ruling caste.[8] For important festive or religious occasions the commoners might be permitted to indulge in more delicate fare.

The basic dress of the ancient Mixtecs resembled that which was typical of central and southern Mexico. Women wore the huipil and wrap-around skirt which are still frequently seen in the Mixtec region. Men wore breechclout, shoulder cape, and the henequen or cotton mantle. There were marked differences in dress depending on individual rank. Rulers, priests, and the nobility wore the more elaborate and richly appointed garb. On ceremonial occasions the apparel of the aristocracy was brilliant with all manner of featherwork, brightly colored embroidery and tapestries, gold and precious-stone earrings, lip and nose ornaments, and rings. Parts of a ceremonial costume were still in the possession of the cacique of Yanhuitlán in 1544–45 and were worn on festive occasions after the Conquest.[9]

Agricultural surpluses, periodic markets, internal geographic and economic diversity, a symbiotic interdependence, and a brisk trade, items which Coe correlates with the rise of urban centers in internally specialized or "organic" civilizations,[10] were all present in the Mixteca. There was, however, an absence of extensive state organization or other social and political institutions that might have induced this kind of development. Despite the presence of many of the components that characterized the great civilizations of Mesoamerica, Mixtec society did not attain the level of urban life characteristic of centers like Tenochtitlán-Tlatelolco, Teotihuacán, Mayapán, Tikal, or Monte Albán. The Mixtec peoples had achieved a high degree of artistic and cultural sophistication, but their creative efforts stopped short of the attainment of the urban stage of development.[11]

[8] Burgoa, *Geográfica descripción*, I, 287; PNE, IV.

[9] AGN, *Inquisición*, 37, exp. 9.

[10] M. D. Coe, "Social Typology and the Tropical Forest Civilizations," *Contemporary Studies in Society and History*, Vol. IV (1961), 65–85.

[11] The subject of urbanization in relation to Mixtec culture is discussed further in Chapter IV of this volume.

Social Organization

Information on pre-Conquest Mixtec social organization is limited. Consultation of available early materials and the recent analyses of Dahlgren and Harvey allows comment on certain features of social life and provides a basis for additional inferences.[12]

The Mixtec community constituted the total social universe for the majority of its inhabitants. At first glance, it would appear that the community was dissected by a two-class system composed of an aristocratic nobility and a massive common class. Closer inspection, however, reveals that the nobility, or aristocracy, must have been subdivided into (a) a ruling-caste family and (b) a supporting contingent of hereditary nobles who served as administrators, assistants, and advisers for the community rulers but who also acted as individual entrepreneurs and were entitled to receive tribute and services from a designated segment of the population.[13] At the broad base of the structure was the common class, which was composed of groups of farmers, tradesmen, artisans, and a servile component of tenant farmers, servants, and slaves. Commerce occupied an important place in Mixtec life, and it is possible that merchants may have enjoyed a superior status to that of the farmers. There is no evidence for the existence of a military class. The priests were drawn from either the common class or from the nobility, and while set apart from the rest of the population by their offices, they seem not to have constituted a special class.

On close examination, the over-all structure of Mixtec society can be arranged in the following manner: at the apex, a privileged kin group composed of the native ruler, his siblings, his mate, his children, and perhaps an elderly parent; next, a more flexible contingent of supporting nobility of indeterminate, but relatively small, size; then, the great mass of *macehuales*, or commoners; and finally, a lesser number of tenant farmers, servants, and slaves who cared for the lands and households of the ruler and high-ranking nobility. Thus arranged, Mixtec society con-

[12] Burgoa, *Geográfica descripción*, I, 376–77, 395–96; Herrera, *Historia*, déc. 3, lib. 3, caps. 12–13; Reyes, *Arte en lengua Mixteca*, 86–88; PNE, IV, 55, 73–74, 127; RMEH, I, 174–78; *ibid.*, II, 135–46, 185–91; JM and MH, 38–45; Dahlgren, *La Mixteca*, 145–66; Herbert R. Harvey, *Términos de parentesco en el Otomangue* (cited hereafter as Harvey, *Términos*).

[13] AGI, *Escribanía de Cámara*, 162.

sisted of four, rather than two, broad classes. In certain areas of contrasting behavior, particularly in the realm of the extension of privilege, it is meaningful to speak of two classes, for clearly dual norms were recognized for the nobility and ruling caste on the one hand and the remainder of society on the other. When considering other segments of social and economic experience—marriage and courting patterns, ceremonial observances, income and acquisition of goods and property, freedom and servitude, and assessment of tribute and/or services—the delineation of four social strata becomes significant. Designation of class level had considerable behavioral implication and was a very important organizing principle among pre-Conquest and colonial period Mixtecs.

There is little evidence for the existence of clans or any other consistent pattern of unilineal organization. Strong ties of kinship did not reach far beyond the boundaries of the community. Although actual relationship must have occasionally extended among members of nearby communities, no organizational principle can be seen to have evolved from an intercommunal bond of consanguinity. Despite the existence of a great web of kinship and mutual recognition that embraced many of the ruling families of the Mixteca, the bonds of authority did not normally carry across lines of community demarcation. Even in the instance of a consolidation of communities through inheritance and royal marriage, no unusual extension of authority is indicated. Each community kingdom, or *cacicazgo*, was regarded as a discrete political entity. It is possible, even probable, that certain lineage ancestors were venerated by several ruling families, but the implication of a commensurate bond of intercommunal authority is slight.

The extended family and the community were key features of Mixtec social organization, and the great majority of contact situations and daily activities were framed within the context of these two units. Descent was reckoned bilaterally by the ruling caste, and inheritance of property and title descended in the same fashion, with the oldest male probably receiving the most favorable consideration. As will be seen in a later chapter on royal succession in the Mixteca Alta, the written documents of the sixteenth century suggest a certain bias for the male line, but, depending on the advantages to be gained, either the male or the female line could be stressed in cases of royal inheritance. Although specific information is extremely limited, it is probable that similar forms of reckoning and inheritance existed among the nobility and the common mass of society. In light of the bilateral principles that governed kin relations and the over-all weakness of organizing principles in general, the Mixtec community probably resembled Murdock's deme in organization. Factors of spatial proximity and kinship worked in unison and with comparable strength to give the Mixtec community its distinctive conformation.

Marked distinctions in marriage forms existed among the various classes. Herrera comments on the elaboration of overtures of betrothal, gift-exchange, and ceremony among the ruling caste and the nobility as opposed to a lack of such observation among the common people. Community endogamy was standard for the common class. This conclusion is based not on specific mention in the sources but upon modern patterns and general impressions gained from the documentation (Appendix D–1). Community exogamy and caste endogamy were characteristic features of marriage among members of the ruling class. This was a consistent pattern. There is, at present, no adequate picture of marriage among the nonruling class nobility. Conceivably, they tended to emulate the behavior of the ruling caste and probably occupied an intermediate position between commoner and ruler with regard to the extension of the universe from which mates were selected. In theory, the nobility practiced class endogamy. Nobles were said to marry nobles, and rulers married rulers.[14] This theme is repeated often in the documentation. The restriction on noble class marriage, however, may have been affected by some degree of upward mobility from the commoner class.

Residence, at least for the ruling caste, was ambilocal. It is probable that marriage among the commoners was governed to considerable extent by spatial proximity. There is no indication that an individual would go beyond the boundaries of a community to secure a mate. In the modern communities of the Mixteca Alta, including Jaltepec, Tilantongo, Yanhuitlán, Nochixtlán, Tejupan, Teposcolula, and Tlaxiaco, there is a pronounced tendency, despite the expanded range of contact made possible by improved communication and transportation, not only to marry within a community but within the rancho in which one is

[14] RMEH, II, 138–39, 161.

born (Appendix D–1). The probability of marriage between related individuals is obviously very high. One might expect the emergence of an organizing principle for cousin marriage or for somehow defining the internal perimeters of the conjugal universe. On the basis of an analysis of kin terms and royal marriages recorded for the Mixteca in the sixteenth century, this does not seem to have been the case.

Herrera indicates that around the time of the Conquest the Mixtec were endogamous.[15] Except that two individuals with the same number in their names (*Four* Flower, *Four* House) could not marry, there were no prohibitions or prescriptions governing marriage between persons of any degree of relationship. Marriage took place among all manner of relatives. Dahlgren's analysis of the pre-Hispanic Mixtec codices indicates that eleven royal marriages are recorded between a male and his brother's daughter (two cases) or a parallel cousin (three father's brother's daughter; four father's father's brother's daughter; and two mother's sister's daughter). There were fourteen instances of marriage either with a sister's daughter (eight cases) or a cross-cousin (one father's sister's daughter; one father's father's sister's daughter; and four mother's brother's daughter), and five instances of marriage to immediate relatives (four sisters; one half-sister with the same mother but different father.)[16]

Basing her conclusions on Caso's work on the Nuttall, Selden, Selden-Roll, Vindobonensis, and Bodley codices, the *Mapa de Teozacoalco*, and the *Lienzo de Nativitas*, Dahlgren shows the frequency of parallel-cousin marriage (a total of thirteen cases) to be nearly equal to cross-cousin marriage (fourteen examples). It is most important to consider that marriages between related individuals shown in the picture manuscripts accounted for only 15 per cent of the total of all marriages. Dahlgren's findings, coupled with those of Harvey and our own analysis of post-Conquest marriage among the Mixtec royalty, leads to the conclusion that there is no evidence for the existence of unilineal exogamic organization among the Mixtecs from pre-Conquest times until after the close of the sixteenth century. Other elements governed marriage

[15] Herrera, *Historia*, déc. 3, lib. 3, cap. 12.

[16] Dahlgren, *La Mixteca*, 149–51.

among Mixtec royalty, and considerations of caste and economic and political advantage overrode kinship factors.

The best information on sixteenth-century kinship terminology comes from the Reyes grammar of 1593. Reyes points out that while there were special terms of address for first cousins, male and female, and that these could also be used for second cousins, male and female, "their customary mode is to call all of them brothers (and sisters) even though they are cousins."[17] This corresponds to modern usage in Rancho San Juan near Huamelulpan (Appendix D–2). Here there are known forms to designate and differentiate cousins from siblings, but informants indicate that they are seldom if ever employed. The normal practice is to extend sibling terms to the cousins, both male and female.

In the Mixtec kinship terminology, which Harvey has classified as of the "Hawaiian type," there were distinct terms for close relatives according to the sex of the speaker. Among brothers, first born, older, younger, and youngest could be distinguished by separate terms. Pike's study shows that modern Mixtecs designate female cousin (male speaker) and male cousin (female speaker) by the same term, indicating that the object of address is of the opposite sex to that of the speaker.[18] Lists of kin terms as taken from sixteenth-century sources are given in Appendix D–3.

Lineage depth and continuity of bloodline were of great importance in the case of the ruling caste. This is evidenced by the great emphasis placed on genealogy and legitimate and proper succession in the surviving Mixtec codices and in the post-Conquest picture manuscripts and documents. While polygyny was allowed for the upper classes, *only the offspring of the principal wife* of a ruler who was herself of the ruling caste and necessarily descended in legitimate fashion from rulers could inherit title from either his or her father or mother. In the event of failure of a ruling line, it was often necessary to go back two or more generations to determine what particular living person stood in the

[17] Reyes, *Arte en lengua Mixteca*, 87.

[18] Harvey, *Términos*; Dahlgren, *La Mixteca*, 147; Kenneth Pike, "Analysis of a Mixtec Text," *International Journal of American Linguistics* (cited hereafter as *IJAL*), Vol. XI (1945), 129–39.

closest degree of relationship to former rulers. (Rules of descent and inheritance among the ruling caste are discussed in further detail in Chapter VI.)

Warfare

There was a rather well-developed pattern of warfare in the Mixtec area during pre-Conquest times. Localized skirmishes were fought between neighboring communities, but there were also many instances of "long-range" warfare: Tilantongo *v.* Teposcolula and the Zapotec; Tejupan *v.* the Chocho; Mitlatongo *v.* Tlaxiaco and Tututepec; Tamazola *v.* Tututepec.[19] The kingdom of Tututepec carried on extensive warfare along the Pacific coast of Oaxaca, in the Mixtec and Zapotec towns of Peñoles, in Achiutla and Tlaxiaco, and in other Mixtec communities. All of these communities fought at one time or another with Mexican armies.

Engagements were fought over disputed boundaries, probably in cases of contested royal succession, and to achieve extensions of tributary dominion. There seems to have been little incentive for acquisition of territory as such by warfare. Here, as elsewhere in Mesoamerica, the taking of slaves for sacrifice was sufficient inducement to warfare. Confronted by the Mexican expansion in the late fifteenth and early sixteenth centuries, alliances were formed among various communities to ward off the common danger. Mixtec armies even allied with the Zapotecs to fight the Mexicans, and in a famous battle near Tehuantepec just before the Conquest the combined Mixtec and Zapotec armies delivered a crushing defeat to the Mexicans.[20]

Although standing armies were not present in the Mixteca Alta, we know that in the case of an attack by the Mexicans just prior to the Spanish Conquest an *ad hoc* army was collected from the hamlets subject to the ruler of Yanhuitlán and presumably from other communities. The army was formed under the leadership of a member of the Tilantongo nobility who had been appointed as a war captain, but conscription and

[19] PNE, IV, 55, 74, 79, 84, 208; RMEH, II, 187; Burgoa, *Geográfica descripción*, I, 352.

[20] *Ibid.*, II, 341–45; J. A. Gay, *Historia de Oaxaca*, I, 187–96.

Codex Nuttall

removal of people from the populated areas were with the full consent of the ruler of Yanhuitlán.[21] This corresponds with statements made by Herrera. (See quotation below.)

Weapons of warfare included bows and arrows, macanas measuring about five and one-half feet in length, spear-throwers, darts, and shields. The nobility wore padded cotton armor and might be elegantly attired for battle. Foot soldiers normally went into battle naked or in breechclout and shoulder cape.[22] Face paint was worn; this, according to Herrera was "to frighten the enemy." Herrera also relates something of the manner and tactics of warfare in the following statement:

> For war they removed the people by barrios, and the captain led them. If there were hills nearby, they ascended them, and they gathered the women, children, and property there where there were fortified walls. And they departed from there in groups of seven, with captains fighting

21 AGI, *Escribanía de Cámara,* 162.

22 PNE, IV; RMEH, I, II.

captains and soldiers fighting soldiers. And if one was killed, another took his place. And thus they performed until they were defeated and taken prisoners or until the war ended in peace or by agreement.[23]

The Mixtec, then, had a fairly well-developed raiding pattern, but there is little resemblance between this brand of sporadic fighting and the highly institutionalized warfare characteristic of the Aztecs and other groups in the Valley of Mexico.

Art and Science

The Mixtecs excelled in the production of great art in miniature, carving and working metal, stone, bone, and wood to perfection. In many ways, the artistic productions of the Mixtecs constitute their most notable material achievement. The finest demonstration of the artistic skill and keen aesthetic sense of the Mixtec craftsman is to be found in the remarkable remains recovered from Tomb 7, Monte Albán.[24] With equal skill they painted on animal skin, native paper, and ceramics. We are fortunate to have half a dozen of the beautiful historical and magico-religious picture manuscripts executed by the Mixtecs of the pre-Hispanic period. Robertson has analyzed the techniques and forms of expression exhibited by the so-called Mixtec school of codical art,[25] and the scholarly studies of their content are manifold.[26] From present archaeological evidence, the Mixtecs do not appear to have been accomplished architects

[23] Herrera, *Historia*, déc. 3, lib. 3, cap. 13.

[24] Alfonso Caso, "*Exploraciones en Monte Albán, temporada 1931–32,*" *Instituto Panamericana de Geografía e Historia Publicación* (cited hereafter as *IPP*), No. 7 (1935); Alfonso Caso, "Reading the Riddle of the Ancient Jewels," *Natural History*, Vol. XXXII (1932), 464–80; Alfonso Caso, "Monte Albán, Richest Archeological Find in America," *The National Geographic Magazine*, Vol. LXII (1932), 487–512; Alfonso Caso, "*Las tumbas de Monte Albán,*" *Anales del Museo Nacional de Arqueología, Historia, y Etnografía* (hereafter cited as *AMN*), Vol. VIII (1933), 641–47.

[25] Donald Robertson, *Mexican Manuscript Painting of the Early Colonial Period.*

[26] See, for example, the following: Alfonso Caso, "*Explicación del reverso del Codex Vindobonensis,*" *Memoria de el Colegio Nacional*, Vol. V (1952), 9–46; Alfonso Caso, *Interpretation of the Codex Bodley 2858*; Alfonso Caso, "The Historical Value of the Mixtec Codices," *Boletín de estudios oaxaqueños* (cited hereafter as *BEO*), No. 16 (1960); Philip Dark, "Speculations on the Course of Mixtec History Prior to the Conquest," *BEO*, No. 10 (1958); Karl Nowotny, *Codices Becker I/II*; Zelia Nuttall, *Codex Nuttall*; W. Lehmann and O. Smital (eds.), *Codex Vindobonensis Mexikanus I*; Mary E. Smith, "The Codex Colombino: A Document of the South Coast of Oaxaca," *Tlalocan*, Vol. IV (1963), 276–88.

or sculptors of great monuments, but future archaeology may alter this view. In the words of Covarrubias:

> In the applied arts the Mixtecs were master craftsmen; they created the finest style of decorative pottery—the Cholula polychrome; produced the most spectacular ornaments of gold, the finest gems of jade, crystal, turquoise, and so forth. In general it can be said that they were little concerned with monumental art, but concentrated on the decorative and precious, with an emphasis on highly developed technique and fine craftsmanship.[27]

While astronomical observation and calculation and a systematic calendar developed or were borrowed from outside, these achievements did not lead to a more highly abstract or practical mathematics. There is, for example, no indication that the Mixtecs knew or possessed the Maya Long Count. Instead, they relied exclusively, as did their immediate neighbors, on the use of repetitive fifty-two-year cycles. The Mixtec calendar, although of a standard Mesoamerican type, lagged one year behind that of the Mexicans.[28]

A sophisticated technology did not evolve among the Mixtecs. They lacked intelligent metallurgy; metals, with the exception of an occasional awl or copper ax, were not put to practical uses. Efficiency in the harnessing and utilization of energy was at a minimum. Human power seems to have been the highest form of the application of energy to work. Tools, work methods, and techniques were rudimentary and oriented toward the output of a single individual. Many technological concepts, such as the utilization of animal power or the principle of the wheel, did not emerge.

Writing did not develop beyond the production of painted or carved pictographs. Phonetic principles were introduced into the Mixtec pictorial manuscripts, but did not evolve beyond a very rudimentary level. While it is probable that the Mixtecs had a system for recording numbers

27 Miguel Covarrubias, *Indian Art of Mexico and Central America.*

28 Alfonso Caso, "*La correlación de los años azteca y cristiano,*" *Revista mexicana de estudios antropológicos*, Vol. III (1939), 11–45; Alfonso Caso, "*Base para la sincronología Mexteca y cristiano,*" *Memoria de el Colegio Nacional*, Vol. VI (1951), 49–66; Alfonso Caso, "*Nuevos datos para la correlación de los años azteca y cristiano,*" *Estudios de cultura nahuatl*, Vol. I (1959), 9–25.

similar, and probably related, to that contained in the Mexican tribute rolls, there is little present evidence in the pre-Conquest codices that they evolved anything beyond the simple cumulative dot system, wherby each unit was designated by a single dot. This reflects a discontinuity in the use of the cumulative bar-and-dot treatment encountered at the Classic Period Yucuñudahui—but lost in later Tilantongo sculpture—and as an isolated point might raise some doubt as to systemic and cultural continuity.

Language

Mixtec is one of the major languages of native Mexico today. It is spoken by more than 150,000 people. The most notable feature of Mixtec is that it is a tone language, which may be defined as "a language having lexically significant, contrastive, but relative pitch on each syllable."[29] Other Mexican languages sharing this characteristic are Mazatec, Amuzgo, Chinantec, Chocho, Cuicatec, Otomí, Tlapanec, Trique, and Zapotec. To further illustrate the importance of tone in language, note the following from Pike:

> Significant pitch distinguishes the meanings of utterances. When pitch is lexical, it distinguishes meanings of words. Thus Mixteco *žūk̨ū* means "mountain," but *žūk̨ù* means "brush," and the only difference between them is that the first word ends in a medium pitched syllable and the second word ends in a low pitched one.[30]

We are most fortunate to have the printed texts of two valuable sixteenth-century works on the Mixtec language. One of these is the Reyes grammar, first published in Mexico City in 1593 and reprinted in Paris in 1890, the work of a Dominican missionary which deals most directly with the dialect spoken around Teposcolula in the early colonial period. The grammar contains parts of speech, limited vocabularies, notes on the dialects of Mixtec, and lists of kinship terms and place names.

The second sixteenth-century source is the great Alvarado dictionary, first published in 1593, compiled by a Dominican friar residing in Tamazulápan but with experience in other areas of the Mixteca. In

[29] Kenneth Pike, "Tone Languages," *University of Michigan Publications in Linguistics,* No. 4 (1948).

[30] *Ibid.,* No. 4 (1948).

Codex Nuttall

compiling this dictionary, Alvarado utilized word lists previously compiled by other Dominican missionaries. A major contribution to the study of Mixtec language and culture was made in 1962 when Jiménez Moreno published a photo-process edition of the 1593 text with a lengthy commentary. In the same volume, Caso presents a partial vocabulary of Mixtec taken from the Reyes grammar and other sources.

After the time of Reyes and Alvarado the study of Mixtec went into a dark age of three hundred years' duration. During the nineteenth century several nonanalytic religious tracts and catechisms in Mixtec were published. Around 1880, Manuel Martínez Gracida, one of the early students of the native life and history of Oaxaca, published two valuable items on place names in Oaxaca with heavy emphasis on translation of Mixtec site designations.[31] In 1892, Seler published a brief article comparing Mixtec and Zapotec.[32]

Another half-century passed before the appearance of a series of scientific analyses of various aspects of the Mixtec language and its relationship to other native Mexican languages. Much of the pioneering work was done by Pike, who has been most concerned with phonemic analysis, the tonal features of Mixtec, and the influence of Spanish on the

31 Manuel Martínez Gracida, *Catálogo etimológico de los nombres de los pueblos, haciendas y ranchos del estado de Oaxaca*; Manuel Martínez Gracida, *Colección de "Cuadros sinópticos" de los pueblos, haciendas, y ranchos del estado libre y soberano de Oaxaca.*

32 Eduard Seler, "*Notice sur les langues Zapotèque et Mixtèque,*" in *8 Congrès International des Americanistes* (Paris, 1892).

language.[33] Mak has been interested in tone and dialectic comparison[34] and, in conjunction with Longacre,[35] has dealt with Proto-Mixtec phonology. Longacre and Millon have been most concerned with the reconstruction of Proto-Mixtec and Proto-Mixtecan and with the relationship of Mixtec to Trique, Chocho, Amuzgo, Popolocan, and Zapotecan.[36] Gudschinsky has considered the relation of Mixtecan and Popolocan in her reconstructions of Proto-Popolocan and Proto-Popotecan.[37] Arana Osnaya has presented articles on the relationship of Mixtec and Trique and has discussed the interesting feature of a special deferential language used in addressing sixteenth-century lords and nobles.[38] Harvey in his outstanding examination of Otomangue kinship terminology has demonstrated a deeply rooted relationship among not only the Mixtecan languages but all of the Otomanguean languages.[39]

A lively debate has grown up involving Arana Osnaya, Swadesh, and Longacre, and recently joined by Jiménez Moreno,[40] regarding the degree of relationship of Mixtec, Trique, and Amuzgo. Longacre takes the position that Mixtec, Cuicatec, and Trique are more closely related than any of the three is related to Amuzgo, which is divergent. Swadesh

[33] Kenneth Pike, "*Una leyenda mixteca*," *Investigaciones lingüísticas*, Vol. IV (1937), 262–70; Pike, "Analysis of a Mixteco Text," *IJAL*, Vol. XI (1945), 129–39; Kenneth Pike, "Tone Puns in Mixteco," *IJAL*, Vol. XI (1945), 129–39; Kenneth Pike, "Mock Spanish of a Mixteco Indian," *IJAL*, Vol. XI (1945), 129–39; Kenneth Pike, "The Flea: Melody Types and Perturbations in a Mixteco Song," *Tlalocan*, Vol. II (1946), 128–33; Kenneth Pike, "Another Mixteco Tone Pun," *IJAL*, Vol. XII (1946), 22–24.

[34] Cornelia Mak, "A Comparison of Two Mixtec Tonemic Systems," *IJAL*, Vol. XXVII (1953), 85–100; Cornelia Mak, "The Tonal System of a Third Mixtec Dialect," *IJAL*, Vol. XXIV (1958), 61–70.

[35] Cornelia Mak and R. E. Longacre, "Proto-Mixtec Phonology," *IJAL*, Vol. XXVI (1960), 23–40.

[36] R. E. Longacre, *Proto-Mixtecan*, Indiana University Research Center in Anthropology, Folklore, and Linguistics, *Publication No. 5*; R. E. Longacre, "Swadesh's Macro-Mixtecan Hypothesis," *IJAL*, Vol. XXVII (1961), 9–29; R. E. Longacre, "Amplification of Gudschinsky's Proto-Popolocan-Mixtecan," *IJAL*, Vol. XXVIII (1962), 227–42; R. E. Longacre and Rene Millon, "Proto-Mixtecan and Proto-Amuzgo-Mixtecan Vocabularies," *Anthropological Linguistics*, Vol. III, No. 4 (1961), 1–44.

[37] Sarah Gudschinsky, "Proto-Popotecan: A Comparative Study of Popolocan and Mixtecan," *IJAL*, Memoir No. 15 (1959).

[38] Evangelina Arana Osnaya, *Relaciónes internas del Mixteco Trique*; Evangelina Arana Osnaya, *El idioma de los señores de Tepozcolula.*

[39] Harvey, *Términos.*

[40] Jiménez Moreno, *Vocabulario*, 40–85.

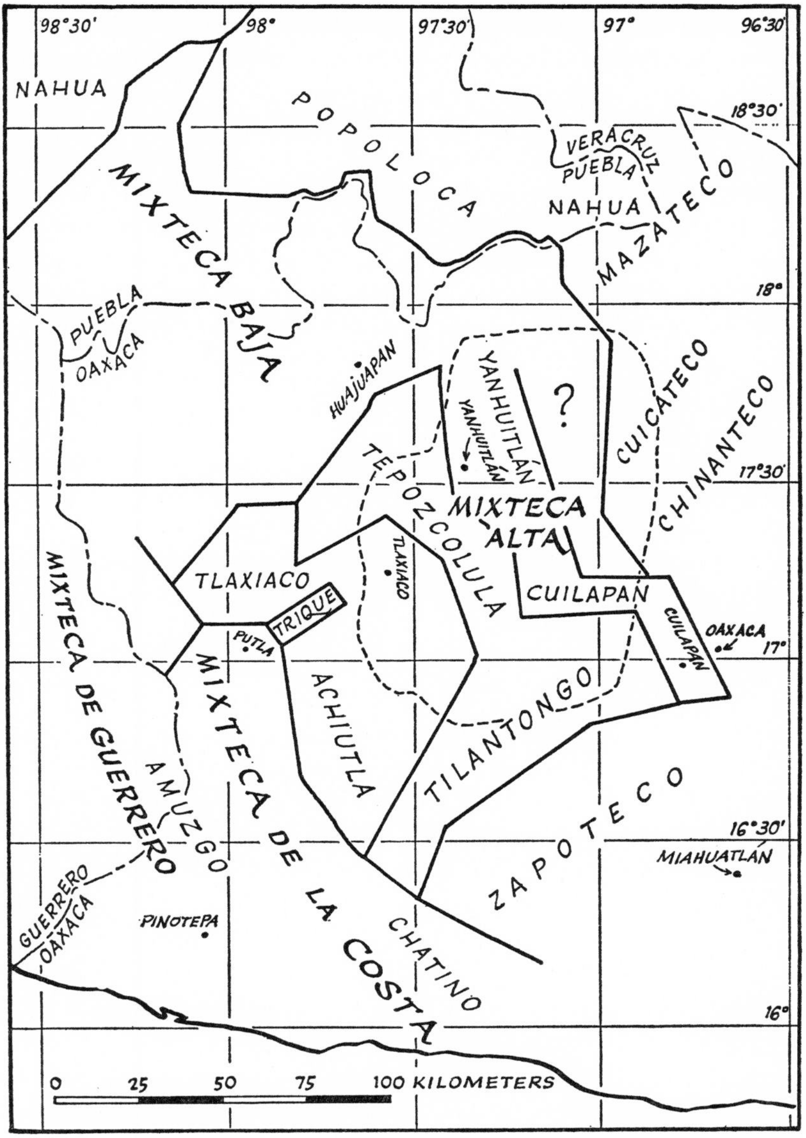

The Jiménez Moreno Linguistic Map of Western Oaxaca

makes a division that combines Mixtec, Cuicatec, and Amuzgo into one group, Mixtecan, and places Trique with Popolocan and Zapotecan to form a second stock called Popoloc-Zapotecan.[41] Proper placement of Mixtec and the Mixtecan family of languages among their immediate and remote relatives requires additional collection and analysis of materials and a more detailed comparison of existing texts.

Jiménez Moreno, after considering available data including that provided by the Reyes grammar of 1593, reduces Mixtec to seven major dialect complexes or divisions. These are considered appropriate for the sixteenth century and may be listed as follows:

1. *Mixteca Baja*: includes dialects of Chigmecatitlán-Tleltempan, Xayacatlán-Tonahuiztla, Tecciztepec, Tepejillo-Iztlán, Cacalotepec-Zapotitlán, Tezoatlán, Silacoyoapan, etc.
2. *Cuauhxochpan-Cuyamecalco*: comprised by those communities.
3. *Yanhuitlán-Cuilapan.*
4. *Tepozcolula-Tilantongo.*
5. *Tlaxiaco-Achiutla*: includes Tlaxiaco, Achiutla-Yucuañe, San Miguel el Grande, San Esteban Atlatlauhca, and Ocotepec; possibly included are Mixtepec and Juxtlahuaca.
6. *La Mixteca de la Costa.*
7. *La Mixteca de Guerrero.*[42]

Jiménez Moreno's map, showing the internal diversity of Mixtec and the geographical relationship of the various dialects, is reproduced in Map 3. Until further evidence becomes available, the Jiménez Moreno classification seems to furnish at least a preliminary framework for consideration of the internal configurations and external relationships of the Mixtec language.

Religion and Ceremony

Religious life was characterized by recognition, possession, and worship of a number of idols and deities closely corresponding to Tlaloc, Quetzalcoatl, Xipe Totec, and others from the Aztec pantheon, but with Mixtec names. These deities and their attributes have been discussed in

[41] Mauricio Swadesh, "The Oto-Manguean Hypothesis and Macro-Mixtecan," *IJAL*, Vol. XXVI (1960), 79–111.

[42] Jiménez Moreno, *Vocabulario*, 40–54.

detail by Caso,[43] Jiménez Moreno,[44] and Dahlgren.[45] In addition, there were idols, gods, and spirits identified with particular regions, communities, or places. Mountain summits, caves, and unusual natural features were venerated and were often marked by shrines.

Very little is known of the actual religious ceremonies of the ancient Mixtecs. Public feasting, fasting, dancing, singing, offering, sacrificing, games, intoxication, and narcotization accompanied calendrically determined and movable religious observances. There is every indication that these were elaborate and colorful ceremonies and that they functioned as one of the principal unifying features of community life. Religious spectacle and ceremony punctuated an otherwise drab existence for the great mass of humanity, but they also had their practical side since they insured the continuation of life through worship and placation of the spiritual world.

The ceremonies accompanying the life crises among the Mixtecs have been discussed by Dahlgren. Herrera, the major source on passage rites, indicates that the peasants, because of their poverty, did not perform the ceremonies at birth, marriage, and death with the customary elaboration of the noble and ruling classes.[46] It seems likely, however, that they attempted to emulate the upper classes.

Birth was observed by bathing the mother and the child in "holy" water. If a boy was born, a dart was placed in his hand, while a girl was given a spindle, both symbolic of future roles. On the third day the placenta was buried in an olla. The mother bathed for twenty days, and there was feasting, singing, and dancing in honor of the God of Cleanliness. There was a feast at the completion of the first year of life. At seven years of age at least some boys went for training in what Herrera calls "monasteries." This would be accompanied by certain ceremonial observances. The next major ceremonial occasion was marriage. Overtures were made through respected third parties, and gifts were offered by the suitor to a prospective bride. If these were favorably received, and

[43] Alfonso Caso, "*Los dioses zapotecas y mixtecas*," in J. Vivo (ed.), *México prehispánico*.

[44] JM and MH.

[45] Dahlgren, *La Mixteca*.

[46] Herrera, *Historia*, déc. 3, lib. 3, caps. 12–13.

after consultation with the priests on the advisability of the match, the wedding would be arranged. Of this Herrera says:

> . . . the priests and nobles with gifts of gold and other jewelry went to the home of the desired girl; and it was customary for armed men to go out on the road to prevent the betrothal of the girl, and they fought and committed robbery, in a most barbarous fashion. In the betrothal there was no ceremony other than to enter the chamber which was covered with mats and decorated with willow branches to obtain consent to marry from the girl.[47]

The actual ceremony of marriage involved the tying together of the mantles of the couple, who were seated on a marriage mat in the fashion of the Mexicans of Tenochtitlán. There were also symbolic acts of cutting the hair and reciprocal feeding of tortillas. The wedding ceremony was always accompanied by feasting.

Death was accompanied by great ceremony and feasting for the ruling class but was a simple affair among the commoners. Herrera gives the following account of the death rites for a Mixtec ruler:

> When the cacique was ill the priests performed great sacrifices, pilgrimages, pious acts, and offerings, and all was conducted with great care and with great purity of conscience. And if he recovered, great feasting and dancing were held in the house of the *Señor* and in the monastery. If he died, the funeral observances were carried out with great pomp. Offerings were placed before the corpse and they spoke to it. A regally dressed slave was placed before the corpse and attended as if he were dead. Four priests buried the corpse at midnight in the mountains, or in the fields, or in some cave together with the slave that had impersonated the dead man, two other slaves, and three women (*mujeres*) who were first made intoxicated and strangled in order that they might serve the cacique in the other world. The dead cacique was enshrouded with many cotton mantles, with a mask for the face, gold rings in the ears, and jewels about the neck, and rings on his fingers, and a mitre on the head. They placed about him a royal mantle, and thus was he placed in the hollow sepulchure without soil being placed above it. Honors were performed every year on the day of his birth and not on the day of death.[48]

[47] *Ibid.*, déc. 3, lib. 3, cap. 12.

[48] *Ibid.*, déc. 3, lib. 3, cap. 13.

So it was with the royal dead. The afterlife was clearly of importance, and belief in the survival of the spirit is indicated by the burial of retainers to attend the deceased lord in another existence. Less pagentry and ceremony but similar concepts must have characterized the rites of transition for the Mixtec commoner.

In the years 1544–45 the cacique and two high-ranking nobles of Yanhuitlán were brought before the Inquisition on charges of heresy and the continuing practice of native religion. The accusation against one of the nobles as quoted below in substantial translation is an important document of the time. It reveals traditional native religious practice and indicates the probable concurrence of pre-Hispanic religious practices with acceptable Roman Catholicism. To be sure, there is no record of a conviction of the three individuals brought before the Inquisition. They denied their guilt, claimed that perjured testimony had been delivered against them, and professed to be unwavering Christians. It is reasonable to assume that they sought to observe and perform assimilable features of the newly introduced religion to which they had been converted for no more than fifteen years. It is also very likely that each participated from time to time in acts similar to those for which they stood accused, and that the testimony of the witnesses, whatever their motives, reflected general experience before and after the Conquest.

The following quotation from the denunciatory statement of Bachiller Cristóbal de Lujo, *promotor fiscal* of the Inquisition, dated January 8, 1546, is the final accusation against Don Juan, a noble of Yanhuitlán. It was presented after testimony had been received and Juan had made the customary three denials of his guilt. The accusation charged:

> Don Juan, after he was taught, baptized, and instructed in the Christian doctrine, reverted to the customs of exercising and performing his pagan rites, ceremonies, adorations, and sacrifices, and of having idols and adoratories for them, both in his house and outside of it in many parts and secret and hidden places, and of having native priests and custodians in charge of them, to care for and venerate the said idols. And Don Juan came often with other caciques and *principales* to honor them. And he sent other people to the market place and to the vendors of the said province to buy quail and pigeons and other birds and dogs to sacri-

fice and offer to their idols with copal, feathers, stones, straws, paper, and bowls, and this was done often. And often he sacrificed blood taken from his ears and private parts with stone needles and blades, offering it to his idols in order to obtain knowledge about them, and to learn of the things of the past from the priests, and to insure fortune and success in his undertakings.

He sacrificed and offered sacrifices, in the said shrines and adoratories of the idols, and in other places, many Indians and slaves in honor of the devil and in reverence for him, and especially, some ten years ago at the death of his mother-in-law when he had a girl sacrificed; and some eight years ago at the time of the great hunger the said Don Juan and some other *principales* ordered that five boys be sacrificed; and some five years ago he ordered the sacrifice of another girl; and about four years ago he killed and sacrificed a boy and buried him in his own house; and some three years ago when there had been no rain he sacrificed two more boys; and there are many other people that he has sacrificed in many and divers times and places as offerings to his idols and demons.

And the said Don Juan, after his baptism, has been in the custom of summoning the *macehuales* of the said province and pueblo of Yanhuitlán who have received holy baptism, and several times he has told them and persuaded them that the doctrine as revealed and taught by the Christians and the baptism that they received were and are a mockery and a lie to which they should pay no attention, but that they should again honor their idols as they once did.

Another thing which he specially advises is to observe and celebrate the days and feasts of their idols as they were accustomed to do in times past, honoring the idol of water which is called Zaaguy, and another that is called Tizones who is the god of the *corazón*, and another called Toyna, and another called Xiton which is the idol of the merchants, these being the feasts which the said Don Juan has celebrated many and divers times, by himself and with others, with their rites and ceremonies, dancing and singing at night as well as by day, consenting to and partaking in the sacrifices and offerings to his idols, invoking the devil and his assistance in the manner of his paganism.

And the said Don Juan, being baptized, and who until now has concealed and participated in heresies, especially those of Don Francisco and Don Domingo, cacique and *principales* of the said pueblo, and of others that were and are native priests, custodians, and guardians of the said idols and their sacrifices and heresies, has remained silent and has likewise concealed information about the persons who have made sacrifices with him, and he with them, and saw them done, and did them jointly and separately, all in contradiction to God our Lord and our Holy Faith.[49]

Much of the same accusation was leveled against Don Francisco[50] and the cacique Don Domingo de Guzmán.[51] These detailed records of inquisitorial investigation and litigation perhaps reveal more about native religion and its lingering persistence than any other ethnological resource. That further investigation will help fill the many gaps in the incomplete picture of Mixtec religion and ceremony is certain, for much remains to be done in this area.

Post-Conquest Change and Continuity

The conquest of the Mixtecs by the Spaniards during the 1520's brought about many changes in their culture. Change, however, was countered by the relative stability of numerous elements and institutions in native Mixtec life. In approaching the study of native cultural development, it becomes apparent that the transformation of Mixtec culture in the sixteenth century depended upon stabilizing factors contributing to the continuity of ancient patterns of behavior as well as forces compelling change. These processes stood in opposition in the reformulation of traditional institutions, and both contributed to the resulting configuration.

The formal religious cult was drastically reduced, and its native priests removed from authority. Autochthonous religion was replaced by Spanish Catholicism and its energetic brotherhood of ministers. Native idols were replaced, or became rechristened, by the cult of Christian saints and fetishes. Blood-offering and human and animal sacrifice were eventually terminated as hopelessly incompatible features of native religion. But native concepts of penance, ritual purification, a supreme deity, offering, confession, communion, and a penchant for colorful religious ceremony found easily assimilable counterparts in Spanish

49 AGN, *Inquisición*, 37, exp. 11.
50 *Ibid.*, 37, exp. 7.
51 *Ibid.*, 37, exp. 9.

Catholicism. Also the great informal substratum of nature spirits, magical practice, and witchcraft continued informally long after the Conquest.

Intercommunity warfare was terminated, and the Spanish judicial system was substituted by the Mixtecs for the rectification of private and public grievances. Diet remained as it had been before the Conquest with only minor additions from newly introduced items. Dress shifted to include hat, trousers, and blouse for men but changed little for women, who have continued to wear their wrap-around skirts and huipiles to the present day. Houses continued to be constructed of thatch, adobe, sticks and poles, and stone. Native civic and religious architecture retained its ancient inventory of construction materials but rapidly assumed Spanish structural forms. Mixtec continued to be the language of all the native population, and Spanish friars found it necessary to learn the indigenous idioms to facilitate their program of conversion.

For the first time in Mixtec history domestic animals, primarily in the form of sheep, goats, and European chickens, became important, and the Mixtecs became herders as well as farmers, hunters, and gatherers. A traditionally neolithic way of life was suddenly confronted by an Iron Age technology and a concomitant improvement in technological efficiency. Foot power was augmented by animal power. But many traditional work patterns, the metate-and-mano grinding complex, the use of the digging stick, and the continuing use of *tamemes*, or human pack-animals, to mention but a few, survived the introduction of European metal technology and endure to the present day in the Mixtec zone.

Native agriculture persisted as the economic base but expanded to include many European fruits, grains, and vegetables. The raising of silkworms on newly introduced mulberry trees, mining, and cochineal production became the three most important industries of the highland region of the Mixteca and made it for a time one of the richest areas of New Spain.

Many elements and institutions originating in native life persisted in more or less unaltered form; other features were slightly or drastically altered; still others were completely eliminated and replaced by newly introduced elements and institutions which were to affect radically the pattern and course of native life. One of the most durable facets of Mixtec experience that was to survive the Conquest and persist through the sixteenth century was hereditary native rule and the community kingdom.

Codex Nuttall

2.

Continuity and Change: The Archaeological Record

THE INCOMPLETE archaeological record suggests that Mixtec culture was the result of a long development in the Mixteca Alta and that this geographical area served as the crucible of the Mixtec tradition of late Mesoamerican times. As yet it is not certain whether Mixtec culture arose directly out of Classic Period configurations that are in evidence in the archaeological remains of the Mixteca Alta or owed the origins of some of its components to areas and traditions that lay outside the area. Probably it was a development out of the Monte Albán-like culture present in the area in the Classic Period with an increment of elements diffused into the Mixteca from the outside, but the evidence is yet inconclusive. Whatever its origins, it is clear that Mixtec culture reached a climax around the fourteenth century, during the renascence of Mesoamerica known as the Postclassic Period. From this time forward there is continuity of tradition right into colonial times.

Notable cultural achievement is evident in partially explored sites at Coixtlahuaca, Tilantongo, Yanhuitlán, Nochixtlán, Teposcolula, Tamazulapan, and Chachoapan-Yucuita,[1] but there has never been a truly

[1] Alfonso Caso, "*Exploraciones en Oaxaca, quinta y sexta temporadas, 1936–1937*," *IPP*, No. 34 (1938); Alfonso Caso, "*Resumen del informe de las exploraciones en Oaxaca, durante la 7a y 8a temporadas, 1937–1938 y 1938–1939*," in *Actas del 27° congreso internacional de americanistas*, II (Mexico, 1947); Alfonso Caso, "The Mixtec and Zapotec Cultures: The Mixtecs," *BEO*, No. 22 (1962); Eulalia Guzmán, "*Exploración arqueológica en la Mixteca Alta*," *AMN*, Vol. I (1934), 17–42; Ignacio Bernal, "*Exploraciones en Coixtlahuaca, Oaxaca*," *Revista mexicana de estudios antropológicos*, Vol. X (1948), 5–76; Ignacio Bernal, "Archeology of the Mixteca," *BEO*, No. 7 (1958); John Paddock (ed.), "Excavations in the Mixteca Alta," *Mesoamerican Notes*, No. 3 (1953); Javier Romero, "*Monte Negro, centro de interés antropológico*," in *Homenaje a Alfonso Caso*.

exhaustive excavation of a single site in the Mixteca Alta. The most thorough explorations were carried out at Tamazulapan, Coixtlahuaca, Yucuñudahui, and at Monte Negro near Tilantongo. Furthermore, there has never been a full-scale survey of surface remains in the Mixteca Alta or even a significant part of it.

Because of the totally inadequate exploitation of the abundant archaeological resources, the origins and course of development of the Mixtec way of life are poorly known. Nearly all knowledge of the latest period of pre-Conquest Mixtec life is derived from historical records and from archaeological materials recovered outside the Mixteca. Many lacunae exist in the chronological and cultural record of the Mixteca Alta of pre-Conquest times. There has been no attempt at solid cultural reconstruction based on archaeological materials from the Mixtec zone itself. The valley of Oaxaca has provided more information on the latest indigenous period than has come from all the sites of the Mixteca combined. As Bernal has been quick to indicate, the Mixteca is one area of Mexico that is most in need of systematic archaeological investigation.

Known or Partially Excavated Sites in the Mixteca Alta

It seems appropriate to include here a summary of the present state of archaeological knowledge of the Mixteca Alta. A number of sites have been visited but not excavated or described in print. Several reports on "unpublished sites" are on file at the National Institute of Anthropology and History in Mexico City. A partial, and usually inadequate, description of a few of these sites is furnished in the *Atlas Arquelógico de la República Mexicana*, printed in 1939. An old but useful source on pre-Hispanic remains is the *Cuadros Sinópticos* of Martínez Gracida.[2] General commentary on the better-known facets of Mixtec archaeology and protohistory may be obtained in the works of Caso, Bernal, Dahlgren, Carrasco, Noguera, Covarrubias, Coe, Nicholson, and Acosta.[3]

[2] Gracida, *Colección de "Cuadros sinópticos."*

[3] Jorge R. Acosta, "Preclassic and Classic Architecture of Oaxaca," in Robert Wauchope and Gordon R. Willey (eds.), *Handbook of Middle American Indians* (cited hereafter as Wauchope and Willey, *Handbook*), III; Ignacio Bernal, "Archaeological Synthesis of Oaxaca," *ibid.*, III; Ignacio Bernal, "Architecture in Oaxaca After the End of Monte Albán," *ibid.*, III; Bernal, "Archeology of the Mixteca," *BEO*, No. 7 (1958); Alfonso Caso, "Lapidary Work, Goldwork, and Copperwork from Oaxaca," in Wauchope and Willey, *Handbook*,

Because of the size and obvious historical importance of the Mixteca Alta, it is deplorable that so little archaeological investigation has been done. Since a systematic survey is lacking, the exact number, distribution, content, and relationship of the sites have not yet been determined. Such a circumstance obviously imposes a severe limitation on the writing of a culture history for the pre-Hispanic era. Insufficient time and funds and the lack of a suitable operational framework have prevented me from conducting the orderly program of excavation and survey that is so obviously required. Preliminary surveys were made in and around Yanhuitlán, Nochixtlán, Tilantongo, Mogote del Cacique, and at Soyaltepec, but conclusive results must await further research.

A list of known sites and complexes in the Mixteca Alta is presented in the pages that follow. Except where all information has been derived from the *Atlas Arqueológico* or from my own field observation, the appropriate sources are listed for each site or zone.

Achiutla (Location: 17° 16′ to 17° 19′ N. Lat.; 97° 29′ W. Long.): Structures, mounds, tombs, and archaeological caves are mentioned. Rickards indicates that there were standing stone walls forming courts. At the end of these walls stands a high mound. Burgoa spoke of sacred caves, adoratories, fortresses, and artificial terraces in the vicinity of Achiutla. There are persistent rumors of a buried treasure at Achiutla that lead the citizens of the community to discourage excavation there. The community is located in rugged mountain terrain and is difficult to reach by motor vehicle.[4]

Apasco (Santa María) (Location: 17° 37′ N. Lat.; 97° 07′ W. Long.): The *Atlas* states only that there are structures here.

Chachoapan-Yucuita-Coyotepec-Yucuñudahui (Location: 17° 30′

III; Caso, "The Mixtec and Zapotec Cultures: The Mixtecs," *BEO*, No. 22 (1962); Alfonso Caso, "Mixtec Writing and Calendar," in Wauchope and Willey, *Handbook*, III; Alfonso Caso, "Sculpture and Mural Painting of Oaxaca," *ibid.*, III; Alfonso Caso and Ignacio Bernal, "Ceramics of Oaxaca," *ibid.*, III; Pedro Carrasco, "*Las culturas indígenas de Oaxaca*," *América Indígena*, Vol. XI (1951), 99–114; M. D. Coe, *Mexico*; Covarrubias, *Indian Art*; *Dahlgren, La Mixteca*; Henry B. Nicholson, "The Mixteca-Puebla Concept in Mesoamerican Archaeology: A Re-examination," in *Congrès International des Sciences Anthropologiques, Compte-Rendu V* (Paris, 1960).

[4] C. G. Rickards, *The Ruins of Mexico*; Burgoa, *Geográfica descripción*, I, 275–76, 348–53.

Codex Nuttall

to 17° 33′ N. Lat.; 97° 16′ to 97° 20′ W. Long.): This archaeological zone was surveyed in 1933–34 by Martín Bazán, Juan Valenzuela, and Eulalia de Guzmán.[5] During 1938, Alfonso Caso and his associates carried out excavations of several days duration in the zone.

Yucuñudahui is a mountaintop site just north of Chachoapan. Several structures were excavated by the Caso party, the most important being a ball court and the so-called *Templo de la Lluvia.* Tomb 1 contained glyphs and ceramics related to Zapotec and Teotihuacán traditions; there was a carved representation of a Tlaloc-like figure; the tomb was in a cruciform shape and had stucco walls containing painted and sculptured scenes and Zapotec-style number glyphs; a roof beam from the tomb yielded a radiocarbon date of A.D. 292 (1652±185).[6] The structure and contents of Tomb 1 of Yucuñudahui compare favorably with

[5] Guzmán, "*Exploración arqueológica en la Mixteca Alta,*" *AMN,* Vol. I (1934), 17–42; Caso, "*Exploraciones en Oaxaca, quinta y sexta temporadas 1936–1937,*" *IPP,* No. 34 (1938); Caso, "*Resumen del informe de las exploraciones en Oaxaca, durante la 7a y 8a temporadas, 1937–1938 y 1938–1939,*" in *Actas del 27° congreso internacional de americanistas,* II (Mexico, 1947).

[6] W. F. Libby, *Radiocarbon Dating.*

Tomb 103 of Monte Albán, and Caso elected to correlate Yucuñudahui, at least this tomb, with Period III–A of Monte Albán. On the terrace system leading down the slopes from Yucuñudahui, Guzmán found plain cream (*rosado*) and red-on-cream to be the most abundant class of ceramics. Also in evidence here were Mixtec fine (*acerado*) gray, brilliant red painted-on-one-side (*rojo, esmaltado brillante por una cara*), and a polished reddish-brown ware (*bayo*).

Behind the present-day settlement of Yucuita is an artificially terraced biconical hill which is laced by an extensive system of tunnels and is topped by a plaza-and-structure complex. A number of foundations, platform-bases, and mounds are in evidence. The larger and smaller nodes of the peak are terraced in a manner somewhat reminiscent of the stepped pyramid. In test pits made in the northern and southern slopes Guzmán encountered the following pottery types: (a) fine polished gray "similar to Zapoteca of Monte Albán"; (b) fine gray from tripodal vessels with serpent-head legs; (c) plain smoothed and polished reddish-brown or tan (*canela*); (d) red-on-cream; (e) brilliant red painted-on-one-side. No polychrome was encountered.

Red-on-cream and gray wares were predominant in all sites within the zone. At a place called *La Iglesia Vieja*, where a colonial structure was built over the foundations of an ancient indigenous structure lying well out from Chachoapan, about ten thousand fragments of polychrome pottery were found in a trash pit in association with a fragment of a Colonial Period painted vase; also found in association with polychrome sherds was the handle of a sixteenth-century Spanish sword. Five copper awls, three bone handles, spindle whorls, and worked bone were also associated with the above-mentioned materials. Caso correlated the polychrome pottery from the *Iglesia Vieja* with the graphic representations in the codices Nuttall, Vindobonensis, and Colombino, and classed both categories as Mixtec.

Caso purchased a plumbate *vaso* said to be from Yucuita and a fragment of a plumbate vessel from Coyotepec. In relatively abundant distribution in the area are worked green stone artifacts and bottle-shaped tombs carved into the rock and called "cellars" (*sótanos*) by the local inhabitants. One of the cellar tombs excavated by Guzmán contained a burial situated in a fetal position and accompanied by reddish-brown or cream ceramics, a cajete (*cazuela*) of dark (*negruzco*) clay, a gray vessel, and a small, polished, black toy olla.

In general, the material from this zone is sketchy and inadequate. Impressionistically, the mountaintop sites of Yucuñudahui and Yucuita appear similar and are probably more or less contemporaneous. Both contain remains dating at least to Monte Albán–III, a period of marked Teotihaucanoid influences. This is a most promising zone for developmental study. Very probably it is a center of continuous occupation from at least the Early or Middle Classic Period of Central Mexico to the present time. Sixteenth-century documentation indicates that the three main communities of Chachoapan, Yucuita, and Coyotepec were in their present locations in earliest colonial times and that there was a congenial relationship between the communities of Yucuita (called Suchitepec in the documents) and Chachoapan. Relations between Coyotepec and the other two towns appeared to be less cordial. I think it conceivable that Yucuita was traditionally closely allied to Chachoapan. Strictly in the realm of speculation, it is possible that the site located atop Yucuita ("Flowery Hill") was once subject to Yucuñudahui. The modern towns of Yucuita and Chachoapan are only about fifteen hundred meters apart, and in recent years they have continued to enjoy a close partnership in cultivating one of the richest and most fertile microzones of the Mixteca Alta.

COIXTLAHUACA (Location: 17° 42′ N. Lat.; 97° 22′ W. Long.): During the 1940's, Bernal carried out a brief but significant excavation in a barrio of Coixtlahuaca.[7] Bernal stresses the point that the excavated site was by no means an urban center but was a small place with the residential area beside or close by the ceremonial center. A total of thirty-nine burials was excavated. The burials fell into four categories: (a) those of true construction; (b) those dug into refuse; (c) tombs with double mortuary chambers; (d) bottle-shaped tombs of the type found at Chachoapan and at other places in the Mixteca Alta. Normally the corpse was placed in a sitting position with knees drawn up and wrapped in a petate. The

[7] Bernal, "*Exploraciones en Coixtlahuaca, Oaxaca*," *Revista mexicana de estudios antropológicos*, Vol. X (1948), 5–76; Esteban Avendaño, MS, Coixtlahuaca, Instituto Nacional de Antropología e Historia; Martín Bazán, MS, Coixtlahuaca, *ibid.*

excavator mentions that all of the funerary customs depicted in the Mixtec codices were found at Coixtlahuaca. Bernal also indicates that the tombs of Coixtlahuaca were quite distinct from those of Monte Albán. Vessels, olla fragments, dog bones, and jade beads accompanied the burials.

The ceramics of the tombs suggested only one period of occupation. One burial was termed "Aztec." While different architectural periods were indicated by the building remains, Bernal could recognize but one ceramic level. In all, thirty-one ceramic types were ascertained. Most of these were of local manufacture; others were of the Aztec culture; some types were of questionable provenience. Aztec–III cramics were found in Burial 4, but nowhere else.

Unpolished red-on-cream made up 29.65 per cent of the total sherds taken from pits and 55.77 per cent of the total vessels from tombs, burials, and offerings. According to Bernal, this is the most abundant variety of typically Mixtec ceramics. It is found at Chachoapan, Teposcolula, and Tamazulapan. Cajetes with compound silhouette are found at Coixtlahuaca and elsewhere in the Mixteca and in Monte Albán–V; Bernal indicates this to be a classic Mixtec type.

Polychrome pottery, similar in style to that from Cholula, was as apparent in lower levels as it was in upper layers and was relatively abundant for a de luxe ceramic. The polychrome motifs were said to correspond to those in the Mixtec codices. Polished gray, also found in Monte Albán–V and in other sites of the Mixteca, was abundant at all levels. A brown ceramic with black slip came from the lowest levels but was generally scarce.

Seven house units were excavated. Bernal states that they were of "typical Mixtec construction," characterized by wall construction of large plain-surface stones with smaller plain and well-worked stones occupying the interstices. All floors were of stucco.

In summary, there is an unmistakable similarity of ceramic types found in Coixtlahuaca and those found in the other known sites of the Mixteca Alta, principally at Tilantongo, Nochixtlán, Teposcolula, Yanhuitlán, and Tamazulapan. In nearly all sites are found unpolished red-on-cream, polychrome, cajetes with composite silhouette, tall tripodal cajetes of polished gray clay, and Aztec–III *molcajetes*. Also, the cellar tombs, called *chaltunes* in Coixtlahuaca, enjoy a wide distribution in the region. Chronologically, Coixtlahuaca is a one-period site coming, as is indicated by the appearance of Aztec–III wares, after Tenayuca of the Valley of Mexico. It is contemporaneous with Tenochtitlán, Monte Albán–V, and Mitla, with a number of other sites in the Mixteca, and with the Mixtec codices. Bernal expresses the opinion that

> [Coixtlahuaca] is not only of the same culture but of the same variant of the Mesoamerican culture that is common to at least all of this region of the Mixteca Alta. . . . The material culture of Coixtlahuaca found in the explorations must be considered as the same as in the other regions of the Mixteca Alta already mentioned. On the other hand, we must affirm that all of this Mixtec culture flourished in the final centuries before the Conquest and that these ceramic types must be considered as late.

It is reported that mounds, structures, and tombs are known from sites at Tlacotepec, Tlapiltepec, Suchixtlahuaca, and Cerro de Veinte Idolos, all in the former district of Coixtlahuaca.

CERRO ENCANTADO (Location: 17° 16′ N. Lat.; 97° 40′ W. Long.): This is a hilltop site located about one kilometer northeast of Tlaxiaco and on the east side of the road running to Teposcolula. There are signs of structures on the upper slopes of the hill. According to reports received in Tlaxiaco in the spring of 1963, tombs were recently opened at this site. Metal, carved stone, and painted pottery were reported to have accompanied osteological material in the tomb.

HUAMELULPAN (Location: 17° 21′ N. Lat.; 97° 41′ W. Long.): Located on the hill called Ayuyucu (?) is a very important ceremonial site containing several structures. Local residents indicate that there are tombs, large and small structures, sculptures, pottery figurines, and a variety of sherds. This site is located immediately adjacent to the Teposcolula-Tlaxiaco road and is clearly visible from the surrounding countryside. Some scientific excavation has been carried out at this site, but a report was not available for incorporation here.

NOCHIXTLÁN (Location: 17° 28′ N. Lat.; 97° 13′ W. Long.): Guzmán surveyed a site, Tinducarrada, just northwest of Nochixtlán. Two high hills were encountered here.[8] Tinducarrada is on the eastern hill and to the west is Pueblo Viejo of Nochixtlán. Characteristic of the site were structure floors of stucco, mounds, artificial terraces, cellar tombs, and abundant surface pottery. The ceramic inventory included plain Mixtec gray, a plain reddish-cream (*amarillo rojizo liso*) ware, brilliant red painted-on-one-side, reddish-brown and *calizo* (?) ware, and red-on-cream. No polychrome was found.

Surface collections were made by the present writer at two locations near Nochixtlán. These materials, on deposit at the University of the Americas, have not been analyzed.

Ñumi (San Juan) (Location: 17° 24′ N. Lat.; 97° 42′ W. Long.): This site is located in the former district of Tlaxiaco. The *Atlas* states only that it contains sculptured pieces.

Loma De Organos (Location: 17° 12′ N. Lat.; 97° 44′ W. Long.): The *Atlas* indicates that this site is located three to four kilometers southwest of Tlaxiaco and that remains include structures, tombs, mounds, and ceramics.

Cerro Partido (Location: 17° 23′ N. Lat.; 97° 5′ W. Long.): This site is near Etlatongo in the valley of Nochixtlán and contains structures.[9] There are other visible features in the vicinity of Etlatongo.

Tamazulapan (Location: 17° 40′ N. Lat.; 97° 35′ W. Long.): During the winter of 1952, a group from Mexico City College excavated at two sites near Tamazulapan.[10] One and one-half weeks were spent by a small contingent at the site of Pueblo Viejo, and a total of three weeks was spent at Yatachio. Yatachio is three kilometers due north of Tamazulapan center and is located on a low hill near the middle of the valley of Tamazulapan. Pueblo Viejo is situated at a higher elevation

[8] Guzmán, "*Exploración arqueológica en la Mixteca Alta*," *AMN*, Vol. I (1934), 17–42.

[9] Benalí Salas, MS, Cerro Partido, in Instituto Nacional de Antropología e Historia.

[10] Paddock (ed.), "Excavations in the Mixteca Alta," *Mesoamerican Notes*, No. 3 (1953); Guzmán, "*Exploración arqueológica en la Mixteca Alta*," *AMN*, Vol. I (1934), 17–42.

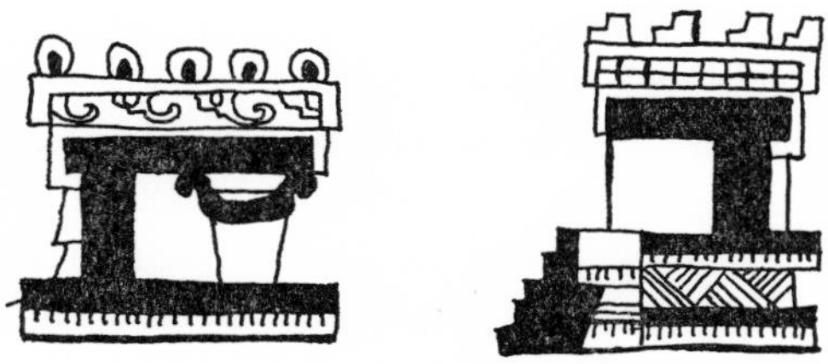

Codex Nuttall

than Yatachio on the point of a promontory bisecting the valley. A report on the work at Pueblo Viejo has not appeared, and there has been only a preliminary report published on the work at Yatachio. Guzmán partially surveyed the Tamazulapan area in 1934.

At Yatachio, five tentative building periods were ascertained: (a) Yatachio–I is said to correspond to Monte Negro, Monte Albán–I, and Zacatenco-Tlatilco-Cuicuilco of the Valley of Mexico; (b) Yatachio–II is said to begin in contemporaneity with Monte Albán–II and Teotihuacan–I and to end around the time of Yucuñudahui, the transition from Monte Albán–III–A to III–B, and the beginnings of Teotihuacán–III; (c) Yatachio–III and –IV persist through Monte Albán–III–B and through Teotihuacán–IV to the beginnings of Tula; (d) Yatachio–V is thought to correspond to the beginnings of Mixteca-Cholula style, Monte Albán–IV, and to be contemporary with Tula; (e) Pueblo Viejo is thought to succeed Yatachio–V and to be contemporary with Coixtlahuaca-Tilantongo, Monte Albán–IV (Zapotec) and Monte Albán–V (Mixtec), the post-Tula cities of Texcoco, Tlatelolco, and Tenochtitlán, and is believed to have persisted until Conquest times.

Dating for Yatachio is based on the appearance of Archaic-type figurines, a structural succession in Mound C, ceramic correspondences with Monte Albán–III, and a lack of polychrome, plumbate ware, and metal objects. The latter indicated to the excavators that final building in Yatachio took place in pre-Toltec times. "Granting the inconclusiveness of the dating," states the report, "it still seems reasonably sure that Yatachio was . . . a site in the Mixteca Alta which was inhabited from early times, before development of the characteristics of late Mixtec art, until a time at least very near the critical one in the development of that art." Excavation at Yatachio failed to cast new light on the origins of

Mixtec art or culture. "Further investigations at Pueblo Viejo may show sufficient continuity with Yatachio to establish the two places as, in effect, a single Mixtec site inhabited from Preclassic times until the conquest by the Spanish."

Pits, a quandrangular court, tombs, burials, walls, high mounds, and artificial terraces were the principal features of Yatachio. Paddock excavated what he thought to be a habitation site on a terrace lying well down the slope of the hill of Yatachio. Obsidian and flint projectile points, blades, an obsidian awl, and Archaic-type figurines were among the objects recovered. The report on the ceramics for Yatachio has not been published. The familiar Mixtec red-on-cream was the prevalent type encountered. Guzmán's surface collection included red-on-cream, a plain cream ware, a highly polished red-painted ware, and some occasional gray sherds. From Pueblo Viejo came polychrome and several Aztec sherds.

Tejupan (Location: 17° 40′ N. Lat.; 97° 25′ W. Long.): This is an important but practically unknown site located at the eastern end of the valley of Tamazulapan. There is a conical mountain to the north of the present center with terraces and apparent structures. A Pueblo Viejo is located on a rise to the southeast of the center. Guzmán obtained a surface collection in the town that included red-on-cream and some plain red and black sherds. Her collection contained no polychrome, but there seems little doubt that it does in fact exist on the surface.[11] There are sites to the south of Tejupan at La Coronita and Miltepec.

Teposcolula (Location: 17° 32′ N. Lat.; 97° 31′ W. Long.): Because of the number of visible surface features and the known importance of this community in the sixteenth century, Teposcolula promises to be one of the most important archaeological zones of the Mixteca Alta.[12] Guzmán visited the main site of the zone located on a mountain rising to the southwest of the center. Here is a mound and plaza complex surrounded by a series of descending terraces. The ridge and the longi-

[11] *Ibid.*, Vol. I (1934), 17–42.

[12] *Ibid.*, Vol. I (1934), 17–42; Benalí Salas, MS, Teposcolula, Instituto Nacional de Antropología e Historia.

tudinal axis of the main building complex run north and south. There are numerous walls of masonry and adobe, and a ball court running north and south with elevations at either end. On the eastern side of the mountain, some distance from the main plaza, ruined walls and structural vestiges dominate that portion of the site.

Examining a terrace on the south side of the site, Guzmán located thick structural walls of horizontally coursed stone coated over with a thin layer of mixed limestone-laden adobe. She also encountered a wall of stones arranged in the alternating form of a woven reed mat.

Guzmán found very little pottery on the surface. What there was included a fine plain-black ware, brilliant red painted-on-one-side, a yellowish-red ware, and red-on-cream. Relative frequencies are not given. A pit dug into the mid-portion of the eastern side of the main plaza revealed a course of well-cut stone resting on a stucco floor, but without associated sherds. In a declivity located on the western slope of the site, Guzmán excavated a layer containing numerous fragments of polychrome, highly polished red with black lines, polished black, a yellowish-red ware, and a coarse black-brown ware; there was a lack of red-on-cream, and polychrome predominated. From a cellar tomb came small cajetes mostly of plain clay (like those from Chachoapan) and several red-on-cream cajetes.

In the spring of 1963 several residents of Teposcolula stated that Teposcolula had been at the above site until the Conquest. The Spaniards, they said, drained a lake at the bottom of the hill and relocated the community at its present site. Guzmán's findings neither corroborate nor disprove this contention, but there is no reference to such a move in the documentation of the sixteenth century. It could well be, however, that Pueblo Viejo on the hilltop did precede a later settlement in the valley at some time in the history of Teposcolula. Of course, it has not yet been confirmed that this mountaintop site was ever more than a ceremonial center; however, it is possible that this site was an occupation center, for such centers were not always located in the valleys as they are today.

There are many sites, including Cerro del Fortín, Monte Verde, and others, in the vicinity of San Pedro y San Pablo Teposcolula and San Juan Tesposolula that are inadequately known.

TILANTONGO (Location: 17° 15′ N. Lat.; 97° 17′ W. Long.): During the 1937–38 excavation season Caso and his associates worked two sites in the Tilantongo zone: (a) Monte Negro, a Preclassic site corresponding closely to Monte Albán Period I in the valley of Oaxaca; and (b) Tilantongo, a Postclassic site related to Monte Albán–V (Mixtec) remains in the valley of Oaxaca.

At Monte Negro, Caso partially excavated a terraced mountaintop site in which he encountered rectangular structures enclosing squared patios, an early appearance of a feature that was to characterize civic and ceremonial architecture in Mesoamerica for two thousand years. In Mound TS were found six circular columns composed of a core of large plain-face stones dressed over with numerous smaller stones arranged to give the columns their cylindrical shape. Two stucco floors were located, but no sloping walls of the type found in Monte Albán were seen.

Everything recovered in Monte Negro has been assigned by Caso to the period of Monte Albán–I; nothing later was found at the site. Included were materials taken from tombs and burials. Clay and technical procedures utilized in ceramics were enough unlike those of Monte Albán proper to indicate that they were of local origin and not imported from the valley of Oaxaca.

The great majority of pottery from Monte Negro was a poorly fired and easily crumbled cream ware (*amarillo rosa*), sometimes carrying a black slip. Also in evidence were a better fired, but less abundant brownish-yellow (*ocre*) ware and a very poorly made gray ware with a dark-gray slip. Vessel types included flat-based cajetes with upturned lips and with base decorations of fine incised undulating lines describing circles and spirals. Other forms were effigy vases, claw vessels, *braseros*, and one *vaso* with a depiction of the rain god projecting from the surface. Caso noted the "Olmecoid" influence in the style of all the effigy figures and assigned all pieces to a Monte Albán–I chronological category, a period running generally from 650 B.C. to 200 B.C.

Other recovered items included shell ornamentation, a bone spatula, two jade earrings, two shell earrings, a bone carved in the image of an alligator with rock-crystal eyes, turquoise mosaic green stone plaques depicting human faces, a Teotihuacán-like *tecali* mask, and a small jade head.

Regarding the importance of Monte Negro in the development of the two great indigenous cultural traditions of Oaxaca, the Mixtec and the Zapotec, Caso concludes: "According to what we know up to now as a result of archaeological research and from the few historical sources which have been preserved, the two great cultures of Oaxaca seem to have been founded upon a basic culture which we find in Monte Negro and Monte Albán I."[13]

At another site adjacent to the church on the southwestern extremity of the present *cabecera* of Tilantongo, brief excavations revealed what must have been Postclassic Tilantongo. Caso believes that sometime before the Conquest, Tilantongo was moved from Monte Negro north to the present site of the town located on a steep-sided hill about four hundred meters below Monte Negro in the valley of Tilantongo. The church, in the construction of which a part of a pre-Hispanic structure was utilized, is located at the tip of a ridge extending south from the present main plaza of the town. Caso trenched into a high mound directly to the west of the church. His partial explorations showed a probable great patio with access to three structures to the west, south, and north. Only a very small portion of the complex which extends north, south, and west was worked. The only results apparent during the spring of 1963 were some rather unsightly gashes in the mounds and terrain of the site.

One of the excavators, Acosta, located superimposed structures, the oldest being a wall of alternating vertical and horizontal stones corresponding in character to Monte Albán–IV and V of the valley of Oaxaca and those recovered by Bernal in Coixtlahuaca. This wall was constructed over a stucco floor which was laid over the natural terrain. Above the wall appeared a carved stone which had formerly been covered with stucco; the stone depicts the god Five Death in a style very similar to that of the Mixtec codices and polychrome pottery; the stone also contained dot number elements but lacked the bar-and-dot treatment encountered in the earlier Tomb 1 of Yucuñudahui. Caso considered the stone to be the finest demonstration of Mixtec sculpture recovered to that time.

The excavated features of Tilantongo, coupled with the appearance

[13] Caso, "The Mixtec and Zapotec Cultures: The Mixtecs," *BEO*, No. 22 (1962).

of polychrome in the exploratory pits, led Caso to conclude that Tilantongo was a very late settlement. It was probably occupied right up to the Conquest. Burgoa mentions a relocation of Tilantongo from an "inaccessible site" to its present position. The protracted transition from Preclassic Monte Negro to Postclassic Tilantongo is not revealed by excavations thus far made in the Tilantongo area.

Northwest of Tilantongo at Rancho del Carmen a cellar tomb which had been carved into rock was located. It measured ninety by seventy-five centimeters with an entrance measuring fifty centimeters in diameter; the tomb differed appreciably from those discovered in the vicinity of Chachoapan. This was a primary adult burial with the corpse in a fetal position and accompanied by vessels.

Another site of probable importance is Mogote del Cacique, some three miles east of Tilantongo center, which I visited during the spring of 1963. This is one of a number of sites on the crest of a mountain range separating the valley and municipality of Tilantongo from the valley of Nochixtlán and the municipalities of Jaltepec and Jaltepetongo (Fig. 1). Mogote del Cacique is a terraced mountaintop site similar in general disposition to Yucuñudahui, Yucuita, Yatachio, Teposcolula, or Preclassic Monte Negro. There are six major structures, including two high mounds, one low mound, two probable platforms, and a probable ball court. There are a number of walls or low ramparts at various locations. The site is terraced for several hundred yards down the south slope. Much of the terraced slope is now under cultivation. There is a heavy concentration of sherds in the ceremonial center with rapidly decreasing quantities at descending elevations. Several probable sacked burials were located well down the southwest slope. Surface collections which I made at Mogote del Cacique and at Tilantongo in the spring of 1963 have not yet been analyzed.[14]

Cerro De La Virgen (Location: 17° 15′ N. Lat.; 97° 42′ W. Long.): This site is located some five kilometers south of Tlaxiaco. It contains

[14] Caso, "*Exploraciones en Oaxaca, quinta y sexta temporadas 1936–1937*," *IPP*, No. 34 (1938); Caso, "*Resumen del informe de las explorcaciones en Oaxaca, durante la 7a y 8a temporadas, 1937–1938 y 1938–1939*," in *Actas del 27° congreso internacional de americanistas*, II (Mexico, 1947); Caso, "The Mixtec and Zapotec Cultures: The Mixtecs," *BEO*, No. 22 (1962); Bernal, "Archeology of the Mixteca," *BEO*, No. 7 (1958); Burgoa, *Geográfica descripción*, I, 372.

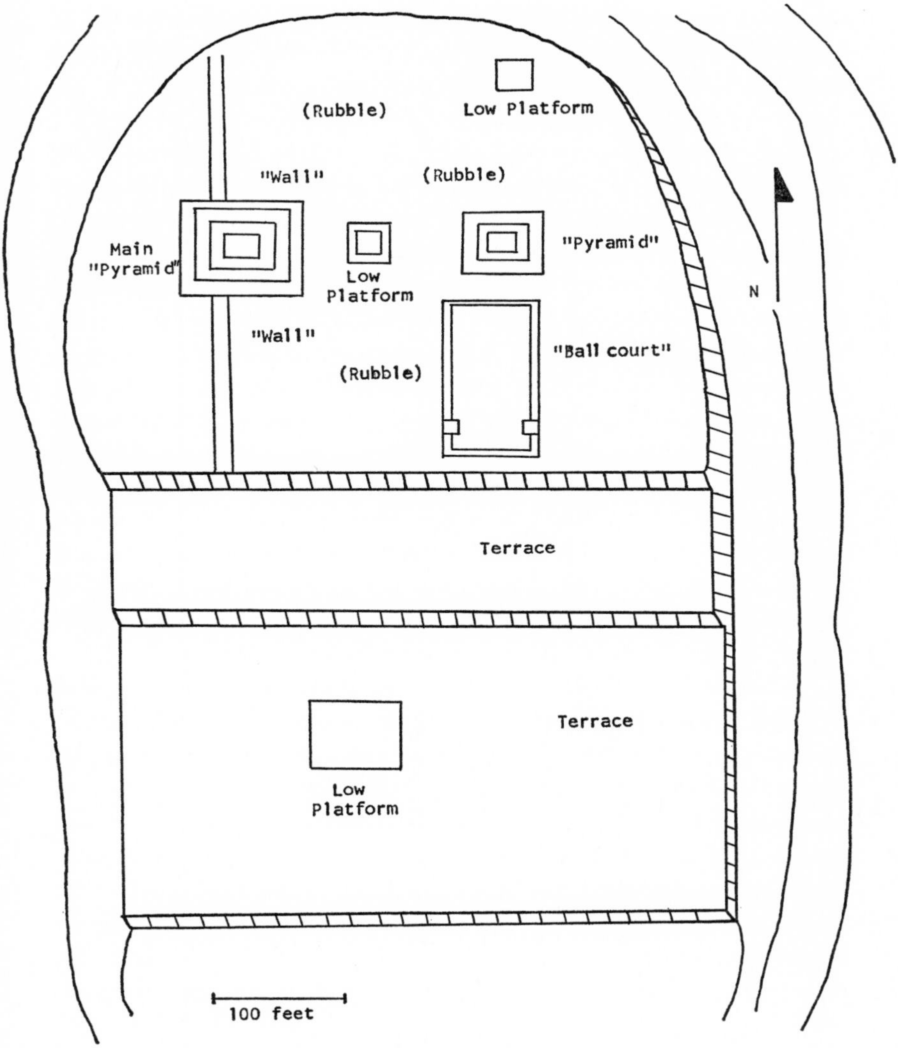

Fig. 1. *Approximate Location of Structures at the Site of Mogote del Cacique*

structures, ceramics, and burials, and is terraced in the manner of Yucuñudahui, Teposcolula, Yucuita, Yatachio, and other Mixtec hill sites. The site is easily approached from Tlaxiaco center.

YANHUITLÁN (Location: 17° 32′ N. Lat.; 97° 21′ W. Long.): Very little is known of this important archaeological zone. My brief survey revealed that there were a number of locations containing signs of structures and/or heavy concentrations of sherds in the fields and foothills surrounding the community center. A general sheet distribution of sherds is noted in the agricultural and grazing lands of the valley floor. Overwhelmingly predominant was a variety of red to brown line, check, curvilinear, and geometric designs on fine cream ware. Some fine gray sherds were encountered. Coarse cream wares were scarce. Numerous fragments of a thick coarse-tempered brown ware were noted in the heavily worked fields lying across the Inter-American Highway to the west of the church and friary. Only one sherd of polychrome was found; it was not in the apparent burial areas but was instead in an open and level field just to the east of the center. Small surface collections were made at three localities, one on the north and two on the east side of the center, but these have not been systematically analyzed.

Guzmán did not visit locations at Yanhuitlán but sent a young man to collect sherds from the foothills west of the center.[15] She reports red-on-cream to be extraordinarily abundant and to be the typical ware for Yanhuitlán. Occasional sherds of gray and plain cream wares were encountered. No other types appeared in her collection. I noted in 1963 that red-on-cream ware was in great abundance at a point just northwest of the small chapel of the *Señor* of Ayuxi on the northern extremity of the center; only a very few pieces of fine gray ware were mixed with the cream sherds. Collections made at other sites revealed considerably more variation, with cream and gray wares lying in more balanced distributions.

In 1963 several crudely excavated pits were noted in the foothills to the north and east of the center. These are normally associated with scattered cut stones and concentrations of large sherds, giving the impression of having been tombs or shrines. This is also the prevalent pat-

[15] Guzmán, "*Exploración arquelógica en la Mixteca Alta*," *AMN*, Vol. I (1934), 17–42.

Market day at Nochixtlán. Note the straw hats worn by Mixtecs; the manufacture of straw hats is a major industry of modern-day Nochixtlán.

A transaction at the market of Nochixtlán.

tern on the natural mound rising near the chapel of Ayuxi. Destructive erosion has cut through many of the hillside sites and deposits of sherds and stone line the banks of streams and arroyos on all sides of the center.

The natives of Yanhuitlán report continuing discovery and excavation of tombs and burials. These burials, they say, are accompanied by "little heads" of green stone, by polychrome, plain, and painted vessels, and by obsidian blades. Vestiges of structures apparent on the lower slopes of the surrounding hills are not impressive; but heavy concentrations of sherds suggest intensive utilization of these areas. No major architectural features were noted in the vicinity of the center, but traces of more remarkable architecture were in evidence on the higher slopes. Aerial photographs clearly reveal structures in these locations. Cerro Jasmín, west of Suchixtlán and north of Tiltepec, contains many obvious structural features, both large and small. Any comprehensive survey of the valley of Yanhuitlán-Nochixtlán should logically start at Yanhuitlán, which lies at the northern extremity of the valley.

YOLOMECATL (Location: 17° 28′ N. Lat.; 97° 54′ W. Long.): Tombs are said to have been found in the vicinity of Yolomecatl. Informants indicated in the spring of 1963 that structural remains, pottery, and greenstone figurines could be found in abundance on the surrounding hillsides and in the fields.

YUCUAÑE (Location: 17° 10′ N. Lat.; 97° 24′ W. Long.): Structures are also said to be in evidence here. This site is in the former district of Tlaxiaco.

The Record Summarized

Two radiocarbon samples from Monte Negro gave dates of 2680±200 and 2518±250.[16] Monte Negro is considered to be contemporary with, and related to, Monte Albán–I remains in the valley of Oaxaca and is therefore representative of the Mesoamerican Preclassic in the Mixteca Alta. The most notable point of nexus between Monte Albán–I and Monte Negro is in the ceramic complex. Regarding Monte Negro pottery, Caso states that it "is very closely connected with that of the first

[16] Libby, *Radiocarbon Dating*, 130.

period of Monte Albán."[17] Monte Albán–I materials have also been recovered in the regions around Coixtlahuaca, Nochixtlán, Huajuápan, and Tamazulapan, leading Bernal to comment: "I think all this shows that the whole area of the Mixteca Alta was occupied at one time by a culture close to that of Monte Albán I."[18]

Until recent years, there was a serious chronological gap between Monte Negro and the Monte Albán–III findings at Yucuñudahui. Cursory excavations at Huamelulpan, a mountaintop site on the road between Teposcolula and Tlaxiaco, have produced a ceramic complex which Paddock has related to Monte Albán–II of the valley of Oaxaca. Bernal indicates that the megalithic construction evident at Huamelulpan is very typical of Monte Albán–II. The gylphic inscriptions at Huamelulpan are also said to correspond to those assigned to the second period at Monte Albán. In regard to these two features, Huamelulpan is contemporaneous with Monte Albán–II, but, as Bernal points out, many additional data are required to make a firm tie between Monte Albán–II and similar manifestations in the Mixteca Alta. A potstand, a typical Monte Albán–II feature, was recovered in the unsystematic excavation at Cerro Jasmín, Tiltepec, in the valley of Nochixtlán. Bernal comments that this probably indicates a correlation with Monte Albán–II, but that the evidence is inconclusive.

The Mesoamerican early Classic in the Mixteca Alta is almost unknown. As of 1958[19] the existence of the early Classic depended on a single thin orange vessel of "undoubted Teothihuacán origin" that was discovered in the excavation of Yatachio.[20] The evidence for the later Classic is not much better. There is only Tomb 1 of Yucuñudahui, which appears to correlate with the middle part of Monte Albán–III chronologically and stylistically. The bar-and-dot system of writing found there is the same as that associated with Monte Albán, and a number of influences which are attributed to Teotihuacán are found at both sites. A radiocarbon sample from a roof beam of this tomb yielded a date of A.D. 292. The Mixtecs become known to us as a people around A.D. 700.

17 Caso, "The Mixtec and Zapotec Cultures: The Mixtecs," *BEO*, No. 22 (1962).

18 Bernal, "Archeology of the Mixteca," *BEO*, No. 7 (1958).

19 *Ibid.*, No. 7 (1958).

20 Paddock (ed.), "Excavations in the Mixteca Alta," *Mesoamerican Notes*, No. 3 (1953).

This information comes not from the archaeological record but from Caso's analyses of the historical codices. It is assumed for the present that Mixtec culture was fully in operation by that time. Whether much earlier archaeological manifestations are to be identified as Mixtec depends on future exploration.

The fourth period in the Mixteca Alta is the best known of all phases of pre-Conquest Mixtec cultural development. It is significant, however, that practically all of our knowledge of this period comes from Monte Albán, a site lying outside the Mixteca, and from historical sources. It is from Caso's excavation of Tomb 7 of Monte Albán that the most important archaeological knowledge of the Mixtecs comes.[21] Beyond the discovery of a late Mixtec complex in association with Spanish materials at Chachoapan and Bernal's excavations at Coixtlahuaca, there has been very little systematic investigation of the period within the Mixtec zone.

Tomb 7 was filled with hundreds of pieces of Mixtec-crafted gold, silver, copper, rock crystal, jade, alabaster, turquoise, obsidian, pearl, amber, and human and animal bones. While the chamber in which the burials and offerings were located was of Zapotec construction—it was common practice for the Mixtecs to re-use Zapotec tombs—the Mixtecs cleared the tomb and filled it with their own dead and with offerings of unmistakable Mixtec authorship. Mixtec mortuary goods at Monte Albán are clearly associated with ceramics found in the Mixteca Alta in such areas as Tilantongo, Tamazulapan, Coixtlahuaca, and Chachoapan and positively articulate with stylistic representations in the Mixtec pre-Conquest codices, all clearly forming a highly developed Mixtec complex. It was the Mixtec culture of this period that penetrated the valley of Oaxaca in late post-Classic times and is termed Monte Albán–V in the Caso-Bernal chronology.

Bernal's systematic excavation at Coixtlahuaca revealed a fifth and final phase in the development of pre-Hispanic Mixtec culture. The penetration of the Mixteca Alta by people carrying a complex of Mexican materials is indicated by the presence of an Aztec burial and post-

[21] Caso, "*Exploraciones en Monte Albán, temporada 1931–32*," *IPP*, No. 7 (1932); Caso, "Reading the Riddle of the Ancient Jewels," *Natural History*, Vol. XXXII (1932), 464–80; Caso, "Monte Albán, Richest Archeological Find in America," *The National Geographic Magazine*, Vol. LXII (1932), 487–512; Caso, "The Mixtec and Zapotec Cultures: The Mixtec," *BEO*, No. 22 (1962).

Tenayuca ceramics. Historical documentation supports the late arrival of the Mexicans in the Mixtec zone. Thus, separate Mixtec and Mexican complexes are represented in the final phase of development before the Spanish Conquest.

The present ordering of available data is most incomplete and provisional. It depends heavily upon abbreviated reports of limited excavations or hasty surveys. Difficulties in interpretation are compounded by the inconsistent terminology employed by the investigators and by my own lack of familiarity with the ceramic collections discussed in the various sources. No adequate understanding of the archaeological history of the Mixteca Alta can be achieved until systematic survey and excavation procedures are instituted within the area itself. There is great need for internal reconstruction that begins at the site level and moves gradually outward to larger cultural-geographical units such as zones and valleys. By logical progression we can then move on to a general consideration of the culture of the Mixteca Alta and the greater Mixteca and their existence within the context of Mesoamerica. As matters now stand, we have only a weak chronological outline and practically no conception of an over-all cultural configuration, or the diversity of related configurations, that characterized ancient life among the Mixtecs. Present knowledge of ancient Mixtec culture has depended very heavily on the rich cache of objects taken from Tomb 7, Monte Albán, analysis of handicrafts and works of art of scattered provenience, and the historical content of the picture manuscripts and Spanish chronicles. Archaeologists should now direct their efforts toward a definition of ancient Mixtec culture, its nature, configuration, distribution, and growth in all phases of development. This can be accomplished by a thoroughgoing program of excavation and survey and a consistent and systematic ordering of old and new data.

A Suggested Course of Action

While fairly good information exists on at least one Preclassic site in the Mixteca Alta, knowledge of this period needs further expansion. Neither the Archaic developments nor the transition from the Preclassic to the Classic are understood. In fact, none of the developmental transitions in the Mixtec area is known. The distribution, variation, and relationship among contemporary sites of all periods should be studied. Each period requires definition. Furthermore, to the extent allowed by archaeological method, we should endeavor to see the gradual changes as well as the less subtle periodic transitions which have been assigned, or will be assigned, to cultural development in the Mixteca Alta.

One of the more urgent needs in Mixtec archaeology is for work on sites that will contribute to a definition of Classic Period culture in the Mixteca and to a discovery of the origins of late Mixtec art styles, polychrome, and other ceramic traditions, and of the total cultural pattern. Practically nothing is known of the Classic Period, and every new excavation of sites pertaining to this period will either provide new data or assist in tying together the few loose pieces now in our possession. The Postclassic must be found, described, and defined from *within the area itself*. I think it safe to assume that an archaeologist might survey or excavate any site in the Mixteca Alta, Mixteca Baja, or Mixteca de la Costa without fear of duplicating earlier work. Bernal made this most clear in the following statement, which adequately describes the present situation:

> The Mixteca is one of the least known areas, archeologically speaking, in central Mexico. Why that is, I really don't know. It is not an outlying area or a difficult place to reach, yet after many years of investigation in Mexico very little is known about the Mixteca Alta, and almost nothing about the Mixteca Baja.[22]

As a general framework for future archaeological investigation in the Mixteca Alta, a suggested course of action is to divide the zone into several cultural-geographical provinces or components. There seems to be a general orientation of various groups of Mixtec peoples along the confines of valleys or adjoining valleys. One gains the impression that the degree of interaction among people sharing a valley, despite residence in separate communities, is far higher than among individuals occupying separate but perhaps adjacent valleys. The documentation of the sixteenth century conveys this impression, and it is reinforced by observation of present-day Mixtecs. The late Mixtec community-kingdom, which we will consider in detail, seems to have functioned

[22] Bernal, "Archeology of the Mixteca," *BEO*, No. 7 (1958).

in a similar fashion. Despite a gradual lessening of authority on the part of the post-Conquest caciques, valley limits tended also to delimit *cacicazgos.*

I believe that the division suggested below might be a useful guide to future research. It remains for archaeology to determine the accuracy of my impressions. Basing his conclusions mainly on historical materials, Bernal has said: "The separation between the valleys obliged each one of them to become a sort of little city-state, if you want to call it that; a sort of unit in itself, a very small unit."[23] He suggests further that these should not be grouped together:

> . . . they were a series of small independent cities, each under the rule of one dynasty. This is exactly the picture that is presented to us in the manuscripts. We see a number of ruling families, each reigning over one (or at certain moments, through marriage and small conquest, two or three) of these cities, in contrast to what we've seen in the Valley of Oaxaca where a single group rules the whole large area.

My only point of contention with Bernal is that I do not believe that the culture of the Mixteca Alta was ever characterized by life in "cities."

Below are listed what I conceive to be five major geocultural components for the Mixteca Alta during at least its later stages of development. Late cultural manifestations reflect a heterogeneity that is not apparent in earlier archaeological materials. This regional diversity may have begun late in the Classic Period while Monte Albán–III–B culture existed in the valley of Oaxaca.

Component 1—The Valley of Yanhuitlán-Nochixtlán: This section of the Mixteca Alta contains the communities and important archaeological zones of Yanhuitlán, Nochixtlán, and Chachoapan-Yucuita. There are in addition many other sites scattered the length and breadth of the valley from Jaltepec at its southeastern extremity to Soyaltepec on the northwestern periphery, and from Coyotepec and Amatlán on the north flank of the valley to Tecomatlán on the south. Notable remains are at Añañe, Suchixtlán, Tillo, Tiltepec, Soyaltepec, Yodocono, Sinaxtla, Amatlán, Jaltepetongo, San Pedro Cántaros, Quili-

[23] *Ibid.*, No. 7 (1958).

tongo, Etlatongo, and other locations. From the standpoint of systematic survey and excavation, these sites are nearly unknown. This valley probably contains the richest concentration of archaeological materials in all the Mixteca Alta, and all are accessible from the Inter-American Highway running through the valley. This component can ideally be studied as a manageable and integral cultural unit, itself divided into a number of subcomponents. Its constituent communities are and have been for many centuries in intimate contact, yet each community with its dependencies, I believe, has been a clearly definable and self-contained but changing unit.

COMPONENT 2—THE VALLEYS OF TEPOSCOLULA AND TAMAZULAPAN: The valley of Teposcolula is narrow and restricted. There are only two major communities within the valley itself, San Juan Teposcolula and San Pedro y San Pablo Teposcolula. The latter is the larger center and is the capital of the district of Teposcolula. San Miguel Tixa, Ixtapan, and Yolomecatl are other important centers that should be included in this component. These five communities seem to have been closely related in the sixteenth century. At that time there was also a high degree of interaction between Teposcolula and Tamazulapan. The ruling families were intimately related, and Teposcolula and Tamazulapan were combined under the same rulers for at least fifty years in the sixteenth century.[24] The *sujetos* of Teposcolula also extended well beyond the limits of the narrow but fertile valley. Again, the valleys of Tamazulapan and Teposcolula can be studied as separate intelligible units, but the probability of their historical interrelationship must be borne in mind and tested archaeologically. On the basis of historical documentation, it seems more logical to assume a close relationship between the valleys of Teposcolula and Tamazulapan rather than the relationship which Paddock postulates to have existed between the valleys of Tamazulapan and Coixtlahuaca.[25] The existence of Chocho-speaking people in the vicinity of Tejupan-Tamazulapan and Coixtlahuaca is, however, a point to be considered in Paddock's favor.

[24] AGN, *Tierras*, 26, exp. 4; AGN, *General de parte*, 1, fol. 200*v*.

[25] Paddock (ed), "Excavations in the Mixteca Alta," *Mesoamerican Notes*, No. 3 (1953).

Component 3—The Achiutla-Tilantongo-Mitlatongo-Teozacoalco Continuum: This is a difficult area to evaluate because it is not well known or described. I have not yet been able to conduct a survey or obtain aerial photographs of the component. I have visited only Tilantongo, but descriptions taken from the sources and from informants indicate that there are a number of communities in proximity to Tilantongo, Achiutla, Mitlatongo, and Teozacoalco that occupy geographical positions analogous to that of Tilantongo.

Tilantongo is quite different from any of the other municipalities visited in the Mixteca Alta. The center sits not in a valley but on a high promontory in the midst of rugged mountains and steep-sided valleys. For the Mixtecs who prefer to farm level terrain, there is very little arable land. Terracing has made available a few small plots that would otherwise not be farmed. Gradual slopes are sometimes cultivated, but steep inclines are avoided. Tilantongo was said to be a rich kingdom in the sixteenth century. To have been so, it would have been necessary to draw on a very large area indeed, for fertile plots must have been few and far between. The municipality of Tilantongo is today one of the largest such entities in the state of Oaxaca. Perhaps there is some coincidence between the modern administrative area and the ancient kingdom which was necessarily an extensive domain.

This component should be considered not as a valley complex, but instead as being comprised by a number of communities situated in a complex of high mountain ridges and peaks rising above narrow, steep-sided and irregular valleys. The component is characterized by radical changes in altitude and differs quite markedly from the other components of the Mixteca Alta, particularly Yanhuitlán-Nochixtlán and Tamazulapan-Teposcolula. It was in ancient times also an area that supported a much smaller population per square mile than any of the other components. The sixteenth-century census records leave little doubt of this. Limits of this component will have to be determined by extensive survey. My general impression is that it may extend from Achiutla in the north to Yolotepec in the south and that it would include such communities as Yucuañe, Diuxi, Tataltepec, Tamazola, Yutanduchi, and Sindihui.

COMPONENT 4—TLAXIACO: The modern villa of Tlaxiaco is surrounded by a number of unsurveyed and unexcavated archaeological sites. The valley occupied by Tlaxiaco itself contains many sites, all accessible from the district capital. Moving beyond the mountains which limit the valley, the District of Tlaxiaco comprises a large area and includes communities in both the Mixteca Alta and Baja. It is the most populous (75,000 to 100,000) of all the districts of the Mixteca, and people from many miles away continue to regard the *cabecera* of Tlaxiaco as an economic, political, and administrative center. The Mexican Instituto Nacional Indigenista has placed its main headquarters here, and regular patrons and vendors of the modern weekly market in Tlaxiaco come from as far away as Ocotepec, Chalcatongo, Putla, San Agustín Tlacotepec, and Atatlauhca.[26]

Again, little is known of the archaeological content of the Tlaxiaco Valley. Probably it can be studied as a unit, as has been suggested for other sections of the Mixteca Alta. Several of the closely allied subjects of Tlaxiaco in the sixteenth century were, however, located outside the valley. The community, as it will be defined in a later chapter, extended beyond the valley in the case of Tlaxiaco.[27] In the 1540's the population of Tlaxiaco community was an estimated 7,500 (based on 1,850 tribute payers), living in the center and thirty-one subject ranchos. The ranchos were located at distances amounting in many cases to three, five, and eight leagues from the center. The population thus distributed may have reached 18,000 (4,500 tribute payers) during the peak years of the 1560's,[28] but declined to some 6,700 (1,678 tribute payers) at the end of the sixteenth century.[29] Tlaxiaco also seems to have maintained a rather intimate relationship with such communities as Achiutla, Atoyaquillo, Cuquila, and Mixtepec, all outside the valley proper.[30] Archaeologists working here in the future should not only test the integrity of the valley as a comprehensible cultural-geographical unit but should also watch

26 Alejandro Marroquín, *La ciudad mercado*, 192–96.

27 PNE, I, 282–83.

28 Luis García Pimentel (ed.), *Relación de los Obispados de Tlaxcala, Michoacán, Oaxaca y otras lugares en el siglo XVI*.

29 ENE, XIII, 42.

30 AGN, *Tierras*, 44; *ibid.*, 2682, exp. 16.

for a probable close relationship of the unit to the expanded area delineated and to the Mixteca as a whole.

COMPONENT 5—COIXTLAHUACA: Except for Bernal's study of a site in Coixtlahuaca center, little is known of this probable center of gravity for the development of Mixtec culture. Coixtlahuaca sits in rather forbidding mountain country. Unlike Tilantongo, it is located in a very narrow valley on a stream bed. The valleys around Coixtlahuaca are restricted, dry, and largely unproductive. To the south of Coixtlahuaca toward Huatla, Apoala, and Sosola, the terrain is very rugged and sparsely inhabited. It would have been difficult indeed for a rich kingdom to have existed at Coixtlahuaca without depending on outside areas of production. Paddock has suggested a close relationship with the valley of Tamazulapan.[31] Historical documents show a higher degree of interaction with communities in the opposite direction, that is, toward Tepenene and as far away as Tlaxila. Coixtlahuaca is central to an extensive province. I believe this to have run largely east and north from the present *cabecera*. Bernal's work on the single location in Coixtlahuaca, however, shows a relationship to other Mixtec sites, particularly in the Nochixtlán and Teposcolula-Tamazulapan components. Paddock, after viewing three surface collections which I made in Yanhuitlán, said that the over-all complex was quite unlike that from Coixtlahuaca and much more closely related to materials from Huitzo in the valley of Etla. Thus there are many problems to be worked out in this component. The fact that the early Spanish chronicles and the Mexican tribute rolls hint strongly of a possible exalted political position for Coixtlahuaca over other communities in the Mixteca must be considered. While I do not believe that such a relationship actually existed, it is a logical problem for further investigation. It is an unfortunate circumstance that, despite the undoubted importance of Coixtlahuaca, the legal documentation of the sixteenth century seems largely to neglect the community. It also is apparently outside the scope of the known Mixtec codices, but prominent in the Codex Mendoza. There seems to be little conclusive evidence throughout the sixteenth century for joining the Coixtlahuaca ruling

[31] Paddock (ed.), "Excavations in the Mixteca Alta," *Mesoamerican Notes*, No. 3 (1953).

Codex Nuttall

family to the other Mixtec rulers. An uncle of Don Gabriel de Guzmán, cacique of Yanhuitlán from 1558 to 1591, is listed as having been cacique of Coixtlahuaca.[32] There are, of course, a number of references in the chronicles to a great king of Coixtlahuaca. In time, the Coixtlahuaca ruling family will probably be firmly woven into the extensive pattern of kinship in the Mixteca. Regardless of these matters, there is nothing to impede recognition of this area as an identifiable component of Mixtec culture.

Concluding Remarks

Admittedly much of what has been stated here is speculative and is based on very little archaeological data. There is only one obvious remedy. The idea that these valleys, valley systems, or continuums constituted intelligible cultural entities (and the nature of their interrelationship) must be tested by the intensive and extensive methods of archaeology. Some extremely important sites outside the Mixteca Alta in the vicinity of such centers as Putla, Juxtlahuaca, Tecomastlahuaca, Tecomavaca, and Huajuápan in the Mixteca Baja, Huitzo in the valley of Etla, and Tututepec and Pinotepa in the coastal portion of the Mixteca have not been considered. These undoubtedly share many features with sites in the Alta from an early date.

The degree of individuality and interrelationship of the five suggested components of the Mixteca Alta can be determined best through a systematic program of research that features flexible concepts and

32 AGN, *Civil*, 516.

methods of investigation. There must be intensive study at particular sites accompanied by broad areal surveys and spot excavations. Any site in the Mixteca will provide a good starting point for a new era of research. The most effective course of action toward construction of a history of Mixtec culture, it seems to me, lies in a method of internal comparison which utilizes either the suggested scheme of cultural and geographical components or a comparable framework that divides the Mixteca Alta into several definable and meaningful units of study.[33]

[33] As this book was going to press, the author, assisted by three students, conducted an archaeological survey of more than one hundred sites in the valley of Nochixtlán-Yanhuitlán. This survey constitutes the initial phase of the projected research outlined in the foregoing chapter. The very substantial data collected in the course of the survey will contribute to the solution of many of the problems posed here, particularly in regards to the many sites found in and around Yanhuitlán, Nochixtlán, Etlatongo, Chachoapan, Yucuita, and other communities of the valley. Unfortunately, these data or significant inferences derived from the data cannot be included in the present work. Nothing discovered in the course of the survey would dictate radical revision of statements made here; on the contrary, the survey uncovered added support for most of the contentions regarding pre-Hispanic and early Colonial cultural development and changing patterns of native settlement. Of course, much additional analysis of collected materials and additional research must be completed before precise statements can be made, and the author intends to make these findings available as soon as possible.

3.
Continuity and Change: The Documentary Record

THE PRE-HISPANIC MIXTECS held a unique position among native Americans in that they attempted to record significant aspects of their history in polychromatic picture-manuscripts. No group in the New World ever invented a phonetic writing system. Thus the Mixtecs with their pictographic system went as far as any other group in developing an adequate system for the graphic representation of concepts. These manuscripts, the Mixtec codices, have been the subject of studies by Caso,[1] Smith,[2] Clark,[3] Dark,[4] and others. Caso long ago demonstrated the historical potentialities of the codices and has since succeeded in identifying a number of the important persons, places, and events in Mixtec history. Through his intensive studies he has been able to construct a chronological sequence of native rulers and their families that extends from the Colonial Period back to A.D. 692. This basic research has prepared the way for full-scale interpretation of the meaning content of these documents, a task requiring a knowledge

[1] Alfonso Caso, "*El mapa de Teozacoalco*," *Cuadernos americanos*, Vol. VIII, pp. 145–81; Caso, "*Explicación del reverso del Codex Vindobonensis*," *Memoria de el Colegio Nacional*, Vol. V (1952) 9–46; Alfonso Caso, "*Lienzo de Yolotepec*," *ibid.*, Vol. III (1957), 41–55; Caso, *Interpretation of the Codex Bodley 2858*; Caso, "The Historical Value of the Mixtec Codices," *BEO*, No. 16 (1960); Alfonso Caso, "*Los Señores de Yanhuitlán*," in *Actas y Memorias 35° congreso internacional de americanistas*, I (Mexico, 1962), 437–48.

[2] Smith, "The Codex Colombino: A Document of the South Coast of Oaxaca," *Tlalocan*, Vol. IV (1963), 276–88.

[3] J. C. Clark, *The Story of "Eight Deer" in Codex Colombino.*

[4] Philip Dark, *Mixtec Ethnohistory*; Dark, "Speculations on the Course of Mixtec History Prior to the Conquest," *BEO*, No. 10 (1958).

of the Mixtec language, use of written documents of the Colonial Period, and ethnological and archaeological research.

While Caso, Miss Smith, and others are proceeding toward increasingly more sophisticated interpretations of the codices, we must at present depend very heavily upon materials that were recorded in various formal chronicles and in administrative and legal documentation during the early Colonial epoch.

The more important published accounts are the chronicles of Burgoa,[5] Herrera,[6] Oviedo,[7] Tezozomoc,[8] Durán,[9] Torquemada,[10] Zorita,[11] the so-called *Anales de Cuauhtitlán*,[12] and *Códice Ramírez*.[13] Even these sources provide scant information on the subject of Mixtec history. Burgoa and Herrera offer the best accounts. The later eighteenth-century efforts of Veytia[14] and Clavijero[15] do little to elucidate or expand upon the work of their predecessors. Supplementing the classic chronicles, we also have the published texts of the *Relaciónes* of 1580[16] for several parts of the Mixteca, which record data concerning both pre- and post-Conquest times. Jiménez Moreno,[17] Dahlgren,[18] Iturribarría,[19] and Gay[20] have utilized some of these writings with varying success.

On the basis of the colonial sources mentioned above, the skilled interpretations of Caso, Jiménez Moreno, and Dahlgren, and unpublished documentation from Spanish and Mexican archives, I will reconstruct a partial history of life in the Mixteca Alta in pre-Spanish times

5 Burgoa, *Geográfica descripción*.

6 Herrera, *Historia*, déc. 3, lib. 3, cap. 13.

7 Gonzalo F. de Oviedo y Valdés, *Historia general y natural de las Indias*.

8 H. A. Tezozomoc, *Crónica mexicana*.

9 Fray Diego Durán, *Historia de las Indias de Nueva España y Islas de Tierra Firme* (cited hereafter as Durán, *Historia*).

10 Fray Juan de Torquemada, *Los veinte i un libros rituales y monarchía indiana*.

11 Alonso de Zorita, *Breve relación de los señores de la Nueva España*.

12 *Códice Chimalpopoca: Anales de Cuauhtitlan y Leyenda de los soles*.

13 J. F. Ramírez, *Códice Ramírez*.

14 Mariano Veytia, *Historia antigua de México*.

15 Fray Francisco J. Clavijero, *Historia antigua de México*.

16 PNE, IV; RMEH, I, II.

17 Jiménez Moreno, *Vocabulario*; JM and MH.

18 Dahlgren, *La Mixteca*.

19 J. F. Iturribarría, *Oaxaca en la historia*.

20 Gay, *Historia de Oaxaca*.

and the sixteenth century. In order to deal as specifically as possible with events, individuals, and historical developments and trends, much of the account will be focused on one important community, Yanhuitlán, located in the heart of the Mixteca Alta.

Legendary Origins

Burgoa[21] presents three versions of the origins of the Mixtec people that were current in Early Colonial times. One tradition stated that the Mixtec sprang from two great trees on the banks of a river near Apoala, high in the mountainous and sparsely populated eastern Mixteca Alta. Nourished by the waters of the stream, the trees grew and produced the first native rulers (caciques), both male and female. From these first rulers grew a population that in time spread over the vast Mixtec kingdom.

A legend, which Burgoa borrowed from Torquemada,[22] was that the first people who settled the mountainous regions of the Mixteca came from the west as had the people who occupied the Valley of Mexico. They settled in the rugged and easily defended mountains around Sosola, also in the eastern Mixteca Alta. Isolated in their mountain retreat, they persevered, multiplied in number, and developed their way of life. Gradually they migrated into the other regions of the Mixteca taking with them their language and culture.

The third tradition, the one favored by Burgoa, holds that the first lords and captains, guided by their gods, penetrated the mountains of the Mixteca from the northwest, presumably after the Mexicans had come into the Valley of Mexico from that direction. They settled in a high and remote plain in the mountains between Achiutla and Tilantongo in the west-central portion of the Mixteca Alta. The plain, bordered by high mountain peaks, was rimmed with impregnable fortifications, and round about for six leagues the region was protected by armed garrisons. Here in the canyons and on the mountainsides they built a great system of level agricultural terraces "like stairways" upon which they grew their crops and which were still in use in Burgoa's time. Burgoa remarked that the appearance of the isolated and fortified moun-

21 Burgoa, *Geográfica descripción*, I, 274–76.

22 Torquemada, *Los veinte i un libros rituales y monarchía indiana.*

tain retreat gave the impression that the first lords and captains were persecuted by a greater power and sought a site that they could defend. They retired behind their defenses where they valiantly fought off intruders. Because they could no longer hunt and gather in the unfriendly countryside, they converted craggy mountains into arable plots, raised crops, and persisted to become the people encountered by the Spaniards at the Conquest. At that time Tilantongo was a great political center, and Achiutla was an important religious place.

Burgoa's account of the origins and early history of the Mixtec peoples furnishes little information concerning developments prior to the hundred years preceding the Spanish Conquest. Caso's studies of the codices have provided considerable data concerning the genealogy of native lords of the Mixteca over a period of some eight hundred years before the coming of the Spaniards, but the pictorial resources have not yet yielded sufficient information for a full history of the pre-Hispanic epoch. Nevertheless, as we move toward the Spanish Conquest, other sources record sufficient data to permit a reasonably detailed discussion of the history of several communities.

We turn now to a general account of Mixtec history in the sixteenth century. As indicated above, this chapter will give emphasis to a single community, Yanhuitlán, an important center in the Mixteca Alta on the eve of the Spanish Conquest and throughout the sixteenth century. By way of introducing our account of Yanhuitlán history, the following section will describe the modern scene in the Yanhuitlán area.

Modern Yanhuitlán

The *cabecera* of the present municipality of Yanhuitlán is located at the northwestern extremity of the valley of Nochixtlán. It is situated at Kilometer 428 of the Mexico City–Oaxaca highway at an elevation of approximately seven thousand feet. Mountain ranges shelter the community on the west, north, and east. Except for the great church and friary which dominate the modern landscape, there is little to suggest the former importance of Yanhuitlán. The half-ruined sixteenth-century religious structure, now a national monument, testifies to past greatness. The unprotected and overgrazed mountain slopes enclosing the community on three sides stand starkly eroded and, for the most part, are

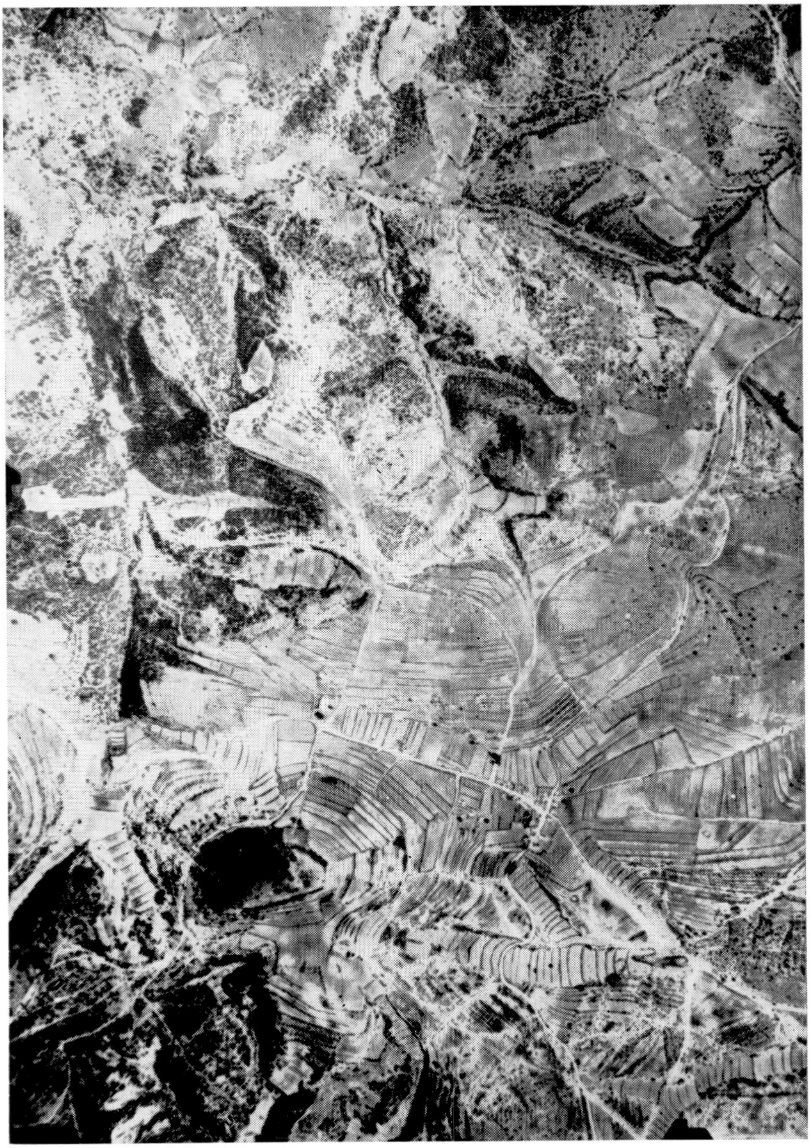

Pre-Hispanic agricultural terraces still in use at Nochixtlán.

MEXICANA AEROFOTO

The weekly market in Tilantongo.

incapable of sustaining plant life. Patches of potentially productive land on the slopes are not cultivated, but are used instead to pasture the numerous herds of goats in the area. There is a lack of the terracing systems that make productive the upper reaches of arroyos in other towns of the valley of Nochixtlán. The natives are content to work the more-or-less level terrain of the municipality, and even parts of this lie fallow. Erosion has claimed huge pieces of formerly arable land. Streams, which annually cut away more terrain, pass on the western and eastern borders of the present center and converge some two kilometers southeast of the populated zone. While there is a tendency for the winters to be dry, the summers usually provide sufficient rain to sustain agriculture. Even in the late spring before the rains the area retains considerable green cover and sufficient pasturage for livestock.

Farming and herding continue to furnish the economic basis of life in Yanhuitlán, but such an existence becomes progressively more tenuous each year. If the community is to persist, improved farming methods and more adequate water and run-off control must be instituted. A number of individuals work outside the community in other parts of Oaxaca or the nation but return regularly or periodically and retain close social ties. Local industries engaged in matwork, ceramic manufacture, and food processing do little more than satisfy local needs and bring little outside capital into the community. The weekly market in Yanhuitlán is small and unimportant.

Presently there are only about one thousand people in the entire municipality of Yanhuitlán which includes the *cabecera* and seven outlying ranchos. This is the same community that during the post-Conquest sixteenth century was the commercial center of the "second richest valley of the whole Bishopric of Oaxaca."[23] Cuilapa in the valley of Oaxaca and Yanhuitlán were the largest towns in Oaxaca around 1570, with each containing about twenty thousand inhabitants. We cannot yet speak with certainty of the pre-Conquest era, but it is probable that Yanhuitlán reached the peak of its economic development during the middle and late sixteenth century. It never again attained the eminence it enjoyed during that period.

[23] Woodrow Borah, "Silk Raising in Colonial Mexico," *Ibero-Americana*, No. 20 (1943), 24.

The Pre-Conquest Period

The importance of Yanhuitlán and its position in Mixtecan or Mesoamerican history prior to the coming of the Spaniards are not clearly discernible. It is known that Yanhuitlán was one of the principal towns within the province of Coixtlahuaca which paid tribute to the lords of the Culhua-Mexica Empire.[24] Coixtlahuaca Province with its component communities is listed on page 21 of the *Matrícula de los Tributos* and is represented on folio 43*r* of the *Codex Mendoza.* Varied tribute was exacted from the province, including periodic assessments of decorated mantles, loincloths, blouses, skirts, warrior's costumes, *chalchihuites* (precious green stones), quetzal feathers, cochineal, and gold dust.[25] There is evidence that subject towns in the area also provided quantities of food, slaves, and possibly some military assistance to the empire.

The *Anales de Cuauhtitlán* indicates that Coixtlahuaca fell to the armies of the Mexican Empire during the reign of Montezuma I, who ruled over Mexico-Tenochtitlán from 1440 to 1468.[26] The *Anales de Tlatelolco* gives 5 Tochtli (1458) as the year of the overthrow of what may then have been the chief "city-state" of the Mixteca Alta.[27] The conquest of Coixtlahuaca receives prominent mention in several of the chronicles made by Mexicans and individuals who utilized Mexicans as informants.

Herrera mentions Montezuma I in connection with the conquest of the Mixteca Alta and of Yanhuitlán in particular. He states that Yanhuitlán was ruled in that time by a powerful cacique, Lord Three Monkey, who had led a strong resistance against the Mexicans. This ruler was said to have been treacherously murdered, and with his death all of his kingdom was subjected to Montezuma.[28]

Two primary sources, the *Anales de Cuauhtitlán* and Clavijero's *Historia,* speak of the original conquest of Yanhuitlán, and both at-

[24] Robert H. Barlow, "The Extent of the Empire of the Culhua Mexica," *Ibero-Americana,* No. 28 (1949), 113–15.

[25] *Ibid.,* No. 28 (1949), 116–17.

[26] *Códice Chimalpopoca,* 66–67.

[27] Heinrich Berlin and Robert H. Barlow, *Anales de Tlatelolco y Códice de Tlatelolco,* 56–57.

[28] Herrera, *Historia,* déc. 3, lib. 3, cap. 13.

tribute the victory to Tizoc.[29] The *Anales de Cuauhtitlán* lists the years of Tizoc's reign as 2 Calli (1481) to 7 Tochtli (1486), and Clavijero indicates that Yanhuitlán fell in the fifth year of this ruler's short tenure, or in 1486.[30] Another reference to Yanhuitlán is made in the great chronicle of Durán. Mexican merchants had been mistreated by the Yanhuitecos, says this account, and in order to remedy the rebellious situation in the area, a punitive expedition was dispatched by Montezuma II.[31] Both Durán and Tezozomoc indicate that the towns of Yanhuitlán and Zozollan (modern Sosola) were attacked as part of the same foray. It is said that prisoners were taken at Yanhuitlán and the town sacked, but that the armies found Zozollan to be deserted.[32] The *Anales de Cuauhtitlan* also mentions that in 1 Tochtli (1506) Zozollan was depopulated in one day "*con pestilencia*."[33] More probably, the population of Zozollan, aware of the arrival of the Mexicans in the region, had fled into the surrounding countryside. The Cuauhtitlán chronicle assigns Yanhuitlán to both Tizoc and Montezuma II; this latter probably indicates a punitive "reconquest" of the same town.[34] The prisoners captured at Yanhuitlán in 1506 were taken to Tenochtitlán where, it is said, one thousand Yanhuitecos perished as sacrificial victims in the feast of Tlacaxipehualistli.[35]

Colonial sources contain a number of references to a single ruler of the entire Mixteca in pre-Conquest times. Unfortunately these references record only scant data concerning the existence of such a supreme ruler of the Mixtecs.

Names that appear as possible candidates for this position are Calci,[36] Francisco Calci,[37] Four Monkey,[38] Nahui Caltzin, or his son Matlacce

29 *Códice Chimalpopoca,* 67; Clavijero, *Historia antigua de México,* I, 306.

30 *Códice Chimalpopoca,* 57; Clavijero, *Historia antigua de México,* I, 306.

31 Durán, *Historia,* I, 454.

32 *Ibid.,* I, 454–56; Tezozomoc, *Crónica mexicana,* 447–51.

33 *Códice Chimalpopoca,* 59.

34 *Ibid.,* 67.

35 Durán, *Historia,* I, 454–56.

36 AGN, *Inquisición,* 37, exp. 7.

37 France V. Scholes and Eleanor Adams, *Cartas del Licenciado Jerónimo Valderrama y otros documentos sobre su visita al gobierno de Nueva España* (cited hereafter as Scholes and Adams, *Cartas*), 297–302.

38 Herrera, *Historia,* déc. 3, lib. 3, cap. 13.

Iztli,[39] and all are associated with Yanhuitlán. Nahui Calztin was "king and cacique of all the Mixteca Alta and Baja." A person named "Ya qui si," or "Ya que se," was also mentioned as the powerful leader of Yanhuitlán just before the Conquest,[40] and a cacique named "Nine House" is prominent in the *Códice de Yanhuitlán*.[41]

Torquemada states that Ce Tecpatl was ruler of the province of Coixtlahuaca when it was overcome by the Mexicans.[42] The Mexicans are said to have sacrificed Ce Tecpatl and replaced him with his brother Cuzcacuahqui. Veytia mentions that around the middle of the fifteenth century Atonalztin was ruler of Coixtlahuaca. This ruler ordered interference with the passage of the Mexicans through the Mixteca. A Mexican army was sent to engage in battle with the ruler of Coixtlahuaca, who had apparently entered into an alliance with forces from Huejotzingo and Tlaxcala. The allies were able to defeat the Mexicans. Later, when the armies of Huejotzingo and Tlaxcala had gone to Tlaxiaco to engage in battle there with the Mexicans, the Mexicans returned and easily defeated the unassisted armies of Coixtlahuaca. Shortly thereafter other areas of the Mixteca fell to the Mexicans.[43] The *Matrícula de Tributos* and the *Codex Mendoza* suggest that Coixtlahuaca had been an important and powerful center, and its ruler might have been the chief of an extensive domain.

The lord of Tilantongo, Yaq Cuaa (Nahui "Mazazi" in Nahuatl), was said to have ruled an extensive area that included Teposcolula, Tlaxiaco, Atoyaquillo, and Teozacoalco. This would imply an extensive domain, but the additional statement that Yaq Cuaa was "one of the *mayores señores* of the province" obviously suggests that there were other "great lords" in the Mixteca, and that the lord of Tilantongo was not necessarily in a position of supreme authority over other rulers. Likewise, the statement that the pueblos "in ancient times were divided among brothers" may indicate that the ruler of Tilantongo had at best only limited authority even over Teposcolula, Tlaxiaco, Atoyaquillo, and Teozacoalco.[44]

Witnesses giving testimony in the Zapotec town of Miahutlán in

[39] AGI, *Escribanía de Cámara*, 162. [40] *Ibid.*, 162. [41] JM and MH.

[42] Torquemada, *Los veinte i un libros rituales y monarchía indiana*, lib. 2, cap. 75.

[43] Veytia, *Historia antigua México*, II, 217–18. [44] PNE, IV, 73.

1547 stated that there had been separate supreme lords in Mexico, in the Mixteca, and in Tehuantepec.[45] These were the three great leaders of central and southern Mexico on the eve of the Conquest. The case for Mexico is clear. We also know that the Zapotec king had moved from the capital of Teozapotlán (Zaachila) to Tehuantepec before the Spanish Conquest. The statement on Tehuantepec probably concerns the Zapotec king. The Mixtec ruler could have been one of the individuals mentioned above in association with Yanhuitlán, Tilantongo, or Coixtlahuaca, or, given the location of the 1547 hearing, the lord of Tututepec, the extensive Mixtec tribute kingdom of the Mixteca de la Costa.

In addition to the statements recorded above, no substantial evidence indicating the existence of a supreme Mixtec monarch with broad authority over an extensive Mixtec-speaking domain has yet come to light. One or more great leaders may have emerged in the pre-Conquest history of the Mixtec peoples. Who they were and the extent and nature of their authority and power are still very much in doubt. We know of one culture hero, Eight Deer (born 1011 A.D.) who ruled Tilantongo from 1030 to 1063.[46] He has a prominent place in the picture manuscripts, which depict his birth, movements, conquests, marriages, family ties, and his death by sacrifice. Other such figures probably appeared, and it would seem that at the time of the Spanish Conquest there were prominent and powerful figures with seats at Yanhuitlán, Tilantongo, Coixtlahuaca, and Tututepec. It is probable, however, that their effective political influence did not extend beyond their personal territorial domains. In all of the sixteenth-century documentation, we find little to preclude the existence, on the eve of Conquest, of a number of separate and autonomous kingdoms. There is evidence that two or more of these kingdoms were sometimes temporarily united under a single ruler (*señor*). But these multiple estates could have also been divided among the ruler's children. This appears to be what actually occurred in the case of Tilantongo, Teposcolula, Tamazola, Tlaxiaco, and Atoyaquillo about the time of the Spanish Conquest.

[45] AGI, *Patronato*, 181, *ramo*. 11.

[46] Clark, *The Story of "Eight Deer" in Codex Colombino*; Caso, *Interpretation of the Codex Bodley 2858*, 37–42; Smith, "The Codex Colombino: A Document of the South Coast of Oaxaca," *Tlalocan*, Vol. IV (1963), 276–88.

Unfortunately, little more can be said at the present time regarding the general pre-Conquest history of Yanhuitlán. The political relationship which existed between Yanhuitlán and the surrounding communities of Coixtlahuaca, Tilantongo, Teposcolula, or Tlaxiaco requires additional study. Despite mention of supreme rulers for "all the Mixteca," not one document has revealed that there was any political or hierarchical tie between Yanhuitlán and the other great communities of the Mixteca Alta. The relationship seems to have been one of kinship and mutual respect, but with each ruler enjoying a high degree of political independence. One document states that Yanhuitlán was one of the "greatest towns of the Mixteca Alta and Baja" but reveals no political nexus with or subservience to any other community. Yanhuitlán was said to have had its own supreme rulers since at least 1000 A.D.[47] The documentary evidence implies that Yanhuitlán was an autonomous community-kingdom for some five hundred years before the Conquest. That it was under the tributary domination of the Mexican Empire for a number of years is not denied. This relationship, however, does not seem to have seriously affected the composition of the community or the right of the rulers to govern and exercise their authority in the traditional manner.

The Spanish Conquest

In November, 1519, Cortés and his soldiers had occupied Tenochtitlán, the Mexican capital, and had taken its ruler, Montezuma II, into their custody. Taking advantage of this situation, Cortés called upon the Mexican sovereign to provide information concerning the source of the tribute, especially gold, paid to him and the associated rulers of the tripartite confederacy by the several towns and provinces under their dominion. In response Montezuma provided maps and native guides for expeditions of Spanish soldiers, which, during succeeding months, were dispatched to several parts of the Mexican domain. One of these expeditions, led by Gonzalo de Umbría, penetrated the Mixteca Alta, visited the districts of Sosola and Tamazulapan, and brought back favorable reports concerning the settlements and resources of these areas.[48]

[47] AGI, *Escribanía de Cámara*, 162.

[48] Francisco López de Gómara, *Historia de la conquista de México*, cap. 90; Oviedo y

Códice de Yanhuitlán

If we may assume that native trails followed the approximate route of the modern highway through natural passes, it seems likely that Umbría proceeded through or close to Yanhuitlán. Any other route from Tamazulapan to Sosola would have required an arduous march through rugged country to the east of the valley of Yanhuitlán-Nochixtlán. This expedition was the first contact of the Spaniards with the Mixteca Alta, and the meeting was apparently peaceful and without remarkable incident.

In July, 1520, the Spaniards had been forced to withdraw from Tenochtitlán. Later in the summer, headquarters were established at Segura de la Frontera (Tepeaca) in the southeastern district of the present state of Puebla, and it was from here that Cortés directed his Second Letter of Relation, dated October 30, 1520, to the Emperor Charles V.[49] At the time this account was written, Spanish soldiers had captured the city of Itzocan (Izúcar de Matamoros), an important place south of Cholula and the Volcano Popocatepetl. Cortés' letter and other

Valdés, *Historia general y natural de las Indias*, lib. 33, cap. 9; Herrera, *Historia*, déc. 3, lib. 9, cap. 1.

[49] Pascual de Gayangos, *Cartas y relaciones de Hernán Cortés al Emperador Carlos V*, 51–157.

sources mention a visit to Itzocan of emissaries from eight of the towns under the province of Coixtlahuaca, who offered allegiance to the Spanish Crown and indicated that four other towns of the same area would soon do likewise.[50] It seems likely that Yanhuitlán was represented in this group.

While the Spanish forces were engaged in the final siege of Tenochtitlán, unrest among the tribes of Oaxaca resulted in attacks on the Spaniards in the Tepeaca area, and this rebellious attitude prevailed for several months after the final defeat of the Mexicans.[51] Specific evidence is lacking as to participation of towns of the Coixtlahuaca and Yanhuitlán districts in these attacks. In 1522, Pedro de Alvarado was dispatched with a sizeable force to restore order and to impose effective Spanish dominion in southern Mexico. An engagement was fought at Itzcuintepec with an entrenched force of Mixtecs.[52] This force probably included Mixtec-speaking groups residing in and around the valley of Oaxaca. With the winning of this battle and a later encounter at Tututepec, Alvarado achieved the final pacification of the Mixtec and Zapotec peoples. By the end of 1522 or early 1523, Spanish suzerainty over the Mixteca Alta had been asserted and never again was seriously challenged.

Population

Four major studies of population trends in the Mixteca Alta during the sixteenth century have appeared in recent years. These investigations were made by Cook and Simpson,[53] Borah and Cook,[54] and Cook and Borah.[55] The findings of these investigators are based upon statistical analysis and manipulation of a mass of data derived from sixteenth-century census, or tribute, records.

[50] López de Gómara, *Historia de la conquista de México*, I, 330; Bernal Díaz del Castillo, *Historia verdadera de la conquista de la Nueva España*, cap. 132.

[51] Herrera, *Historia*, déc. 3, lib. 3, cap. 9.

[52] *Ibid.*, déc. 3, lib. 3, cap. 9.

[53] S. F. Cook and L. B. Simpson, "The Population of Central Mexico in the Sixteenth Century," *Ibero-Americana*, No. 31 (1948).

[54] Woodrow Borah and S. F. Cook, "The Population of Central Mexico in 1548," *Ibero-Americana*, No. 43 (1960).

[55] S. F. Cook and Woodrow Borah, "The Indian Population of Central Mexico, 1531–1610," *Ibero-Americana*, No. 44 (1960); S. F. Cook and Woodrow Borah, "The Aboriginal Population of Central Mexico on the Eve of the Spanish Conquest," *Ibero-Americana*, No. 45 (1963).

In 1948, Cook and Simpson arrived at an estimate of 11,000,000 for the total population of Central Mexico, defined as the area extending from the Isthmus of Tehuantepec northwestward to Sinaloa and Zacatecas, at the time of the Spanish Conquest. In 1960, Cook and Borah increased the estimate to 16,800,000. More recently they have postulated a population of 25,000,000 in 1519–20, the highest estimate of population on the eve of the Conquest that has ever been made.

All of the Cook-Simpson-Borah computations indicate a drastic decline in population in the sixteenth century after 1519. Epidemic diseases of Old World origin, for which the Indians did not have an acquired immunity, swept through Mexico, the worst occurring in the 1540's and 1570's. These are regarded as major causes of the rapid decline of the native population, but there were doubtless other contributory factors which may have reflected a disorientation of indigenous society and economy resulting from the Spanish Conquest.

Cook and Simpson postulated a population of approximately 6,400,000 for the 1540's, contrasting with their estimate of 11,000,000 for 1519. Cook and Borah have a figure of 6,300,000 for 1548, a correction from their previous estimate of 7,800,000.[56] For the years 1565–70 Cook and Simpson made a population estimate of 4,400,000 and for 1597 an estimate of 2,500,000. For these same periods, 1565–70 and the late 1590's, Cook and Borah arrive at populations of 2,650,000 and 1,370,000 respectively.[57] All of the Cook-Simpson-Borah computations indicate a steady decline of Indian population from 1519 to the end of the sixteenth century. This view has been challenged by Kubler, who accepts a sharp reduction in population prior to 1550 but believes that the decades of 1550–70 period were characterized by an increase, followed again by a decline during the years 1570–1600.[58] In support of this thesis Kubler argues that the widespread construction of massive churches and friaries

[56] Borah and Cook, "The Population of Central Mexico in 1548," *Ibero-Americana*, No. 43 (1960).

[57] Cook and Borah, "The Indian Population of Central Mexico, 1531–1610," *Ibero-Americana*, No. 44 (1960).

[58] George Kubler, "Population Movements in Mexico, 1520–1600," *The Hispanic American Historical Review*, Vol. XXII (1942), 606–43; George Kubler, Review of "The Population of Central Mexico in the Sixteenth Century" (by S. F. Cook and L. B. Simpson), *The Hispanic American Historical Review*, Vol. XXVIII (1948), 556–59.

during the decades 1550–70 could not have been carried out during a period of continuing decrease in the supply of Indian labor.

In any case, there can be no doubt that a drastic reduction in the Indian population of Central Mexico occurred between 1519–20 and 1600. Estimates of the rate or percentage of this decrease will depend in large measure upon the total population postulated for the eve of Spanish Conquest. The Cook-Borah estimates of 25,000,000 for 1519–20 and 1,370,000 for the late 1590's would indicate a decline of 90 per cent![59]

I am not prepared at present to accept or refute the Cook-Simpson-Borah population estimates since I believe, that any sound approach to the problem of population trends in the sixteenth century must, in the first instance, take into account all available data for specific areas and local conditions which may possibly reflect some deviation from postulated norms and trends for larger geographical regions, that is, to proceed step by step from particulars to general conclusions. Such a procedure would conform with the views already expressed, i.e., study of the development of Mixtec culture should begin with an investigation of its several geographical-cultural components. It is recognized that the Cook-Simpson-Borah computations of total population at stated periods in the sixteenth century are founded on a mass of detailed data for individual communities in the sixteenth century, but on the basis of extensive archival investigations, I believe the data for the Mixteca Alta utilized in the Cook-Simpson-Borah studies, while adequate for their broad and comprehensive studies, are incomplete and have not been related to changing economic trends in this part of Central Mexico.

Elsewhere I estimated the population of the state of Oaxaca as approximately 1,500,000 at the time of Spanish Conquest.[60] Of these, 500,000 were probably Mixtec-speakers.[61] Unfortunately, at present I can-

59 Cook and Borah, "The Aboriginal Population of Central Mexico on the Eve of the Spanish Conquest," *Ibero-Americana*, No. 45 (1963).

60 Ronald Spores, "The Zapotec and Mixtec at Spanish Contact," in Wauchope and Willey, *Handbook*, III.

61 Professor Borah, in a letter to the author, indicated that according to yet unpublished studies by Borah and Cook, the pre-Hispanic population of the Mixteca Alta alone was 700,000. This seems a high figure, given the total ecological picture in the Mixteca Alta, but could conceivably be closer to reality than my own figure of 500,000 for all three Mixtec areas combined. My figure of 500,000 was based on estimates derived from the earlier Cook-Simpson-Borah studies. Until the data is published, I choose to hold to the more conservative estimate.

not be more precise with reference to total population figures for the Mixteca. Additional comment on general demography must await the completion of research now in progress.

The Population Profile for Yanhuitlan

The population profile for sixteenth-century Yanhuitlán is not necessarily typical.[62] Although there seems to be considerable variation among the Mixtec communities (Appendix D–4), at least one other major community of the Mixteca Alta, Tlaxiaco, had a population profile that closely resembled that of Yanhuitlán.

The earliest population report for Yanhuitlán and its subsidiary settlements, dated about 1548, states that the community comprised 12,207 individuals of age three years and above. This figure doubtless reflects a decline in population since 1519–20. For the period 1565–70 it is reported that the population of Yanhuitlán community included 6000 *tributarios*, or tributary units. The same report indicates that for the bishopric of Oaxaca, this figure was equaled only by Cuilapa.[63]

Any estimate of population based on the number of *tributarios* must take into account methods of tribute assessment. During the decade of the 1560's a married Indian (*casado*) with wife and family was counted as one tributary unit (*tributario*). Widowed persons, male and female (*viudos* and *viudas*), and unmarried adults of both sexes (*solteros* and *solteras*), not subject to parental control, were counted as half tributary units. Thus the number of *tributarios* listed in the contemporary records for a given community did not represent the total number of persons subject to tribute, but instead a computation of *casados* as full tributary units and of *viudos*, *viudas*, *solteros*, and *solteras* as half tributary units. For example, in a community with 400 *casados* and 100 *viudos*, *viudas*, *solteros*, and *solteras*, the total number of *tributarios* for assessment purposes would be 450. In each community a certain number of persons

62 Professor Borah, who read an early version of this volume, disagreed on several points in the author's discussion of population trends in the Mixteca Alta. Indeed, the documents pertaining to sixteenth-century population are subject to varying interpretations. Recognizing that my deductions are subject to challenge, I have chosen to adhere to my current interpretation.

63 García Pimentel (ed.), *Relación de los Obispados de Tlaxcala, Michoacán, Oaxaca y otros lugares en el siglo XVI*, 64.

were exempted from the payment of tribute. These usually included caciques and some members of the local native nobility, village officials during their terms of office, the aged and infirm, and a considerable number of *mayeques* (serfs or tenant farmers) attached to the lands of the caciques and nobility.

In order to estimate total community population on the basis of a recorded number of *tributarios*, it is necessary to use some multiplying factor that will take into account the minor children of *casados*, *viudos*, and *viudas* and the number of persons exempt from tribute. Students of colonial Mexican history have utilized multiplying factors ranging from three to five. I believe it's best, however, to adopt a compromise factor of four, which was also used by Cook and Simpson.[64] On this basis the figure of 6,000 *tributarios* for the Yanhuitlán community in 1565–70 would represent a total population of 24,000. Cook and Borah postulate a population of 17,160 for the same period, but this figure is based on a multiplying factor of 3.3 and different reports regarding the number of *tributarios* for the community.[65]

Whether a population figure of 24,000 for Yanhuitlán in 1565–70 is accepted, or the lower estimate of Cook and Borah,[66] it is apparent that these figures indicate an increase of total population during the decades 1550–70 as compared with the figure cited above for the 1540's. This increase, it should be noted, does not conform to the Cook-Simpson-Borah hypothesis of an unbroken population decline in Central Mexico subsequent to 1519–20. On the other hand, it may lend support to Kubler's thesis of an upswing in population during the decades of the 1550–70 period. But again needing emphasis is the point of view that I gave earlier: conditions in local areas may have deviated from general norms and trends. A population increase for the Yanhuitlán community from the 1540's to 1570 could very well reflect improved economic conditions in this area. At least they were concomitant features in community development. Later in this chapter I will present evidence to support my contention that in the twenty-five-year period after 1550 the Yanhuit-

64 Cook and Simpson, "The Population of Central Mexico in the Sixteenth Century," *Ibero-Americana*, No. 31 (1948).

65 Cook and Borah, "The Indian Population of Central Mexico, 1531–1610," *Ibero-Americana*, No. 44 (1960).

66 *Ibid.*, No. 44 (1960).

lán community enjoyed a greater degree of economic prosperity than in earlier or later Colonial times.

During the last decades of the sixteenth century (1570–1600) the population of Yanhuitlán, like that of other areas of Central Mexico and the Mixteca Alta, was characterized by sharp decline. The epidemics of the 1570's, which ravaged many areas of Mexico, were probably a major factor, but a recession in native economy may have been a contributing cause. Population estimates for the years 1595–1600 range from 9,460 to 12,000.[67]

The population profile for Yanhuitlán during the sixteenth century is one of probable stability from 1500 to the 1530's. Disease and other factors brought about a decline prior to 1548. The next two decades show a population increase. This was accompanied by a decided upswing in the total economy of the community. How much of this population growth was internal and how much was the result of immigration remains in doubt. In the wake of new epidemics in the 1570's and a declining economy, the population again decreased before the end of the century. By 1600 the number of people in Yanhuitlán had been reduced by some 50 per cent from the peak years of 1565–70, and was somewhat less than in 1548.

Encomienda and Tribute

The encomienda system, a major feature of Spanish colonial administration in the New World, dates from A.D. 1499 when the first grants of encomienda, or *repartimiento*, were made by Christopher Columbus in the Island of Española. With expansion of Spanish enterprise in the West Indies the system was subsequently extended to Puerto Rico and Cuba. It has now been established that encomienda was not a method of land grants to Spanish conquerors and colonists.[68] In the West Indies grants of encomienda authorized the recipients of these favors (encomenderos) to enjoy the labor services of a stated number of Indians.[69]

[67] *Ibid.*, No. 44 (1960), 84; AGN, *Tierras*, 2941, exp. 28; Burgoa, *Geográfica descripción*, I, 286.

[68] Silvio Zavala, *Estudios indianos*, 207–305.

[69] Silvio Zavala, *La encomienda indiana*, 1–35.

In Mexico the first grants of encomienda were made by Cortés in 1522 as a means of rewarding the services of his soldiers in the conquest of the Aztec confederacy. After the removal of Cortés as governor of the colony in 1526, his successors continued to grant encomiendas to Spanish conquerors and colonists. Although Emperor Charles V and his advisers expressed opposition to the extension of the encomienda system to Mexico, they soon found it expedient to condone it as a basic feature of colonial society and economy. In 1536 the Crown also recognized the right of succession to encomienda grants for a second life, that is, for a legitimate heir of an original holder to inherit the encomienda grant. Six years later, in the famous New Laws of 1542, the Crown promulgated a reform program, which prohibited new grants of encomienda and denied, contrary to the Law of Succession of 1536, the inheritance of encomiendas for a second life. The New Laws of 1542 provoked such serious opposition in Mexico and also in Peru that the Crown found it expedient to revoke these restrictive provisions, with the result that the encomienda henceforth was a permanent feature of Spanish colonial administration and society. Subsequent legislation permitted, in the case of Mexico, inheritance of encomienda grants for a third and fourth life.[70]

As indicated above, grants of encomienda in the West Indies called for the labor services of a stated number of Indians. In Mexico the Spaniards found a native society characterized by a system of tribute based upon periodic payments of tribute to the Aztec rulers by Indians residing in subject communities. Consequently, Cortés and his governmental successors in Mexico made encomienda grants on the basis of pueblo units, or portions thereof, and authorized the payment of both tribute and labor service to encomenderos. During the 1520's there was no limitation on the amount of tribute and labor an encomendero might require of a town assigned to him. This resulted in serious abuses, and colonial officials, in accordance with royal directives, established, during the decades 1530–50, fixed periodic quotas of both tribute and labor. The tribute schedules called for payment in items of local production. In gold-producing areas the schedules often called for the payment of stated quantities of gold dust, strips or disks of gold, or gold jewelry; in other

[70] *Ibid.*, 1–35; L. B. Simpson, *The Encomienda in New Spain.*

places the schedules called for stipulated payment of stated quantities of cotton textiles (mantas, huipiles, *camisas*, etc.) and/or a variety of agricultural produce. Labor service might include the cultivation of fields of maize and/or wheat, and the assignment of Indians as household servants.[71] A royal order of 1549 decreed the elimination of labor as part of the encomienda obligation. Henceforth the encomienda became a system of tribute only for the benefit of conquerors and colonists.[72]

After 1550 new schedules were formulated which eliminated labor service and progressively simplified the tribute payment. By 1565 standard annual payments in cash (*pesos de oro común*, or silver pesos) and maize had been established in most of Central Mexico. This assessment was based on the number of tributary units (*tributarios*) and the payment by each unit of one peso and a half *fanega* of maize (about eight-tenths of a bushel). Thus the encomendero of a town with five hundred *tributarios* would receive an annual tribute of ₱500 and 250 *fanegas* of maize. In many towns an additional assessment was also made of one or two *reales* (one-eighth or one-fourth of a peso) per *tributario* for local community expenses. These additional payments were often designated as *sobras*. These assessments were used into the later decades of the sixteenth century, when new assessments had to be made because of population decline.

When labor service was eliminated as part of the encomienda obligation, it became necessary to adopt other means for providing Spanish colonists with an adequate supply of native workers. This was effected in large measure by a system of forced Indian labor for wages, generally designated as *repartimiento*. In Mexico it was also known as *cuatequil*, in Peru, as *mita*. The operation of this system of forced labor in Mexico has been described by Simpson[73] and by Zavala and Castelo.[74]

Numerous grants of encomienda in the Mixteca Alta were made by Cortés and his successors during the 1520's. In 1523 the community of Yanhuitlán was granted by Cortés to his cousin Francisco de las Casas.

[71] F. González de Cossío (ed.), *El libro de las tasaciones de los pueblos de la Nueva España.*

[72] Zavala, *La encomienda indiana*; Simpson, *The Encomienda in New Spain.*

[73] L. B. Simpson, "Studies in the Administration of the Indians in New Spain, III," *Ibero-Americana*, No. 13 (1938).

[74] Silvio Zavala and M. Castelo, *Fuentes para la historia del trabajo en Nueva España.*

This mark of favor to a relative, who had not participated in the successful campaign against the Aztec, illustrates the nepotism practiced by Cortés as governor of the colony. Subsequently, Las Casas achieved fame, perhaps notoriety is a better word, by his sea expedition in 1524 to Honduras, where he participated in the murder of Cristóbal de Olid, whom Cortés had sent to occupy that region. In 1529, when Las Casas was absent in Spain, the First Audiencia of Mexico revoked the grant and placed it under direct royal jurisdiction. Las Casas promptly instituted legal proceedings to regain his title to the encomienda,[75] which was confirmed in 1537.[76] In later years he was frequently at odds with the Church and offered little assistance to the Dominicans in their first efforts to establish a friary in Yanhuitlán.

At the death of Francisco in 1546, his son Gonzalo succeeded to the title of encomendero. The younger Las Casas was at first little better disposed toward the clergy than had been his father. Before 1550, however, a reconciliation appears to have taken place, for Gonzalo is known to have lent his support to the ambitious building program of the Dominicans beginning about that time. In 1580, Gonzalo departed for Spain and left the encomienda in care of his son Francisco II. The latter succeeded to the encomienda at the death of his father in 1591. Francisco remained as encomendero until at least 1622.[77]

The first record of a tribute assessment for Yanhuitlán dates from the early 1530's, when the town was temporarily a possession of the Crown and paid tribute to the royal treasury of New Spain. The schedule called for the payment of ₱120 in gold dust (*oro en polvo*) every eighty days, or ₱540 each year. In addition, the Indians had to provide food for the local royal officials (*corregidor and alguacil*).[78] This modest requirement, in terms of the large population of the community, may possibly be explained by the fact that during this early period assessments for Crown towns were often less harsh than those of encomienda towns.

Revision of the tribute schedule occurred—perhaps more than once—

[75] AGI, *Justicia*, 117, num. 1.

[76] JM and MH, 13.

[77] *Ibid.*, 15.

[78] González de Cossío (ed.), *El libro de las tasaciones de los pueblos de la Nueva España*, 58.

Teposcolula. Note the cabecera *and pre-Hispanic structures on the surrounding hills.*

MEXICANA AEROFOTO

The Mixtecs of Tilantongo bear the symbolic body of Christ to Calvario *in observance of Good Friday.*

after Francisco de las Casas regained his title in 1537, but the next date for which we have specific record of a schedule for Yanhuitlán is 1548, two years after the death of Francisco. This assessment required tribute and service as follows:

1. An annual payment of 782.5 in gold dust. Each year the Indians were also required to cultivate and harvest for their encomendero a field planted with fifteen *fanegas* of maize.

2. Daily payments of four turkeys, two European hens, a small jar of honey, four hundred cacao beans, two cakes of beeswax, a bundle of sandlewood (*tea*), six hundred maize tortillas, thirty eggs, a half *fanega* of maize, one plate each of salt, chili, and tomatoes, ten loads (*cargas*) of firewood, and ten loads of fodder.[79] The daily assessment also included the service of ten Indians in the pueblo.[80]

The 1548 schedule represents a much heavier burden on the Indians than that of the early 1530's. The annual gold payment had been increased by 45 per cent. It would be difficult to calculate a money value for the daily payments in kind, but the Indians must have regarded them as onerous and also as a veritable nuisance. In addition to the payments in gold and in kind, they were now required to give labor service in the pueblo and to cultivate a field of wheat.

In order to draw a comparison between contributions made by Yanhuitlán and other communities in the Mixteca Alta during the 1540's some additional assessments are given. These are taken from the *Suma de Visitas*,[81] the *Libro de las Tasaciónes*, and from AGI, *Patronato*, leg. 182, *ramo*. 40.

1. Nochixtlan. Assessment of September 7, 1546:₱40 in gold dust every sixty days (₱240 annually) "and no more."

2. Teposcolula. Assessment of July 20, 1546:₱50 in gold dust every twenty days (₱900 annually), the value of which is to be paid in cash (*reales*), plus a field of wheat of three *fanegas* to the planting.

3. Teozacoalco. Assessment of July 30, 1545: one peso in gold dust daily, plus small amounts of chili and beans.

[79] A *carga* in these cases probably was the amount of wood or fodder an individual Indian could carry on his back.

[80] PNE, I, 131.

[81] PNE, I.

Specific assessments of tribute for Yanhuitlán after 1548 are not available. The *Libro de las Tasaciónes*, which lists assessments at different periods for many towns in New Spain, contains only one entry, that of the 1530's, for Yanhuitlán. Post–1548 schedules for Yanhuitlán doubtless reflected trends in other areas, viz., elimination of labor service and gradual standardization of the tribute payments, culminating in the 1560's in an annual assessment of one silver peso and a half *fanega* of maize for each *tributario*.

As noted in the section on population, Yanhuitlán and its subject settlements had six thousand *tributarios* in 1565–70. On the basis of the standardized tribute assessment of the 1560's, the encomendero of Yanhuitlán would have received ₱6,000 in cash and three thousand *fanegas* of maize worth ₱1,500,[82] or a total of ₱7,500 annually. Although some Spaniards in New Spain enjoyed larger encomienda revenues, the encomendero of Yanhuitlán in 1565–70 received a handsome annual income from this source on little or no investment. By comparison, the *corregidores* of Indian towns received salaries ranging from ₱200 to ₱600. Gonzalo de las Casas would have been obliged, of course, to make fairly substantial payments in support of the missionary friars resident in Yanhuitlán and for his share (one-third according to colonial law) of the cost of building the massive church and friary then under construction. But his encomienda revenue must have been augmented by income from other sources, such as the flourishing silk industry in which he probably had considerable interest.

Of course it was economically advantageous to the encomendero for his community to have as large a population as possible, for this was the basis upon which tribute was assessed and collected. As already noted, the population of Yanhuitlán declined by some 50 per cent between 1570 and 1600. As the population dwindled, so did the revenue of the encomienda. With a declining population, the Indians were quick to complain of their inability to meet tribute assessments, and the necessary adjustments were made by the Spanish officials. It must have been of great concern to Gonzalo de las Casas and his son Francisco to watch their main source of income decline steadily and drastically. A document

[82] Based on Woodrow Borah and S. F. Cook, "Price Trends of Some Basic Commodities in Central Mexico, 1531–1570," *Ibero-Americana*, No. 40 (1958).

of 1596 records the number of *tributarios* as 2,475.[83] The gross encomienda income would at that time have amounted to only ₱3,862.5, or about one-half of what it had been in the peak years of 1565–70.

Economic Enterprise

The money economy of Yanhuitlán in the sixteenth century was basically dependent upon three industries. Because of ample water and fertile lands, it was possible to conduct extensive general agriculture throughout the valley of Yanhuitlán and on the terraced hillsides of its perimeters. There was continued cultivation of the pre-Conquest crops of beans, maize, chili, and squash, but new crops and new industries were introduced with considerable success by the Europeans. Cereal grains were very important additions to the agricultural complex. The principal sources of income, however, were silk, cochineal, and sheep.

Some time after 1531, Hernando Cortés, who had experimented with sericulture in other parts of the New World, gave to María de Aguilar, his cousin and the wife of Francisco de las Casas, some seed worms. These silkworms produced about one pound of eggs, and from this began the great Mixtecan silk industry of which Yanhuitlán became the principal center.[84] This fact takes on added significance when it is known that the Mixteca Alta, according to evidence provided by Borah, was the most important silk producing area of New Spain.[85] From the 1530's to 1580, the period of the great silk boom, the entire valley of Yanhuitlán and the Mixteca Alta were devoted to silk culture. Mixtecan silk became known in Europe, and although silk production declined in the rest of New Spain after 1555, it remained of the utmost importance in Yanhuitlán until near the end of the sixteenth century.[86]

Before 1580 the annual output of "clean well-prepared raw silk" in the Mixteca Alta was twenty thousand pounds.[87] Much of the success of the silk venture, of course, is attributable to the Dominican friars, among them Domingo de Santa María and Francisco Marín, who instructed the Indians and fostered sericulture throughout the region.[88] Silk was of

[83] AGN, *Tierras*, 2941, exp. 28.

[84] Borah, "Silk Raising in Colonial Mexico," *Ibero-Americano*, No. 20 (1943), 24–25.

[85] *Ibid.*, No. 20 (1943), 24.

[86] *Ibid.*, No. 20 (1943), 26–31.

[87] *Ibid.*, No. 20 (1943), 87.

[88] *Ibid.*, No. 20 (1943), 25.

such great importance and interest that the second encomendero of Yanhuitlán, Gonzalo de las Casas, wrote an extensive treatise on silk raising, the first of its kind in the Spanish language. It was printed in 1581 under the title *Arte para Criar Seda.*[89]

By 1580 sericulture in Nochixtlán and Yanhuitlán had become the main "cash producing industry."[90] With the advent of the 1590's, however, annual silk production in the Mixteca had fallen to fifteen hundred pounds and was steadily declining. The Mixteca Alta had ceased to be the great center of sericulture. Despite viceregal attempts to revive the industry in 1605, and at later times, silk was never again to play a vital part in the economy of Yanhuitlán or of the Mixteca Alta.[91] The exhaustion of the labor supply through the great plague of 1575–85, competition from the China trade, and the excessive demands of the clergy and civil officials contributed to the demise of the industry, and with its termination the Mixteca was deprived of its most important economic asset.[92] Silk, probably more than any other single enterprise, had brought to Yanhuitlán a level of prosperity that would not again be attained.

Silver was the leading export of New Spain in 1600. Ranking next to silver, according to Raymond Lee, was cochineal.[93] By the end of the sixteenth century some 250,000 to 300,000 pounds of *grana* (dried cochineal) valued at ₱500,000 to ₱600,000 moved annually through Veracruz en route to European clothmakers.[94] A native Mexican dye had in the span of eighty years become "one of the most important New World exports to the Old World."

The *Codex Mendoza* shows that the Culhua-Mexica Empire required yearly a total of eighty-five *talegas* (bags) of cochineal from its tributaries. Of this amount twenty bags came from the Cuilapa area of Oaxaca, and twenty bags came from other Zapotec towns. The remaining forty-five bags came from the Mixteca Alta. The Tlaxiaco-Achiutla area produced five bags, and the twelve towns of the province of

[89] *Ibid.*, No. 20 (1943), 51–52.

[90] *Ibid.*, No. 20 (1943), 31.

[91] *Ibid.*, No. 20 (1943), 87.

[92] *Ibid.*, No. 20 (1943), 94.

[93] Raymond Lee, "Cochineal Production and Trade in New Spain to 1600," *The Americas*, Vol. IV (1948), 462.

[94] *Ibid.*, Vol. IV (1948), 472.

Coixtlahuaca were required to supply forty bags annually.[95] According to this document, the Mixteca Alta was the principal supplier of this dyestuff.

During the sixteenth century at least three towns of the Mixteca Alta continued to figure prominently in the raising of the tiny insect *Coccus cacti*, or *Dactylopius coccus*, of which some seventy thousand were required to produce a dried pound of *grana*. These towns were Tamazulapan, Nochixtlán, and Yanhuitlán.[96] Gonzalo Gómez de Cervantes, writing at the close of the sixteenth century, mentions the Mixteca Alta as an important *grana* center and states that the Spaniards had greatly increased pre-Conquest production.[97] Unfortunately, the exact figures on *grana* raising for Yanhuitlán cannot be ascertained through presently available sources. It can be assumed, however, that the care and raising of the microscopic dye-producing insects continued to play a major role in contributing to the prosperity of Yanhuitlán in the sixteenth century.

Of lesser importance than silk and cochineal to Yanhuitlán's economy was sheep raising (actually both sheep and goats). By a royal cedula of 1551 the Indians were permitted to raise livestock.[98] Under this cedula, Indians, after obtaining the required permit, were allowed to raise any stock animal that was being raised by the Spaniards. Contrary to Burgoa's statement in the early seventeenth century that all manner of European livestock was in evidence around Yanhuitlán,[99] herding in the Mixteca Alta was directed primarily toward sheep.

Miranda indicated that there were, in all, some 300,000 sheep in the Mixteca, and that of sixty-one registered flocks, forty-four were in the Mixteca Alta and seven in the Baja.[100] It is estimated that there were well over 200,000 sheep in the Alta late in the 1500's. The principal centers were Coixtlahuaca, Nochixtlán, Tejupan, Teposcolula, Tlaxiaco, and Yanhuitlán.

95 *Ibid.*, Vol. IV (1948), 452.

96 *Ibid.*, Vol. IV (1948), 451, 464.

97 Gonzalo Gómez de Cervantes, *La vida económica y social de Nueva España al finalizar el siglo XVI*, 164.

98 *Recopilación de leyes de los Reynos de las Indias*, lib. 6, tít. 1, ley. 22.

99 Burgoa, *Geográfica descripción*, I, 286.

100 José Miranda, "*Orígenes de la ganadería en la Mixteca*," *Miscellanea, Paul Rivet octogenario dictata*, 794–95.

Although livestock raising was permitted after 1551, it was only rarely that concessions were granted to Mixtecans for the raising of *ganado mayor* (cattle and horses). For this class of animals Miranda could locate only two licenses, both for horses, which had been granted for the Mixteca Alta. Rights to own and raise livestock were generally denied to commoner Indians until very late in the sixteenth century, and then only limited concessions were allowed.[101] For the most part, livestock raising in the Mixteca Alta was beneficial almost exclusively to the cacique and to the indigenous nobility. Any communal benefit which might have been derived through tribute relief, remarks Miranda, was counteracted by injury to fields through destruction and impoverishment of tillable lands by erosion, the inevitable sequel to "the irrational and immoderate raising of sheep."[102]

The Church

The missionary program in the Mixtec and Zapotec areas of New Spain was carried on mainly by members of the Dominican Order. The first Dominicans, a group of twelve friars, arrived on the North American continent in 1526. Death soon claimed five, and four others left the colony of New Spain within a short time. In 1528 twenty-four new missionaries arrived, and with these reinforcements the Order was able to embark upon a wide-ranging missionary effort in central and southern Mexico. The Dominican corps of missionaries was steadily enlarged by new contingents which arrived in 1535 and later years, and also by the admission of new members who took their vows in Mexico. By the mid-1500's the Dominicans were the second largest missionary group—second only to the Franciscans—in New Spain. Before 1535 the Dominicans in Mexico had been subject to the jurisdiction of the province of Santa Cruz with headquarters in Española. As a result of representations made by Fray Domingo de Betanzos, a member of the first group that arrived in 1526, the General Chapter of the Dominican Order authorized the creation of a separate province of New Spain, the province of Santiago de México. Betanzos was elected as the first provincial at a meeting of the provincial chapter held in Mexico City in 1535. The

[101] *Ibid.*, 787.
[102] *Ibid.*, 796.

Códice de Yanhuitlán

province of Santiago exercised jurisdiction over all of the Dominican establishments in Mexico until 1592, when a separate province, the province of San Hipólito, was created for the Oaxaca area.[103]

The first Dominican missionaries entered the Mixtec and Zapotec areas of Oaxaca in 1529–30. The colonial chronicles relate that these pioneers were Fray Gonzalo Lucero and Fray Bernardino de Minaya.

103 Fray Agustín Dávila Padilla, *Historia de la fundación y discurso de la Provincia de Santiago de México.*

According to Burgoa, Fray Gonzalo engaged in missionary effort throughout the Mixteca, whereas Fray Bernardino was principally occupied with the construction of a church and friary in the town of Antequera (modern Oaxaca de Juárez).[104] It would appear, however, on the basis of data recorded in the inquisitorial processes of 1544–45, that it was Fray Bernardino who established the first mission in Yanhuitlán, and that during his short term of service there (1529–30) he baptized some of the Indian leaders, including Don Juan and Don Francisco, later identified as governors of the town, and Don Domingo, who later served as cacique-regent of the community.[105]

Apparently within a year (probably in 1530) this mission was abandoned, and missionary effort at Yanhuitlán and at other towns in the Mixteca Alta was not resumed until after the establishment of the independent Dominican Province of Santiago in 1535.[106] After 1535, however, the Dominicans carried on an active missionary program throughout both the Mixtec and Zapotec areas and gained such a preponderant influence in church affairs in these regions that Licenciado Jerónimo Valderrama, visitor-general of New Spain, asserted in a letter addressed to the king in 1564 that the Dominicans, rather than Bishop Bernardo de Albuquerque, constituted the real controlling force in the diocese of Oaxaca.[107]

The Dominicans resumed their missionary work in Yanhuitlán in 1535 or 1536. During the succeeding five years, a convent, or friary, was established, and the contemporary documents record the names of several friars who served there as missionaries. Of these, the most distinguished was Fray Domingo de Santa María, author of a grammar of the Mixtec language, who resided in Yanhuitlán during the year 1540–41, and subsequently held office twice as provincial of the Dominican Province of Santiago.[108]

During these early years (1535–36 to 1541), the Dominicans took active measures to combat and eradicate the continuing practice of native religion in Yanhuitlán, especially by prominent Indian officials of the

[104] Burgoa, *Geográfica descripción*, I, 42, 52.

[105] AGN, *Inquisición*, 37; JM and MH, 21, 37–47.

[106] *Ibid.*, 21.

[107] Scholes and Adams, *Cartas*, 297–302.

[108] JM and MH, 22.

pueblo. It is apparent, however, that in these activities and in other phases of their missionary effort, they encountered some opposition from Francisco de las Casas, the encomendero of the pueblo. Because of the hostility of the Indian officials and the encomendero, the Dominican provincial, Fray Pedro Delgado, instructed Father Santa María in 1541 to transfer his friary from Yanhuitlán to Teposcolula.[109]

From 1541 to 1546–47 the mission at Yanhuitlán was administered by secular clergy.[110] It was during this same period that Don Francisco and Don Juan, governors of the pueblo, and Don Domingo, the acting cacique, were subjected to inquisitorial process on the charges of the continuing practice of native religion. The records of these cases, preserved in the Inquisition section of the Archivo General de la Nación, México, provide the basis for a very interesting chapter in Yanhuitlán history. Much of this material will be presented later.

The Dominicans returned to Yanhuitlán in 1546–47 and had permanent charge of the mission thereafter. Coinciding with the return of the Dominicans was the succession of Gonzalo de las Casas to the title of encomendero, and it appears that Gonzalo eventually gave more active and positive support to the missionary program. During the years following 1547, the Dominicans established such a wide measure of influence in local affairs that a Spanish resident of Yanhuitlán, Alonso Caballero, was prompted to send a lengthy complaint concerning their activities to the visitor-general of New Spain, Licenciado Valderrama. This document, dated 1563, describes the Dominicans as the directing force in community affairs and accuses them of using their position for economic exploitation of the Indians. Some of the charges made by Caballero were that the Dominicans were forcing the Indians to work long hours in the stone quarries for little or no pay, assessing fines for missing Mass or fiestas, carrying on monopolies in certain commodities, charging excessive prices for goods and services, and conspiring with the caciques to exploit the Indians.[111]

The Dominican foundation at Yanhuitlán was a place of great missionary activity from 1550 onward. It served a large population and

109 Jiménez Moreno, *Vocabulario*; JM and MH.

110 *Ibid.*, 22.

111 Scholes and Adams, *Cartas*, 297–302.

Codex Nuttall

ranked high among the great convents of the colonial period. During the last half of the sixteenth century the importance of the foundation is illustrated by the fact that general chapter meetings of the province of Santiago were held there in 1558, 1570, and 1591.

Around 1550 the construction of the massive church and friary, which today dominate the landscape at Yanhuitlán, was initiated. This monumental example of sixteenth-century church architecture, in the opinion of Kubler, cannot antedate 1550 and was, in all probability, begun in the year 1550.[112] Construction continued for about twenty-five years, and Burgoa writes that the project required the services of more than six thousand Indians, working in shifts of six hundred, to carry stone, water, and lime, in addition to a considerable staff of skilled workers and artisans.[113] It is evident that the building of the structure placed a heavy burden on the labor force and natural resources of the area. Indeed, it was in part such exploitation of native labor that prompted Alonso Caballero to make his criticism of the Dominican Order in Yanhuitlán.

Contrary to common belief, the convent was not built on an ancient pyramidal structure. The huge platform, although it may conceal lesser pre-Conquest structures, was put down under the direction of the

[112] George Kubler, *Mexican Architecture of the Sixteenth Century*, II, 390.
[113] Burgoa, *Geográfica descripción*, I, 291–92.

friars.[114] Burgoa implies that the base was a creation of the friars, and he speaks of the problems involved in its construction.[115] The entire edifice was completed around 1580 after the introduction, in the later stages of building, of an Italian architect by Gonzalo de las Casas. The Italian and the great religious artist, Andrés de Concha, applied the finishing touches to the masterpiece.[116] Despite the ravages suffered during the Wars of Mexican Independence and the recent revolution, when the church was employed as a fortress, much of its majestic beauty has been preserved to the present day.

114 Kubler, *Mexican Architecture of the Sixteenth Century*, II, 390.

115 Burgoa, *Geográfica descripción*, I, 292.

116 Kubler, *Mexican Architecture of the Sixteenth Century*, II, 535; Burgoa, *Geográfica descripción*, I, 293.

4. The Mixtec Community in Transition

DURING THE PRE-HISPANIC era the population of the Mixteca Alta was concentrated in a number of dispersed, nonurban communities. Typically, the Mixtec community was composed of four major components: a relatively compact civic and commercial center; one or more outlying hamlets; a ceremonial precinct; and farming and collecting lands. This loosely nucleated entity constituted the catalyst for the formation of Mixtec culture and served as the guide to its development during the centuries preceding the Spanish Conquest. The initial section of the present chapter is devoted to consideration of the nature and composition of the Mixtec community as it appeared prior to the arrival of the Spaniards,[1] and a later section will

[1] The present interpretation is based largely upon sixteenth-century historical documentation and suffers from a lack of detailed archaeological verification. The Mixtec region has not yet been subjected to extensive archaeological survey of the type conducted by Sanders in the Mexican highlands (William T. Sanders, "The Central Mexican Symbiotic Region," in Willey, *Prehistoric Settlement Patterns in the New World*) and in the Maya region (William T. Sanders, *Prehistoric Ceramics and Settlement Patterns in Quintana Roo, Mexico*), by Willey in the Belize Valley of British Honduras (Gordon R. Willey, *et al.*, *Prehistoric Maya Settlements in the Belize Valley*), by Bullard in the Petén (W. R. Bullard, "The Maya Settlement Pattern in Northeastern Petén, Guatemala," *American Antiquity*, Vol. XXV), by Willey in the Viru Valley of Peru (Gordon R. Willey, *Prehistoric Settlement Patterns in the Viru Valley, Peru*, BAE *Bulletin No. 155*), or by Adams in the Diyala Plain of Iran (Robert M. Adams, *Land Behind Baghdad*). Offered in the present chapter are inferences based on sixteenth-century sources, available archaeological reports, and impressions drawn from air photography and cursory survey of much of the area by automobile and on foot. A detailed settlement-pattern survey planned by the author for the near future will most probably result in some revision of the model presented herein.

be devoted to demonstrating what happened to the community after foreign influences began to penetrate the area.

Prior to consideration of the major components of the community and their variations, a description of Mixtec dwellings would be worthwhile. According to early written accounts, Mixtec dwellings were small cell-like units with flat roofs, lacking windows, and facing onto an open patio or courtyard.[2] The houses were constructed of adobe, worked stone, lime mortar, wooden beams, and planking. Packed earth or adobe served as flooring material. Structures of this general type appear in the picture manuscripts and are reported in archaeological context in Coixtlahuaca.[3] Wood, mud, and thatch appear to have been utilized for dwelling construction in certain areas where it was possible to take advantage of readily available materials, and more substantial building materials were not easily obtainable.[4] Ceremonial structures, although normally raised on platforms or somehow distinguished from other buildings, seem to have utilized the same materials and general plan of construction as dwellings.[5] The ruler's house in Yanhuitlán, for example, was credited with having a number of patios and many rooms, elaborately furnished and decorated, but the basic materials, the plan of the rooms, and the general architecture did not depart radically from conventional patterns. While more substantial evidence of pre-Hispanic domestic architecture must await future archaeological investigation, it is possible to discuss the major components of the community in detail.

The Pre-Hispanic Community

The Center: The concentrated civic and commercial center was composed of dwellings, commercial buildings, some kind of market plaza, and other structures (Fig. 2, No. 1). Centers were usually located on level or gently sloping ground lying at the margin between steep mountain slopes and relatively level valley farm lands. The center was divided into wards, or barrios, from two to fifteen in number. Some of

2 PNE, IV, 56, 77, 81, 86.

3 Bernal, "*Exploraciones en Coixtlahuaca, Oaxaca,*" *Revista mexicana de estudios antropológicos*, Vol. X (1948), 75–77.

4 PNE, IV, 64; Dahlgren, *La Mixteca*, 134.

5 Herrera, *Historia*, déc. 3, lib. 3, cap. 12; AGN, *Tierras*, 400, exp. 1.

the wards were occupied by families devoted to the service of the community ruler; others were taken over by free commoners who were farmers, merchants, or artisans; also residing in the center were the hereditary ruler and his family and members of the local nobility. There is at present no good evidence that the Mixtec barrios constituted discrete kinship or corporate property-holding units of the type reported for other areas of Mexico.[6] The documents make frequent mention of barrios as residential and political units but make no reference to kinship as an organizing factor.

The community of Tejupan consisted of a center without dependencies. The center was divided into barrios, and each was governed by a noble appointed by the ruler-cacique.[7] A similar division of the center into precincts, each supervised by members of the nobility, was the pattern in Yanhuitlán,[8] where there were more than twenty barrios, and at Tecomastlahuaca just northwest of Tlaxiaco in the Mixteca Baja.[9] The Teposcolula center was also divided into barrios, but little is presently known about the actual composition of this community. Yanhuitlán and Tecomastlahuaca were quite different in make-up from Tejupan, for both were communities composed of large centers and numerous dependent settlements. To reiterate, nowhere in the Mixteca Alta is there an indication that the precincts of the center were kin-based or kin-determined structures of the type ascribed by Caso[10] to the Post-classic urban development in the Valley of Mexico, nor is there an indication that the barrios were corporate land-holding units.

Probably the barrios of a Mixtec pueblo were more or less contiguous districts comprising the compact pueblo center. It is likely, moreover, that the barrios were associated with certain agricultural lands in the vicinity of the center, but presently available documentation does not

6 Alfonso Caso, "Land Tenure Among the Ancient Mexicans" (trans. by Charles Wicke), *American Anthropologist*, Vol. LXV (1963), 861–78.

7 PNE, IV, 55.

8 AGI, *Escribanía de Cámara*, 162, lists twenty-three barrios; AGN, *Civil*, 516, designates fourteen barrios that are devoted to service of the cacique, but does not indicate the number of additional barrios making up the community center.

9 AGN, *Tierras*, 26.

10 Alfonso Caso, "*Los barrios antiguos de Tenochtitlan y Tlatelolco*," *Memorias de la Academia Mexicana de la Historia*, Vol. XV (1956), 7–63; Caso, "Land Tenure Among the Ancient Mexicans," *American Anthropologist*, Vol. LXV (1963), 861–78.

elucidate this point. The barrios were distinguished from the outlying ranchos. The latter were settlement areas clustered at varying distances from the center. Thus the compact center was ringed about by several dependent but semiself-sufficient ranchos. The center with its barrios and the more sparsely occupied and dispersed clusters of dwellings and structures making up the ranchos characterized the Mixtec community in the sixteenth century. I suspect that archaeological investigation will verify the existence of this pattern of relationship for many years before the Conquest.

It is known that certain barrios were set aside in pre-Conquest times to furnish services, rather than tribute, for the rulers. This does not mean that all of the barrios of the center were so designated. Certain ones must have been assessed tribute in the fashion of the outlying dependencies. In 1580 there were 309 *tributarios* in the fourteen service-barrios of Yanhuitlán, indicating a population of perhaps 1,250.[11] This would be only a very small fraction of the total population. Either a part of the population of the service-barrios was not included in this figure, or the great bulk of the population would have to be accounted for outside the listed fourteen service-barrios, that is, in the other barrios and on the ranchos. An earlier document indicates that there were twenty-three barrios in Yanhuitlán.[12] The proportion of the total community population actually residing in the barrios of the center as opposed to that living in the outlying ranchos must for the present remain in doubt. It is essential, however, that the barrio be distinguished from the rancho. These are separable geographic, political, and demographic components.

THE HAMLETS: At least half of the communities of the Mixteca Alta, and all of the larger ones, had a number of outlying dependencies. These carry the designations *sujetos*, *estancias*, or ranchos and were integral components of the Mixtec community (Fig. 2, No. 2). Dependencies are indicated by place glyphs on the pre-Hispanic picture manuscripts and by glyphs and Spanish glosses after the Conquest.[13] Each *sujeto* con-

[11] AGN, *Civil*, 516.

[12] AGI, *Escribanía de Cámara*, 162.

[13] *Ibid.*, 162; Smith, "The Codex Colombino: A Document of the South Coast of Oaxaca," *Tlalocan*, Vol. IV (1963), 276–88.

sisted of a number of dwellings clustered in an open and rather informal pattern. Groups of buildings within a cluster were often separated by open fields or narrow stretches of land. The hamlets of a community were separated from each other and from the center by open fields and irregular terrain at distances ranging from one to several kilometers. Often, hamlets were isolated from their center by ranges of mountains or hills.

On the basis of a 1582 suit[14] brought against Yanhuitlán by its subject *estancia* Tecomatlán, some generalizations can be drawn about the nature of the relationship which existed between a community center and its *sujetos*.

1. Only the center (*cabecera*) was entitled in pre-Conquest and early colonial times to have its own cacique. Where a community center existed, a cacique resided and governed, and the seat of the cacique's power was in a community center. The record states specifically and repeatedly that "each pueblo that was a *cabecera* had its cacique and *señor natural*." *Estancias* and pueblos subject to the cacique of a center had no caciques, only *principales*. The cacique appointed a noble to rule over and collect tribute in each *sujeto*.

2. The duties owed to the cacique by the natives of the *estancias* and subject pueblos were: obedience, tribute, "royal and personal services," assistance in warfare (pre-Conquest), and assistance in public works such as temple (pre-Conquest) and church (post-Conquest) construction. After the Conquest the people of the subject *estancia* of Tecomatlán came to the *cabecera* of Yanhuitlán to hear religious instruction, to attend church, to bring their tribute, and to engage in personal services and perform communal works, "and they did all that they were ordered to do in the manner in which the other subject pueblos and *estancias* have accorded these things to Yanhuitlán. And thus it was done in antiquity."

3. Justice in civil and criminal matters was dispensed in the center for the entire community. Official community business was transacted in the center, and the principal market facility was located there. The main ceremonial precincts were located either adjacent to the center (pre-Conquest) or coincided with the center (post-Conquest).

4. The possessions (*sujetos*) of Yanhuitlán were recorded on a

[14] AGI, *Escribanía de Cámara*, 162.

Celebrating Easter in Tilantongo. A feast of tortillas, masa, chili peppers, and barbecued goat is enjoyed by citizens of the community, former residents who have returned for the Easter season, and an anthropologist.

Tilantongo. A modern dwelling in the foreground, the sixteenth-century church constructed over a pre-Hispanic ceremonial site on the right, and the Preclassic center of Monte Negro located atop the mountain in the background.

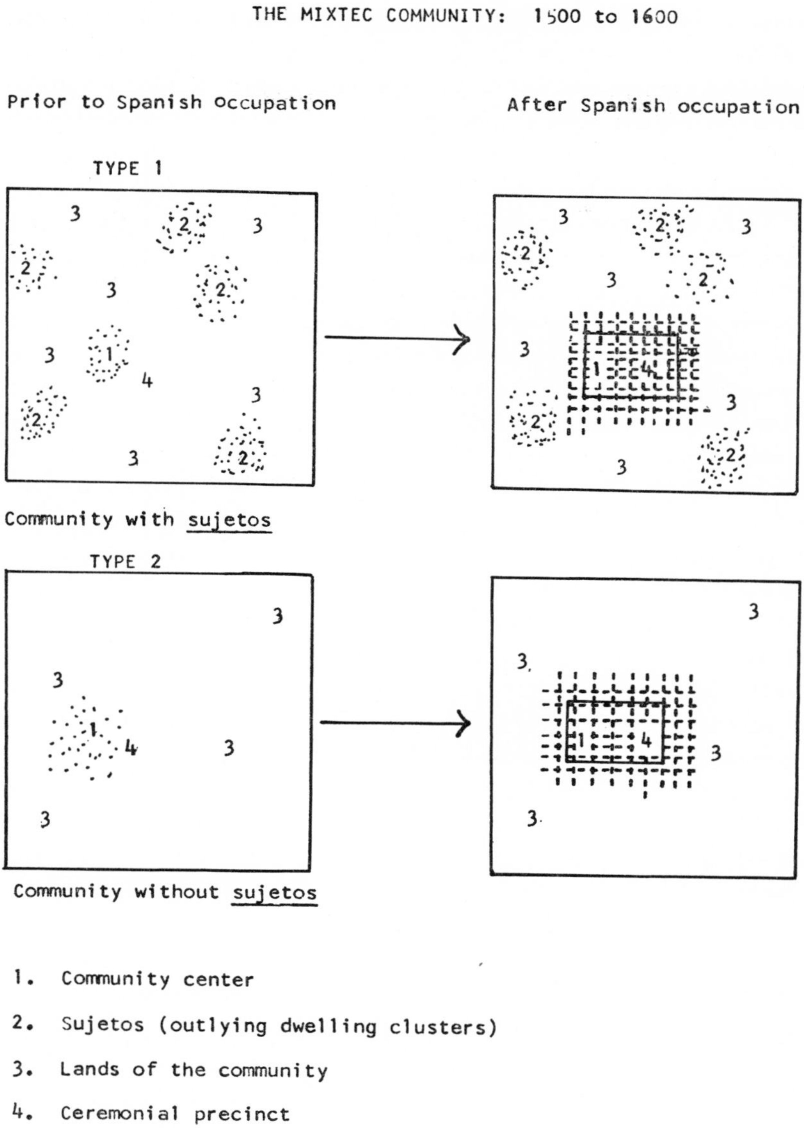

Fig. 2. *The Mixtec Community, 1500–1600*

pintura together with a succession of twenty-four caciques who had ruled the community over the preceding five hundred years. In 1582 this ancient document was kept in the community strong box located in the center. A witness from Tilantongo indicated that it was customary for each community center to maintain these documents, and that such a custom had been observed in Tilantongo.

5. In post-Conquest times the subject *estancias* had no right to elect their own officials. Appointments of governors, alcaldes, *regidores*, and other officials came from the community center and seem to have been largely at the discretion of the cacique and *principales* of the center. Of the two alcaldes appointed to the Indian *cabildo* of Yanhuitlán, one customarily came from the center and the other from one of the *estancias*. Post-Conquest custom accorded well with the ancient practice of the ruler appointing members of the nobility to govern the components of the community. The nobility could act only with the full approval of the ruler, and it was through the nobility that the ruler traditionally maintained power over his community.

The Ceremonial Precinct: The third component of the Mixtec community was the ceremonial center which was usually located adjacent to the concentrated center (Fig. 2, No. 4). This zone was most often situated on a mountain or hilltop, in a cave, at a spring, or in association with some unusual natural configuration. Such a pattern is exemplified at Monte Negro, Yucuñudahui, Teposcolula, Yatachio, Tiltepec, Yucuita, Mogote del Cacique, and Huamelulpan. Lesser shrines were located in dwellings, particularly in the residences of the community ruler and the nobility.[15]

Mountains, high and lofty crags, and the more remarkable features of nature were sacred to the Mixtec as the source of rivers, and as being near the heavens and intimately associated with the elements and fertility. At the same time, caves, springs, and other openings of the earth's surface were related to the spiritual underworld. The origin tales of the Mixtec recount the miraculous appearance of the ancient ancestors from streams of water, from rocks and mountains, caves and trees in high and

[15] AGN, *Inquisición*, 37, exp. 5; Herrera, *Historia*, déc. 3, lib. 3, cap. 12; PNE, IV, 78–79, 84.

Codex Nuttall

secluded regions.[16] Spectacular natural features were the repositories of spirits of good and evil and for the souls of ancestors real and imagined. Such features and forces were the ultimate sources and sustainers of life. Logically, Mixtec shrines would appear in these places, aloof, secluded, and sacred, grotesque or lovely. There are many such features and places in the Mixteca Alta.

It is clearly revealed in the early Spanish documentation that major sacred places were located outside the civic and residential precincts in the surrounding countryside.[17] Ceremony, worship, offering, and animal and human sacrifice frequently took place in these zones which were associated with some kind of ceremonial architecture. Unfortunately little is known of the nature of these Postclassic ceremonial constructions or how they were utilized. There were, in addition to the communal ceremonial compounds, shrines located in houses and in public buildings and palaces, each with its idols or paraphernalia.[18] The more notable of these were attended by priests acting in the service of the ruler. Certain of these sacred places were perhaps dedicated to a cult of personal ancestor worship or to individual or lesser ranking members of the supernatural

[16] Burgoa, *Geográfica descripción*, I, 274–76.

[17] PNE, IV, 77–80, 82–87; AGN, *Inquisición*, 37; AGN, *Tierras*, 44; Burgoa, *Geográfica descripción*, I, 337.

[18] AGN, *Inquisición*, 37.

hierarchy. It is even possible that ancient, genealogical picture manuscripts were somehow involved in a cult of ancestor worship. The great ceremonial places, prime catalysts of community integration, however, were not directly incorporated into the residential centers but were more likely to be located adjacent to the sacred natural features or zones.

While the pattern described is probably typical of Mixtec communities, there are strong indications of less than total conformity with the pattern. Bernal's findings at Coixtlahuaca—where the ceremonial center was immediately adjacent to the residential center—are at some variance with the typical configuration which I have proposed. Achiutla and Tilantongo had community centers located in high, rather inaccessible positions, and apparently residential districts were tightly clustered around religious precincts. Achuitla and Tilantongo are otherwise exceptional in their unusual placement on high irregular slopes. This is atypical for other areas. In the case of Coixtlahuaca, Achiutla, and Tilantongo there seems to have been a closer association between residential and ceremonial centers than was true for other Mixtec communities. These were important religious and political centers, probably occupying rather special positions in Mixtec culture, which may well account for the somewhat anomalous configuration of the community centers. It is possible that future research may reveal a closer spatial affinity between civic and religious precincts in other Mixtec centers. Suggestive of this is the documentation of 1550 which mentions a ceremonial structure near the site of the present convent and plaza in Yanhuitlán.[19] The same documentation, however, more frequently emphasizes the existence of important ceremonial sites in the lands outside the center, and it seems most improbable that the central site constituted the main ceremonial precinct for the community.

The Lands: The fourth component of the Mixtec community consisted of the lands surrounding the center, the hamlets, and the religious precinct (Fig. 2, No. 3). These lands were devoted to agriculture or were utilized for the hunting of wild game and for the collecting of vegetal materials, minerals, and wood for construction and fuel. Topographically, the Mixteca Alta is characterized by an interlacing network of steep-

[19] *Ibid.*, 37.

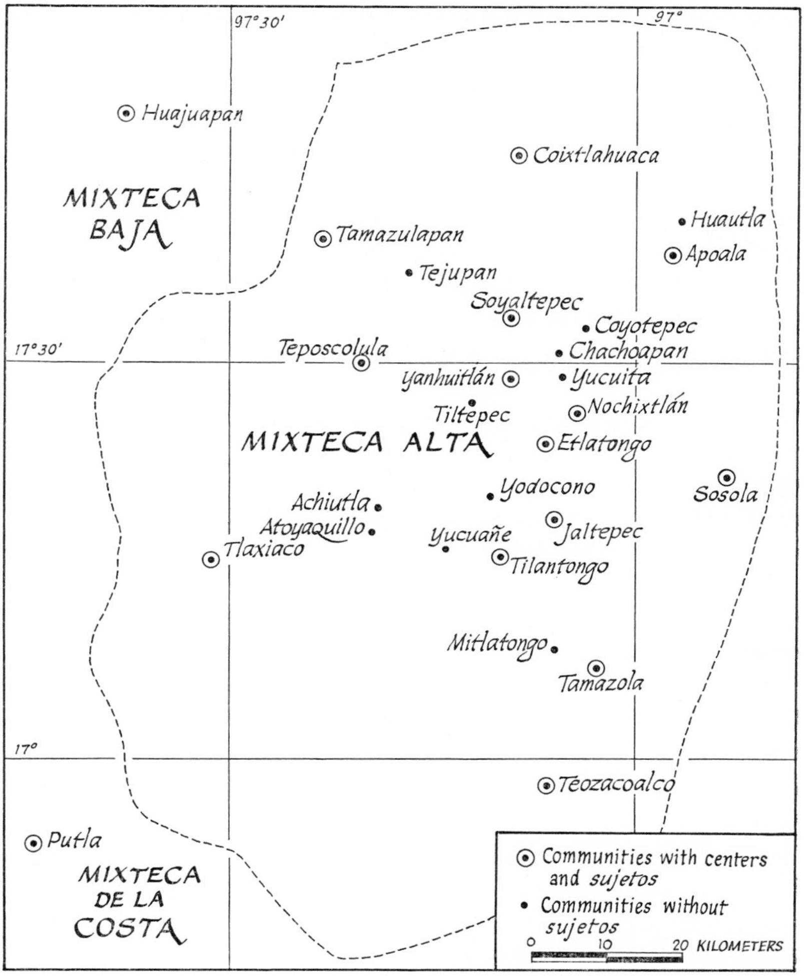

Communities of the Mixteca Alta, 1500–1600

sided mountains, ridges, buttes, and narrow dissected valleys. With the exception of lower slopes and arroyos which were often terraced to form level farm plots, steeply inclined lands apparently were not farmed. Since there is little open valley land available in the Mixteca Alta, such a custom of farming only valley lands imposed a severe limitation on the extension of Mixtec agriculture. This limitation of agricultural potential could well have had a pronounced effect in limiting the direction and development of Mixtec culture. High slopes could have been cultivated, as they have been in the Huasteca, in Chiapas, in Zapotecan Oaxaca, and in other parts of Mexico, but the Mixtec were apparently disinterested in utilizing these areas for agricultural purposes.

MIXTEC SETTLEMENT TYPES: The combination of these four components, a civic and commercial center, several outlying dwelling clusters (hamlets), a ceremonial precinct, and farming and collecting lands, constituted the large community in the Mixteca Alta from 1500 to the time of effective Spanish occupation around 1530.

I have examined sixteenth-century documentation for twenty-four communities in the Mixteca Alta. Thirteen of these communities were of the center-with-hamlets type, Mixtec Settlement Type 1. The earliest records containing information on settlement type date from the 1540's, but formal chronicles and records of litigation leave no doubt that these were well established pre-Conquest patterns. This type of community existed at Tamazulapan (six *sujetos*), Zoyaltepec (four *sujetos*), Apoala (ten *sujetos*), Etlatongo (eight *sujetos*), Tamazola (fourteen *sujetos*), Nochixtlán (four *sujetos*), Zozola (one *sujeto*), Jaltepec (six *sujetos*), Tilantongo (five *sujetos*), Teposcolula (six *sujetos*), Yanhuitlán (sixteen *sujetos*), Tlaxiaco (thirty-one *sujetos* [?]), and Teozacoalco (thirteen *sujetos*).[20]

The three-component community pattern consisting of a concentrated center, ceremonial precinct, and farming and collecting lands, but without dispersed residential districts, or hamlets, appears in eight of the twenty-four cases: Tejupan, Chachoapan, Huatla, Mitlatongo, Atoya-

[20] PNE, I; *ibid.*, IV; AGN, *Tierras*, 24, exp. 6; *ibid.*, 44; AGI, *Escribanía de Cámara*, 162; Caso, "*El mapa de Teozacoalco*," *Cuadernos americanos*, Vol. VIII, pp. 145–81; JM and MH; AGN, *Tierras*, 400.

quillo, Yucuañe, Achiutla, and Tliltepec. In this type of community the entire population is concentrated in only one center. The second Mixtec pattern can be designated a center-without-hamlets community, or Mixtec Settlement Type 2.

Clear patterns have not been established for three of the twenty-four communities studied: Coixtlahuaca, Coyotepec, and Yodocono. It is probable that Coixtlahuaca is of Type 1 and Coyotepec and Yodocono of Type 2, but the evidence is yet insufficient for a definite conclusion in this regard.

At the Spanish Conquest, Mixtec communities ranged in size from two or three hundred to several thousand inhabitants. Four communities, Coixtlahuaca, Teposcolula, Yanhuitlán, and Tlaxiaco, had pre-Conquest populations approaching or exceeding ten thousand. In each case, however, the population was widely distributed over a community territory of forty to sixty square kilometers, and in the case of Tlaxiaco, Yanhuitlán, and Teposcolula the bulk of the population was resident not in the centers but rather in the outlying hamlets. Neither pre-Conquest surface architecture—evident in such sites as Teposcolula, Yucuita, Tamazulapan, Tilantongo, Chachoapan, Achiutla, Tlaxiaco, and Coixtlahuaca—nor early sixteenth-century population figures suggest a population in a single cluster that would be sufficient to warrant the designation "urban" for any settlement in the Mixteca Alta. This holds true whether one uses as a model of the urban center Teotihuacán, Monte Albán, Xochicalco, Tikal, Uxmal, Tenochtitlán, or Chanchan or turns to Old World examples in Mesopotamia, the Indus Valley, or Mediterranean Europe and Africa.

It is clear that at the Spanish Conquest, the two community patterns, Mixtec Settlement Types 1 and 2, were found to exist among groups of people speaking the Mixtec language, carrying what has been described as Mixtec culture, and residing in the region called the Mixteca Alta. Since there is no adequate archaeological evidence available at present, it is uncertain as to how far back in time one can project these patterns. I believe that the configuration of Mixtec culture as it was known at the time of the Spanish Conquest was formed and functioning at a time no later than A.D. 1000, that is, most of the elements present in Mixtec culture at the time of the Spanish occupation were already present by that date. This conclusion is drawn from statements in the available sixteenth-century documentation, from the analyses of native picture manuscripts, and from the very incomplete archaeological record.[21] The linguistic evidence gathered and interpreted by Longacre and Millon indicates that speakers of the Mixtec language may have resided in the Mixteca Alta for the past three thousand years and that the Mixtec cultural pattern, with some exceptions, had already begun to form by 1000 B.C.[22] Oral traditions recorded by Torquemada,[23] Herrera,[24] and Burgoa[25] would tend to suggest a more recent arrival or emergence of the Mixtec people in the Mixteca Alta. Alfonso Caso has traced the royal genealogies in the pre-Hispanic picture manuscripts to their mythical origins around A.D. 692.[26] Archaeological evidence would indicate that during the seventh and eighth centuries, and prior to this time, the residents of the Mixteca Alta were in possession of a culture that was rather closely related to that in evidence at Monte Albán in the valley of Oaxaca. The nature of the relationship existing between the peoples of the Mixteca Alta and the valley of Oaxaca has not yet been adequately studied. Despite the existence of lacunae in the archaeological record, I am confident that it is proper to project the community structure that was in evidence at the Spanish Conquest back to A.D. 1000, or back to the early Postclassic Period in Mesoamerica. This seems a valid contention, regardless of the fact that certain communities in the Mixteca Alta seem to have been integrated politically with communities in the Mixteca de la Costa sometime during the eleventh century.[27]

COMPARATIVE DATA: Mixtec Type I communities correspond generally to what Willey has called settlement type "C" in the Lowland

21 AGI, *Escribanía de Cámara*, 162.

22 Longacre and Millon, "Proto-Mixtecan and Proto-Amuzgo-Mixtecan Vocabularies," *Anthropological Linguistics*, Vol. III, No. 4 (1961), 1–44.

23 Torquemada, *Los veinte i un libros rituales y monarchía indiana.*

24 Herrera, *Historia.*

25 Burgoa, *Geográfica descripción.*

26 Caso, *Interpretation of the Codex Bodley 2858*; Caso, "The Historical Value of the Mixtec Codices," *BEO*, No. 16 (1960).

27 Smith, "The Codex Colombino: A Document of the South Coast of Oaxaca," *Tlalocan*, Vol. IV (1963), 276–88.

Maya zone.[28] This designates a community composed of a center with dispersed residential districts or hamlets. The principal difference between the Mixtec and the Maya patterns is that in the Mixteca Alta the ceremonial precinct was not central to the civic and commercial center, whereas in the Maya type "C" pattern these functions were combined in a more strongly nucleated fashion. Mixtec Type 2 communities generally coincide with Willey's Lowland Maya settlement type "A," a concentrated and restricted town. It is clear that none of the twenty-four communities for which data has been accumulated possessed a pattern resembling Willey's Lowland Maya type "B," a community center surrounded by widely scattered dwellings.

Turning to other areas of Mesoamerica, we find that Sanders speaks of the Valley of Mexico at the time of the Spanish Conquest as being "divided into scores of semiautonomous city- or town-states, which in general organization of population were not very different from the late-sixteenth-century 'pueblo' and the modern *municipio*—especially the larger *municipios*."[29] In broad outline this pattern resembles that which was present in the Mixteca Alta at the Conquest, except that I see a far more intensive social, political, and economic interaction among the components of the Mixtec community than Sanders recognizes for his Valley of Mexico "town-states." After an examination of the area from the central Mexican plateau to the Guatemalan Highlands, there seems to be no close parallels between the pre-Hispanic Mixtec community and the dispersed villages, compound villages, or concourse centers or their pre-Colombian antecedants.[30]

Among the Zapotec of Oaxaca, Schmieder depicted a pre-Conquest pattern of nucleated communities with all dwelling houses clustered in a center and with farm lands spread out around the residence center.[31] This pattern was held to exist for both the Valley and Mountain Zapotec.

28 Willey, "Problems Concerning Prehistoric Settlement Patterns in the Maya Lowlands," in Willey (ed.), *Prehistoric Settlement Patterns in the New World*, Viking Fund Publications in Anthropology, No. 23.

29 Sanders, "The Central Mexican Symbiotic Region," *ibid.*

30 S. F. Borhegyi, "Settlement Patterns in the Guatemala Highlands: Past and Present," *ibid.*; E. M. Shook and T. Proskouriakoff, "Settlement Patterns in Mesoamerica and the Sequence in the Guatemalan Highlands," *ibid.*

31 O. Schmieder, *The Settlements of the Tzapotec and Mije Indians, State of Oaxaca, Mexico, University of California Publications in Geography*, Vol. 4 (1930).

The Mixe, residing north and east of the Zapotec in a rugged mountain setting, are credited with an ancient pattern of widely scattered houses or very small house clusters located on separate plots of land. This dispersed settlement contrasts sharply with the compact configuration of the Zapotec community.

The Chinantec had a vacant ceremonial center with the population scattered over a broad territory and living on dispersed farms or in hamlets.[32] The Cuicatec appear to have grouped their houses along streets in compact centers.[33] It is possible, however, that the latter case reflects a post-Conquest innovation. No clear pattern has yet emerged for the Nahuatl-speaking peoples to the west and south of the Mixtec zone. In the case of the Mixteca Baja and Mixteca de la Costa, it is by no means certain that the settlement patterns corresponded to those in the Mixteca Alta. There were sharp environmental disconformities existing among the three Mixtec areas, and it is very possible that settlement patterns may have differed appreciably. Only additional comparative study can fully reveal the nature of settlement in the remaining areas.

The foregoing discussion has been focused on the patterns of settlement in the Mixteca Alta on the eve of the Spanish Conquest with particular emphasis on the conformation of the community from 1500 through the 1520's. Community patterns in areas outside the Mixteca Alta have been mentioned so that Mixtec patterns can be viewed within the context of pre-Conquest Mesoamerica. Next, consideration must be given to the development of the community after Spanish influences had begun to affect native patterns.

The Mixtec Community Under Spanish Influence

Initial contact between native peoples and Europeans occurred in the 1520's. Effective penetration by Spanish administrative officials, encomenderos, and Catholic priests did not begin until around 1530. Subsequent to 1530 pronounced external influences were felt in the Mixteca Alta, and important internal changes began to occur.

In an effort to bring about more effective subjugation, administra-

[32] PNE, IV, 59.

[33] *Ibid.*, IV, 175.

Codex Nuttall

tion, exploitation, and Christianization of the Mixtec, Spanish authorities introduced several changes in the patterns of native settlement. These processes were set in motion after 1530 and continued in operation during the remainder of the sixteenth century. After about 1580 there was a solidification of the settlement pattern that was to remain in effect until recent times.

The community center remained the pivotal component of the community, but as new construction was instituted under Spanish auspices, a rectangular grid, quadrangular, or checkerboard arrangement of intersecting streets and building alignments, was introduced. A civic-religious plaza was placed at the center of the settlement, and streets emerged in four directions from the plaza. Probably there was an increasing concentration of settlement in the center as a result of the new alignment. In the fringes of settlement, as in the modern *cabecera*, buildings tended to occupy a rather random distribution peripheral to the rectangular plan of the central core.

The hamlets were little affected by the Spanish occupation. They were allowed to retain the random cluster arrangement of pre-Conquest times. Indeed, this is a pattern that is seen in the ranchos of the modern

Mixtec *municipio*. Little or no effort was made by Spanish officials to realign the hamlets. The community centers, rather than the dependencies, figured in plans for reorganization. The attention of the population of the hamlets continued to be focused on the community center, where were located the market, the mission and the clergy, Spanish administrative and judicial authority, and the traditional native ruler who continued to be recognized and to perform his role much as he had before the Conquest. Tribute and labor services continued to be delivered to the center as in pre-Conquest times.

The ceremonial precinct was moved from a location adjacent to the civic center into the center itself. In actual practice the ancient ceremonial center was abandoned and was replaced by the Catholic mission. The ceremonial unit and the civic and commercial units were combined into a central plaza complex which has characterized the community center, or *cabecera*, throughout the Spanish and Mexican national periods to the present time.

When Spanish Catholicism penetrated the Mixteca Alta after the Conquest, the church was placed at the center of the town. This was a departure from the pre-Conquest custom of making the town a point of transition from the sacred universe, as symbolized by remarkable features of nature, to the fields and ranchos that characterized and supported everyday existence. Concepts of the sacred and secular were combined under Spanish leadership in a fashion that possibly resembles an ancient pattern. This principle was more clearly reflected on new patterns of settlement. The architectural manifestation of this is observable in Mexico to the present day, despite years of liberating legislative reform which has sought to separate the function of civic government and religious institution. The palace, *ayuntamiento*, or civic offices occupy one or another side of the great central plaza, the main church taking up position on the opposite side. All is integrated into a civic-religious plaza complex. It is found everywhere in Mexico and is the pattern in Jaltepec, Nochixtlán, Yanhuitlán, Teposcolula, Tamazulapan, Tlaxiaco, Chachoapan, Yucuita, Tejupan, and in Coixtlahuaca. It is most certainly not the case in Tilantongo where the church is quite removed from the civic and residential center.

The civic-religious plaza with an enveloping residential zone is unquestionably the modal pattern of the modern *cabecera* of the Mixteca Alta. The subject ranchos, quite naturally, are well removed from the center itself. Under the Spaniards, ceremonial religion was made convenient by the placement of the church, the most impressive piece of architecture on the horizon, in the midst of the population center. Where possible, small chapels were constructed in outlying spots, possibly to coincide with ancient shrines or temples. These can yet be seen in a number of locations about the Mixteca Alta and Baja (notable examples at Tilantongo, Nochixtlán, Yanhuitlán, and Huajuápan). The result of one such attempt to "rechristen" an old religious center may be in evidence at Tilantongo where the friars sought to take advantage of the "good will" reposing in an ancient religious center. Modern Mitla in the valley of Oaxaca affords something of a parallel example where the church occupies a seat directly over and among ancient ceremonial structures, while the population and civic center is well removed from the site of the present church.

Community lands continued to be utilized for agriculture, for hunting, and for collecting. For the first time, however, community lands were devoted to the herding and grazing of livestock, particularly sheep and goats. New crops, increased requirements for production of native and European crops, livestock, minerals, cochineal dyestuff, and silk, and the introduction of a superior Iron Age technology and animal power allowed a far more effective realization of the productive potential of community lands. The result was an unprecedented economic florescence in the Mixteca Alta around the middle of the sixteenth century.

I have seen nothing in the documentation of the sixteenth century which would indicate that the major communities of that time were in other than locations which they presently occupy. Concentration (*congregación*) of native settlements in the Mixteca Alta did not begin until 1590, and because of the numerous complaints registered with the viceregal authorities and the reticence of the small communities to give up their homes make it doubtful that many of these congregations, which were made primarily for the benefit of the clergy and for greater ease of administration, were ever effected. Such communities as Yucuita, Huatla, and Coyotepec in the vicinity of Nochixtlán[34] and a number of communities in the vicinity of Yanhuitlán and Teposcolula[35] apparently won permanent stays of congregation orders. The futile attempts of the Spaniards to bring about these concentrations of population were most evident at the end of the sixteenth century.

In the aftermath of the Spanish occupation of the Mixteca Alta, the traditional community center underwent realignment; the ceremonial precinct was combined with the civic and commercial center and relocated as part of the pivotal plaza complex; new crops, new industries, and a more effective technology brought about a rapid upturn in native economy at mid-century. The rise in economy was accompanied by a rise in population which was at its century high around 1560. Changes at these loci of community culture, however, need not necessarily be taken as indications of a full-scale reorganization of other community patterns and relationships. Social and political ties, traditional means of production and consumption of most consumer goods, many basic technologies, diet, basic family organization, and concepts regarding the nature of existence represent continuities in Mixtec culture. These served to dampen the effectiveness of external influences on the total society and to impede the processes of acculturation. The high degree of social interaction between the hamlets and the center seems not to have diminished in the least as a result of the Spanish Conquest, and, except for the changes I have mentioned, the basic configuration of the Mixtec community was preserved throughout the sixteenth century and may be found in much of the Mixteca Alta at the present time.

Summary

In conclusion, there were two types of community patterns in the Mixteca Alta from 1500 to 1600: Type 1 consists of a center with hamlets; Type 2 is the center without hamlets. Out of a total of twenty-four communities studied, there were thirteen, and probably fourteen, instances of Type 1 communities, and eight, and probably ten, instances of Type 2 communities. In general form, these two patterns persisted from pre-

[34] AGN, *Tierras*, 1520, exp. 2.

[35] AGN, *Libro de congregaciones*.

Colonial times to the end of the sixteenth century. The main changes that occurred during the Spanish-occupation period were a realignment of the community center into a checkerboard or grid pattern, the incorporation of the ceremonial center into the civic center–plaza complex, and a probable tightening of the arrangement of structures and the general plan of the center. Very little change, if any, took place in the outlying hamlets, and the close relationship between the hamlets and the center remained about the same as in pre-Hispanic times. The sixteenth-century community, in slightly altered form, exists today in the modern Mixtec *municipio*. The old native rulers, the regular clergy, the tribute and labor service systems, and the flourishing economy of the middle and late sixteenth century have disappeared, but the two types of community that have been described remain as major organizing influences in Mixtec life. The extent to which one thousand years of change and continuity in community composition correlate with changes and continuities in the over-all behavior of the Mixtec people is a matter that has only begun to be appraised.

Codex Nuttall

5.
Native Rule in Sixteenth-Century Mexico

AFTER THE CONQUEST and occupation of Mexico and other New World colonies, the Spanish monarchs found it expedient and useful to permit the continued observance of native customs that were not inconsistent with concepts of royal supremacy, the Christian religion, and European standards of social and moral conduct. This policy prompted them to recognize the status of the pre-Conquest native rulers and nobility and their descendants, to grant them honor and privilege, and to incorporate them as an important element in the system of colonial administration.[1]

In the documents of the Colonial Period the native rulers were designated as caciques or as *señores naturales*. The term cacique was of Arawakan derivation and designated a local chieftain in the Antilles. From the West Indies the Spaniards carried the term to the mainland areas of America, where it was employed to designate the native rulers of conquered towns. The term *señor natural* appears in medieval Spanish documents, in which it was used with reference to the kings of Castile and feudal lords who were recognized as legitimate, hereditary princes. Consequently the term, as employed in colonial documents should not be translated as "native lord" but as "natural lord," i.e., an Indian ruler or chieftain who enjoyed status by virtue of legitimate and hereditary

[1] Charles Gibson provides incisive commentary on the position and function of the native nobility in the Valley of Mexico during the Colonial Period (*The Aztecs Under Spanish Rule*, 154–65); his studies of the nobility of Central Mexico and those of Roys for the Maya region have furnished the guidelines for all subsequent study of the subject, the present chapter included.

descent in a direct line of succession from pre-Conquest native rulers.[2] In the colonial records members of the native nobility of lower rank than the caciques were usually designated as *principales.*

Early History of Native Rule in New Spain

Gibson has stated that in Central Mexico "the transitional period of the 1520's has thus far offered no documents consistently to explain the *caciques'* colonial origins or to connect them with pre-colonial antecedents in the Aztec aristocracy."[3] In the case of Yucatán, however, Roys believes that the first caciques were the native chiefs whom the Spaniards found in conquered areas and towns.[4] In Yucatán the Maya term *halach uinic* designated the pre-Conquest ruler of a native territorial province, and the term *batab* described the chieftain of an individual town. After the Conquest some of the *halach uinicob* continued to exercise authority over areas comprising several towns (as in the case of the pre-Conquest district of Mani), and the *batabob* governed their towns as they had done before the Conquest. The local nobility (*almehenob*), designated as *principales* in Spanish documents, continued to have control over the common class. The *halach uinicob* and *batabob* were often described in colonial documents as caciques and/or governors of specified districts and pueblos.

Until the 1550's there was considerable confusion in the writings of Spanish officials in Mexico regarding the meaning and application of the term "cacique." The terms "cacique" and "governor" were frequently employed interchangeably, and in many instances no functional distinctions in the use of these terms were recognized. Viceroy Mendoza, in his letter of instruction to his successor Velasco I, dated 1550, stated that the office of pueblo governor is "certainly different from that of cacique,"[5] but he did not elaborate on this point. The first viceroy spoke

[2] Robert S. Chamberlain, "The Concept of Señor Natural as Revealed by Castilian Law and Administrative Documents," *The Hispanic American Historical Review*, Vol. XIX, pp. 130–37.

[3] Gibson, "The Transformation of the Indian Community in New Spain: 1500–1810," *Journal of World History*, Vol. II (1955), 587.

[4] Ralph L. Roys, *The Indian Background of Colonial Yucatán.*

[5] DII, VI, 502.

of the confusion which existed in the election and succession by inheritance of governors and caciques, although his report implied that governors were elected for one or two years and that the position of cacique was based upon inheritance.

In any case the Spaniards quickly found that the indigenous system of native rule and government in local areas afforded advantages from the standpoint of their own designs of political, economic, and religious domination in their New World colonies. This is clearly revealed in a royal decree of June 19, 1558, as stated in the *Recopilación:*

> The *audiencias* must have knowledge of the law of the *cacicazgos*, and if the caciques or their descendents claim succession in them and the jurisdiction that they formerly had, and if they seek justice, the *audiencias* shall proceed according to that which is ordered; and at the same time they should officially inquire into custom in this respect; and if it is apparent that some are unjustly deprived of the *cacicazgos*, jurisdictions, rights, and rents to which they were entitled, they shall make restitution to them, and give judicial notice to the parties concerned; and the same shall be done if pueblos have been deprived of the right that they have had of selecting caciques.[6]

This provision and similar legislation coming out of Spain at mid-century reflected the controversies which had raged during the 1540's and had given rise to positive steps in favor of the Indian, who should be treated as a rational being with recognized rights. As Gibson states it, the prevailing attitude was that "Indian properties were to be preserved; Indians were not to be reduced to slavery; existing Indian rulers were to be respected as 'natural lords' [*señores naturales*]."[7]

In central Mexico the local communities operated autonomously with locally constituted hierarchies of offices and institutions.[8] Pre-Conquest tribute provinces, as listed in the *Codex Mendoza*, offer little evidence of the existence of an intercommunity political organization in the towns subject to the empire of the Culhua-Mexica beyond that es-

[6] *Recopilación de leyes de los Reynos de las Indias*, leg. 2, tít. 7, lib. 6.

[7] Charles Gibson, "The Aztec Aristocracy in Colonial Mexico," *Comparative Studies in Society and History*, Vol. II (1960), 169–96.

[8] Gibson, "The Transformation of the Indian Community in New Spain: 1500–1810," *Journal of World History*, Vol. II (1955), 588; Gibson, "The Aztec Aristocracy in Colonial Mexico," *Comparative Studies in Society and History*, Vol. II (1960), 169–96.

tablished for tribute purposes. *Calpixques* and garrisons were stationed in certain towns of the empire, but their major function was to ensure the steady flow of tribute to the rulers of the tripartite confederacy. There is no conclusive evidence that these "regional capitals" exerted political control over individual communities of the tributary provinces, nor do we have a clear picture of the relationships of towns within such independent "tribute empires" as Tututepec in southern Oaxaca,[9] Teotitlan del Camino on the Oaxaca-Puebla border,[10] or in important areas like Michoacán, northern Veracruz, and Guerrero. Thorough study of archaeological remains and historical documentation should greatly expand the knowledge of the interrelationship of the hundreds of communities of Central Mexico before and after the Conquest.

Local rulers and their activities do not become prominent in the documentary record until the 1540's. For the remainder of the sixteenth century we have an extensive corpus of legislation, especially viceregal decrees, and litigation relating to caciques and *cacicazgos*. Conflicts over cacique titles, property, and privilege were taken for adjudication to Spanish administrators, who gained the confidence of petitioners, and soon there evolved a formal system of investigation into the claims of local caciques seeking to establish or defend their rights to *cacicazgos*. This represented a growing willingness on the part of the Indians to make appeal to formal statute and to utilize the system of Spanish courts for settlement of disputes formerly handled by concensus or by intercommunity warfare.[11]

Litigation might be instituted on any one of several occasions: to obtain goods and services to which a claimant believed himself entitled by tradition; at the death of a former cacique and the succession of his nearest kin; when a contest arose over land jurisdiction among individuals or communities; when a cacique saw his position threatened by possible usurpation; and at the time of the marriage of a cacique to a *cacica* apparent.

Spanish administrators and jurists required satisfaction of tradi-

[9] RMEH, I, 114–20; PNE, IV, 158, 232–51; Heinrich Berlin, *Fragmentos desconocidos del Códice de Yanhuitlán* (cited hereafter as Berlin, *Fragmentos*).

[10] PNE, IV, 213–31.

[11] For discussion see Gibson, "The Transformation of the Indian Community in New Spain: 1500–1810," *Journal of World History*, Vol. II (1955), 586.

tional native custom before substantiation of a petitioner's claim to cacique title and privilege. This was in accordance with legislation enunciated from time to time by the Crown. For example, a royal cedula of 1550 directed the *audiencia* of Mexico to make a careful inquiry into the mode of cacique succession in pre-Conquest times, i.e., whether succession was by virtue of inheritance or some other method in the local communities, and also to inquire into the privileges that caciques had formerly enjoyed.[12] Another royal decree, dated December 20, 1553, called upon Viceroy Velasco and the *audiencia* to conduct a thoroughgoing investigation of the tributes paid by the Indians of New Spain to Montezuma and to their local caciques, and also to make inquiry into pre-Conquest methods of cacique selection and/or succession and the powers and authority enjoyed by caciques in their respective communities.[13] In response to this cedula several reports were eventually made to the Crown, including the famous treatise of Licenciado Alonso de Zorita entitled *Relación Breve y Sumaria de los Señores . . . en la Nueva España*.[14] These royal orders reflected implicit recognition of cacique rights and status. More explicit statements are recorded in cedulas of 1557 and 1558, which directed colonial authorities to protect, by appropriate legal and judicial process, the proven and hereditary rights of caciques to their *cacicazgos*, properties, and privileges.[15] Finally, a royal order of July 19, 1614, reiterated the right of hereditary succession "according to ancient law and custom."[16] That Spanish officials in Mexico made a serious effort to make actual practice conform to this royal legislation is indicated by litigation of the sixteenth century and the findings of courts in matters of cacique recognition and succession.

Establishing Title to Cacicazgos

The paramount consideration in cases of cacique succession during the sixteenth century was the requirement of direct legitimate descent from a line of native rulers. Simply to be of noble birth, that is, of the *principal* class, was insufficient. Moreover, royal legislation of 1576 stipu-

12 Puga, *Provisiones cédulas instrucciones . . . para el gobierno de la Nueva España*, 122.

13 Scholes and Adams, *Cartas*, 19–23.

14 Zorita, *Breve relación de los señores de la Nueva España.*

15 *Recopilación de leyes de los Reynos de los Indias*, leyes 1–2, tít. 7, lib. 6.

16 *Ibid.*, ley 3, tít. 7, lib. 6.

lated that no person of mixed European and Indian blood could be a cacique.[17] Bloodlines were closely guarded to insure that a male of the cacique class married only a female of the same class, and vice versa. Marriages involving members of the cacique class required consultation and approval not only of the families concerned but also of the *principales* under the control of the families. These requirements were carefully observed in the Mixteca Alta. Documents pertaining to royal succession in the rest of Central Mexico also seem clearly to reflect similar requirements.

There were certain accepted procedures that were followed in establishing *cacicazgo* claims before Spanish judicial authority. For purposes of demonstrating the initial phases of litigation, a typical example of a claim from the last quarter of the sixteenth century will be employed. It is representative of the numerous claims to cacique succession in Central Mexico presented during the Spanish portion of the sixteenth century.

A viceregal order, dated December 29, 1582, states that Don Melchor de Castañeda of Quautlatlauca had made report to the viceroy declaring that the cacique of that pueblo had died without legitimate issue.[18] Since Castañeda was the brother of the former cacique and his closest legitimate heir, he wanted to be named cacique of the said pueblo. The viceroy therefore ordered the *corregidor* of Quautlatlauca to investigate and determine whether Castañeda was "*por linea recta y legítima y derecha sucesión*" entitled to the *cacicazgo*, or if there were heirs who were more closely related to the decedent and more entitled to the *cacicazgo*. The *corregidor* was to send the results of the investigation to the viceroy. In the interim, there was to be no change of status in the pueblo.

A somewhat abbreviated form of such an order was dispatched to the *alcalde mayor* of Yanhuitlán on October 27, 1580.[19] The official was directed to investigate the legitimacy of the succession of Don Pedro de Velasco as cacique and *señor natural* of the pueblos of Tamazola and Chachoapan in the Yanhuitlán district. Fortunately, this order is accompanied by the complete record of investigation carried out by the *alcalde mayor*, which was eventually forwarded to the viceroy.

17 *Ibid.*, ley 6, tít. 7, lib. 6.
18 AGN, *Indios*, 2, exp. 322.
19 AGN, *Tierras*, 3343, exp. 12.

On December 10, 1580, Don Pedro de Velasco was informed by the *alcalde mayor* of the investigation, and on December 11 the natives of Chachoapan and the witnesses scheduled to appear were notified. Because of a change in the office of *alcalde mayor* for Yanhuitlán, nothing more was done on the matter until August 2, 1581, when Don Pedro filed a petition with the new *alcalde mayor* requesting that an investigation be initiated to verify that he was cacique of Chachoapan and Tamazola. On October 4, 1581, the natives of Jaltepec and Tamazola were informed by the public secretary of the forthcoming hearing, and witnesses were summoned. An identical procedure took place in Chachoapan on October 8, 1581, where the hearing was held before Hernando de Múxica, the *alcalde mayor* of Yanhuitlán.

Fourteen witnesses were called to testify in this hearing. All stated that Don Pedro was the legitimate heir to the *cacicazgo* of Tamazola and Chachoapan. The testimony of all witnesses was directed toward the matter of the genealogical rights of the claimant. It was established and confirmed through testimony that Don Pedro was the legitimate son of the former cacique, Don Matías de Velasco. Don Pedro was shown to be the grandson of the former cacique, Don Diego de Velasco Ninco (Nuqh), and his wife, Doña María Cocuahu. Don Diego had inherited the *cacicazgo* of the two towns from his older brother, Don Domingo Cuncusi, who had died without children. There is no dissenting testimony, and at the end of the record of the hearing, the *alcalde mayor* endorsed the succession of Don Pedro, stating that the *cacicazgo* pertained to him without contradiction and by "*legítima y recta linea.*" This certification was sent to the viceroy, who would take final action.

No viceregal approving order could be located for the above case. Don Pedro was confirmed in his claim, however, and it is likely that the order issued in his favor resembled one issued on December 16, 1592, in favor of Lázaro Hernández of Pizándaro.[20] This order states that Don Lázaro had petitioned to be recognized as cacique and for the privilege of enjoying services pertaining to the title, that the investigation had been conducted, and that Don Lázaro had been found to be the legitimate son and heir of his father, the former cacique, Don Juan Cari. The viceroy then declared that Don Lázaro was cacique of Pizándaro and ordered

[20] AGN, *Indios,* 6, *la parte,* exp. 397.

Codex Nuttall

that he be furnished sufficient Indians for the maintenance and repair of his house and certain maize fields and cotton fields. No mention was made of lands other than those to be worked by the Indians for the cacique, nor was there any specific delegation of the cacique's duties or powers.

Cacicazgo *Composition*

Throughout the sixteenth century a native lordship, or *cacicazgo*, consisted of a number of interrelated elements. Provisionally, it can be defined as the sum and combination of all traditional rights, duties, privileges, obligations, services, lands, and properties pertaining to the title of a native ruler, natural lord, or cacique, whose right to the title was established by verification of direct descent from antecedent supreme lords of designated areas. Entitlement was validated through recognition by a body of local and regional nobility and implicit acceptance by the population subject to the rule of the lord. As the most eligible member of a single legitimate cacique family, the lord was the supreme native authority in his community and its dependencies.

As presently employed, the terms "ruler," "natural lord," and "cacique" refer to local, or community, supreme hereditary leaders of native society and not to pre-Conquest heads of state, or empire seated in

Tenochtitlán, Texcoco, Tzintzuntzan, or Tututepec. The power and wealth of the emperors and the extent of their tributary domains were far greater than was true of the local, or community, kings with whom we are presently concerned. Gibson has shown, however, that many of the same institutional concepts and forces characterized both the empire states and the local kingdoms. No implications of hierarchy between the two are necessarily suggested.

In the Valley of Mexico outside the great urban centers, the post-Conquest caciques may be equated with the pre-Conquest *tlatoque*, as local hereditary lords, there being only one legally entitled family of such rank in each community. Only one cacique and his *cacica* wife were recognized at a given time.[21] The same concepts were characteristic of native rule in the Mixteca Alta before and after the Conquest. Consanguineal and affinal ties bound many of the *cacicazgos* in the Valley of Mexico into a great royal kindred, and the same appears to have been true in the Mixteca Alta.[22]

During the first two decades following the Spanish Conquest, most of the native ruling families in the Valley of Mexico retained their traditional titles, prerogatives, and property without serious challenge. Although the Conquest generally eliminated centralized Indian authority, and also the military and priestly ranks, "native succession methods continued to operate, vacancies were immediately filled (often, to be sure, under Spanish sponsorship), and a continuity of office holding was maintained during the period of shock."[23] Stability in nonmilitary and nonreligious native institutions is clearly suggested, and the tendency toward preservation of native political organization is indicated for other parts of New Spain, including Yucatán,[24] Tlaxcala,[25] and Oaxaca.

The fall of the tripartite confederacy in the Valley of Mexico signaled the collapse of imperialism in this area, but as Gibson states, there was:

[21] Gibson, "The Aztec Aristocracy in Colonial Mexico," *Comparative Studies in Society and History*, Vol. II (1960), 169–96.

[22] Caso, *Interpretation of the Codex Bodley 2858*.

[23] Gibson, "The Aztec Aristocracy in Colonial Mexico," *Comparative Studies in Society and History*, Vol. II (1960), 169–96; Gibson, *The Aztecs Under Spanish Rule*, 154–65.

[24] Roys, *The Indian Background of Colonial Yucatan*.

[25] Gibson, *Tlaxcala in the Sixteenth Century*.

> the survival or partial survival of its separate elements, especially in the individual towns with their Tlatoque. It was in these towns, the connecting political bonds of which had been destroyed, that the Indian nobility was to find its most effective adjustment to colonial life.[26]

It is also noteworthy that in Texcoco and Tacuba (Tlacopan) descendents of pre-Conquest ruling families continued to enjoy cacique status, but with authority limited to the immediate districts of these communities. A similar situation evolved in the Tarascan state, where descendents of the reigning *caltzontzin*, or emperor, had cacique status only in the Tzintzuntzan-Patzcuaro district;[27] in other Tarascan communities local lords were recognized as caciques.

In short, the breakdown of central authority in the pre-Conquest empires was not carried over into the local community kingdoms. In these areas, following the initial shock of conquest, there was a rapid adjustment to the imposition of Spanish dominion. At the community level native political institutions survived with a high degree of continuity during the sixteenth century. In these areas *cacicazgo* composition was generally characterized by the features discussed above.

Post-Conquest Indian Government

After the Spanish Conquest the Indian communities continued to enjoy a considerable degree of self-rule exercised by a *gobernador* (governor) and *cabildo* (town council), a varied group of officials both Spanish and Mesoamerican in origin, and royal dynasties tracing lineage to pre-Conquest antecedents. Many facets of native life, such as formal religion, militarism (characteristic of certain areas, but not of others), and a strong merchant class were suppressed, but the Spaniards gave active support to a traditional inclination and ability of the Mesoamerican Indians to govern themselves. Gibson, who has given special attention to this feature of Spanish colonial administration, has suggested that there was a conscious redirection of native society, whereby the fervor of Mesoamerican religion was directed into the acceptable mold of Christianity, and energies which formerly found an outlet in intercommunity war-

[26] Gibson, "The Aztec Aristocracy in Colonial Mexico," *Comparative Studies in Society and History*, Vol. II (1960), 169–96.

[27] AGN, *Tierras*, 29, exp. 3.

fare were channeled into litigation so amply provided by the Spanish judicial system. He has characterized the functioning of the system of native self-rule in the middle of the sixteenth century as follows:

> From the Spanish point of view, mid-century Indian government was a most practical and economical institution; it maintained itself without expense to the royal treasury; it required the presence of only a few Spanish officials; it preserved local order; it handled all the details of tribute exactments; it came rarely into conflict with Spanish authority. It fulfilled the program assigned to it in Spanish colonial theory. For the most part it was tractable and cooperative, even enthusiastic, in adjusting itself to Spanish control. The common assertation that Spanish government ruled through native caciques expresses the over-all situation, while it ignores the diverse motivations, the elaborate Hispanization in cabildo form, and the complexity of aboriginal political hierarchies.[28]

The governor and *cabildo* were agencies of local control set alongside the cacique system. Personnel for these offices was very largely derived from the native nobility, the *principales*, an element of society which the Crown carefully sought to preserve in the sixteenth century. This reflected a desire to maintain existing channels of power and control over the native population. (The position of the caciques in relation to these new agencies of government will be discussed later.) Thus authority at the local level was to remain where it had been traditionally, that is, in the hands of the nobility. Only the directing force at the top of the hierarchy had been shifted or extended. Whereas power in pre-Conquest times had been vested in local kings or princes, the chain of authority now extended from the local *cabildo*, governor, or cacique through an *alcalde mayor* or *corregidor* to the viceroy and *audiencia* and, ultimately, to the Spanish Crown. From the standpoint of the native in the Indian community, however, authority descended from the traditional source, the native lords, princes, or caciques, and the supporting nobility.

The Indian Cabildo

One of the first official acts after the conquest of a province in New Spain was the establishment of the *cabildo* composed of a group of

[28] Gibson, *Tlaxcala in the Sixteenth Century*, 123.

Spanish officials. This was a time-tested Spanish institution of municipal government. When it was decided that Indian self-government was to be fostered, the *cabildo* was introduced to the Indian communities. As established in the mid-sixteenth century, these municipal corporations, exclusively Indian in composition, were normally comprised of a governor, two *alcaldes*, and four *regidores* chosen by the local nobility.[29] In addition there was a group of lesser officials, assistants, and religious servants, who while not an actual part of the council were essential appendages and were instrumental in carrying out effective administration. The second group included *mayordomos*, *escribanos* (scribes), *alguaciles* (police officers and custodial workers), and *cantores* (singers in the church). There is no indication that an elaborate system of rotation between secular and religious offices, as is now found in Guatemala and other parts of the Maya zone, was in operation in the nonurban communities of Central Mexico during the sixteenth century. The exact means of succession to a *cabildo* post is not entirely clear. It seems likely that there was some method of "turns" in the pueblos which would allow for a respite between terms of service, but this requires further study.

The three main *cabildo* offices required viceregal approval subsequent to nomination in the pueblos. Salaries for officers came from the *sobras de tributos*. As nearly as can be determined from examination of a number of *tasaciones* issued during the last thirty years of the sixteenth century, salaries depended to a large extent on the relative importance of the community as an economic and religious center.[30]

The town council met regularly and dealt with problems of local government, economy, and social life. It cared for community properties, preserved privileges among the local nobility, assisted in tribute collection, and could make appeals to the viceroy or to the king. The *cabildo* could enact local legislation in matters not covered by Spanish law, and it was the medium through which Spanish law reached the Indian.[31] Authorities within the *cabildo* and lesser municipal officials and servants were

29 Gibson, "Rotation of Alcaldes in the Indian Cabildo of Mexico City," *The Hispanic American Historical Review*, Vol. XXXIII (1953), 212–23.

30 AGN, *Indios*, 1–6.

31 Gibson, *Tlaxcala in the Sixteenth Century*, 114–15.

charged with maintaining the peace, assuring attendance at religious functions, and seeing to compliance with orders from Spanish officials.[32] The *alcaldes* had specific authority to order arrests and to exercise minor judicial power.[33] The *alguaciles* and other subordinate officials performed their functions and duties under the general direction or by order of the town council. (Appearing in Appendices C–6 and C–7 are viceregal decrees which furnish some indication of the duties of *alcaldes* and *alguaciles.*)

Chávez Orozco[34] and Gibson[35] have described the organization and function of the native *cabildos* of Mexico City and Tlaxcala, and have shown that in these urban centers certain procedures, especially with reference to the election and rotation in office of *cabildo* members, reflected features of pre-Conquest native government that were carried over into post-Conquest times. It would be hazardous, however, to utilize their findings as a basis of generalization for other areas. There has been inadequate study not only of the functioning of specific *cabildos* but also of the over-all nature of Indian government in other towns of New Spain in the sixteenth century. This gap in our knowledge is in large part due to a lack of data of the type Chávez Orozco and Gibson have assembled for Mexico City and Tlaxcala. It also suggests a lack of interest in this phase of native life by anthropologists and historians. A very notable exception to this trend is of course Roys's study of native government in colonial Yucatán.[36] For the Mixteca Alta and other parts of New Spain further study in depth, based upon archival investigation, is needed to clarify many features of *cabildo* organization and function.

The Native Governor and the Cacique

If there was an indigenous counterpart for the native governor in

32 Luis Chávez Orozco, *Manifestations of Democracy Among Mexican Indians During the Colonial Period*, 4–5.

33 Clarence H. Haring, *The Spanish Empire in America*, 174.

34 Chávez Orozco, *Manifestations of Democracy Among Mexican Indians During the Colonial Period.*

35 Gibson, *Tlaxcala in the Sixteenth Century*, 108–12; Gibson, "Rotation of Alcaldes in the Indian Cabildo of Mexico City," *The Hispanic American Historical Review*, Vol. XXXIII (1953), 222–23; Charles Gibson, "*El sistema de gobierno indígena de Tlaxcala, México, en el siglo XVI*," *América indigena*, Vol. X (1959), 86–90.

36 Roys, *The Indian Background of Colonial Yucatan.*

Codex Nuttall

Central Mexico it does not emerge clearly in the documentation. The position seems to have been almost completely a Spanish creation that was adapted to conditions which existed in Central Mexico after the Conquest. It is difficult to draw sharp lines between the roles of offices owing their origins to the Old World and those which arose in Mesoamerica. There was overlap and fusion, and no clear-cut division of authority or unconditional granting of official powers. This undoubtedly stems from the desire of the Spaniards to centralize authority and to institute a series of checks at the lower echelons of government service.

Soustelle comments on certain divisions of power at the highest level of government in pre-Conquest Tenochtitlán. From the era of Montezuma I, the emperor, *Tlatoani*, seems to have shared much of the responsibility of governing the empire with a vice-emperor, the *Cihuacoatl*. Montezuma I appointed his brother Tlacaelel to this post, and he held it through the reign of at least three Mexican rulers. To the *Cihuacoatl* were delegated powers over the military, and he exercised the role of supreme judge in criminal offenses. The *Cihuacoatl* was also a kind of overseer of royal properties and acted for the emperor in his absence.[37]

There may be certain parallels between the offices of *Tlatoani* and *Cihuacoatl* in Mexico-Tenochtitlán and the post-Conquest cacique and

[37] Jacques Soustelle, *La vida cotidiana de los aztecas en vísperas de la conquista* (trans. by Carlos Villegas).

Indian governor. Too little is yet known of the relationship between the two Mexican offices, and it is not certain whether the differences between the post-Conquest positions of cacique and governor represented a degree of continuity of Mesoamerican custom. With so little knowledge of pre-Conquest political structure, it would be unwise to infer a division of power at the top generally for pre-Conquest Mesoamerica or that such a division penetrated the provincial areas in and around the empire of the Culhua-Mexica. There is no evidence that such a situation existed at any time in the Mixteca Alta or Mixteca Baja in the years just prior to the Spanish Conquest. Power was vested specifically in a single native lord who was assisted by a corps of native nobility.

Regarding the distinctive nature of certain offices and the problem of continuity from pre-Conquest into colonial times, several examples can be cited. In 1559 the natives of Coxcatlán, Puebla, in order to protect their title to certain lands, drew up a most interesting document. This document is presented first in Nahuatl. Immediately succeeding is a copy of the same document in Spanish. The most significant aspect of this document for present purposes is its use of native terms in the Nahuatl text and the Spanish equivalents of the corresponding Spanish text.

Nahuatl Text	Spanish Version
Don Luis, *tlatoani*	Don Luis, cacique
Don Pedro, *gobernador*	Don Pedro, *gobernador*
(several) alcaldes	(several) alcaldes
(several) *regidores*	(several) *regidores*
(several) *tequitlato*	(several) *tequitlatos*
(collectively, for above individuals) *pipiltin*	(collectively) *principales*[38]

Plainly, two Nahuatl terms, *tlatoani* and *pipiltin*, have Spanish equivalents, and one term, *tequitlato*, is retained in the Spanish version. Three terms in Spanish have no Nahuatl equivalents. Several conclusions might be drawn from this, at least as regards Coxcatlán.

1. There was continuity for the concept and the role of *tlatoani*, which the Spaniards translated to "cacique," the term employed in the

[38] AGN, *Tierras*, 51, exp. 2, ff. 71*v*–74.

Antilles to describe a native chieftain or community leader, that is, the term "cacique" was sufficiently generalized to be applicable to the office of *tlatoani.*

2. There was no concept in Nahuatl comparable to that conveyed in the Spanish term "*gobernador.*" It was simply a creation of the new dominant group, perhaps not completely original but sufficiently so to have no equivalent in Nahuatl. The same is true for the terms *alcalde* and *regidor.*

3. The term *tequitlato* refers generally to a tribute collector and a procurer of native labor or servants. The Spaniards, according to our interpretation, adopted the existing system of tribute and service. The *tequitlato* was a functioning member of that system. He was known to all, and since the Spaniards had no more acceptable an equivalent based on their own previous experience, the term was retained to designate tribute collector and labor procurer.

4. It is of interest to note that the body of *pipiltin* is given the equivalent term *principales.* This implies a reasonable continuity of the concept and function of the native nobility under Spanish administration. Of course, there is great room for interpretation here, for obviously there were great changes effected in the function of the body of *pipiltin.* Most important, the warfare which provided the stepping stone for many into the *pipiltin* class was now gone as were certain other means of upward mobility. The class, from this standpoint, was frozen from the time of the Conquest, but there were likely other channels open for ascent to the noble class aside from birth. Acquisition of land or wealth through mercantilism or through the attainment of official power within the Spanish scheme of administration and government might have furnished means of rising from the massive common class to the privileged ranks of the *principales.*

Now it is true that the Nahuatl terms themselves were subject to local interpretation. A *tlatoani* may have been quite a different thing in Tenochtitlán than in Coxcatlán, and, undoubtedly, precise function was quite different. I believe, however, that *tlatoani, tequitlato* (or the alternate term, *calpixque*), and *pilli* (singular) or *pipiltin* (plural) were sufficiently precise terms to allow an application of the meanings assigned by the early chroniclers writing of the Valley of Mexico, Tlaxcala, and northern Puebla, to such places as Tepeji de la Seda,[39] Coxcatlán in southeastern Puebla, and to Cuauhtitlán on the eastern shore of Lake Texcoco.

None of this is startingly new. Many have perceived the above conclusions from the statements of Zorita, Ahumada, and other commentators. These are simply some additional facts aimed at providing a basis for statements regarding continuity and change in native social and political organization of the sixteenth century. By the same token, these instances are listed not necessarily for their general applicability but to demonstrate what occurred in at least one Nahuatl-speaking community and to provide hints of what *might* be generally true for Central Mexico in the sixteenth century. There is a great deal to be learned of pre-Conquest social and political life from the study of such post-Conquest documents.

During the seventy-five years of Spanish domination up to 1600, it was customary that the individual named to the community's most important elective position, governor, would come from the nobility. Of eighteen viceregal approvals for the election of governors dated from 1542 to 1596 and drawn from all over Central Mexico, seventeen orders clearly specify that the governor-elect was an *indio principal*. The other order stated that the individual was an *indio cacique*, so in actuality all were drawn from the noble class.[40]

[39] *Ibid.*, 9, la parte, exp. 1.

[40] The discussion of the Indian governorship is based on extensive examination of documents from AGN, *Indios*, and AGN, *Mercedes*. Eighteen viceregal approvals of governors from a wide area and covering the period 1542–96 were extracted for special consideration. These documents with their dates and towns are listed as follows:

AGN, *Mercedes*, I, exp. 108—Chiautla, 1542
Ibid., 1, exp. 202—Xacapango, 1542
Ibid., 1, exp. 490—Teozacualco, 1542
Ibid., 2, exp. 258—Ciudad de Michoacan, 1543
Ibid., 2, exp. 410—Talistaca (1543)
Ibid., 3, f. 44—Tacuba, 1550
Ibid., 3, f. 65—Tezuntepeque, 1550
Ibid., 3, f. 116—Matalzingo, 1550
Ibid., 3, f. 147—Elosuchinca, 1550
Ibid., 3, f. 177—Tetela, 1550
Ibid., 4, f. 169*v*—Tapalcatepec, 1555
Ibid., 4, f. 255—Azcapuzalco, 1555

An Aerial view of Yanhuitlán.

MEXICANA AEROFOTO

Yanhuitlán. The Dominican church and friary, constructed in the sixteenth century.

INSTITUTO NACIONAL DE ANTROPOLOGÍA E HISTORIA

The procedure in operation during the period 1540 to 1600 was that the governor would be elected by the *cabildo*, the *principales*, or by the natives of the pueblo through their electors. Any or all of these factions could be involved in the election depending on the time and location. The choice was then submitted to the viceroy for approval. The viceregal approbation would outline to the governor-elect the general terms and requirements of his office. A typical example is the approval and delegation of duties favoring Don Antonio as governor of Tacuba issued on April 20, 1550. This order reads as follows:

> I, Don Antonio de Mendoza, Viceroy, etc., for the present, in the name of His Majesty, name as governor of the pueblo of Tacuba, you Don Antonio *indio principal*, heedful that you were elected and named for the said office by the *principales* and natives of the said pueblo, and I command the alcaldes and *principales, alguaciles,* and natives of the said pueblo, that during the time that you shall have the said office, they shall hold and obey you as such governor and comply with your orders and come at your calling. You shall exercise care of the good government of the said pueblo and look after and provide the things which touch upon the service of God, Our Lord, and of His Majesty and see that the natives of the said pueblo go to hear and learn the Christian doctrine and the Divine Offices, prohibiting and forbidding the making of drunken orgies, sacrifices or other idolatries or public sins. And moreover, you shall not permit the *macehuales* to give or be charged tributes exceeding that which they are assessed. For the reason stated, and in order that you may understand and be acquainted with the rest of the things and cases that you, as such governor, may use and exercise, I give you complete power, and you shall hold the said office for the time that it is the will of His Majesty or myself in his royal name, and I order the natives of the said pueblo to give to you for your support all that pertains to you as governor, and nothing more, according to the *tasación*. Heedful of the said election and because of the end and death of Don Francisco, former governor of the

Ibid., 4, f. 268—Matalcingo, 1555
Ibid., 4, f. 325—Suchitepeque, 1556
AGN, *Indios*, 1, exp. 178—Mizquitlán, 1578
Ibid., 2, exp. 356—Aculma, 1583
Ibid., 3, exp. 437—Xalpantepec, 1591
Ibid., 6, la parte, exp. 301—Tepetlaoztoc, 1592
Ibid., 6, la parte, exp. 1164—Mixquitlán, 1596.

said pueblo, I give you the said office for the said time. Done in Mexico on April 20, 1550. Don Antonio. By order of his Lordship, Antonio de Turcios.[41]

It is clear that the governor was elected not only for his ability to govern the pueblo and to head the *cabildo* but, as well, for the respect which he commanded in his community. That the post was a significant one is evident. "Always in the sixteenth century," comments Gibson, "the native governor was the most important powerful single figure of Indian political life."[42] While this may have been true for Tlaxcala, the statement cannot be applied to the general area of New Spain in the sixteenth century. Certainly in the Mixteca Alta and Mixteca Baja—one could say Oaxaca in general—there was one figure who eclipsed the governor in importance. This was the cacique. Despite this, the governor emerges everywhere as either the first or second most important person in the Indian community. There is a high degree of continuity in requirements and specification of duties for the governor throughout the Spanish period.

Isolated cases of direct viceregal appointment to complete the term of an infirm or deceased governor were in evidence during the century. The position of Indian governor, however, was an elective office requiring final viceregal approval.[43] While there are cases of a son or nephew of a former governor being elected to office, the position was not hereditary.[44] There are two instances of the election of the minor son of a deceased governor for whom the viceroy designated a regent until such time as the youth was of sufficient age to assume the governorship.[45] The implication is that although the office was an elective one, there was an inclination on the part of native *cabildos* and *principales* to favor direct succession, possibly a carry-over from pre-Conquest times. There was no requirement, however, during the century that the governor be descended from or related to former governors or pre-Conquest rulers, quite in opposition to what was true for caciques throughout the period.

41 AGN, *Mercedes*, 3, f. 44.

42 Gibson, *Tlaxcala in the Sixteenth Century*, 104.

43 Examples of direct appointment, apparently without election: Chiautla (1542), AGN, *Mercedes*, 1, exp. 108; Cuitlahuac (1583), AGN, *Indios*, 2, exp. 967.

44 AGN, *Mercedes*, 3, f. 116, f. 147.

45 *Ibid.*, 3, f. 320; *ibid.*, 4, f. 244.

In the case of caciques the hereditary right of succession was the most significant requirement.[46]

Gibson has stated that after the viceroy instituted Spanish offices in the Indian communities of the Valley of Mexico and Tlaxcala, the caciques often established themselves as governors.

> The office of *gobernador* entitled a *cacique* to regular services and salaries supplied by the town, and even when *caciques* did not hold the gubernatorial offices they frequently appeared on the municipal payrolls for reasons of hereditary status alone, receiving stated amounts of maize or other tribute and specified services from the community. Even in a substantial community, however, gubernatorial salaries were small in comparison with *caciques'* traditional perquisites in tribute and service, and the salaries did not in themselves offer sufficient inducement to enter into formal office holding after the Hispanic model. What the governorship provided was a further position of local authority, one created and endorsed by the viceroyalty and one that furnished its holder with local judicial authority and some other powers that a *cacique* could not comfortably allow to fall into non-*cacique* hands. Most of all the governorship entrusted its holder with the control of royal or *encomienda* tribute collection in the community. *Gobernadores,* whether *caciques* or *principales,* were charged with the collection of these taxes and with their delivery to Spaniards.[47]

There is no reason to believe that exactly the same incentives did not induce Mixtec caciques to seek the governorship of their pueblos with equal enthusiasm.

The combination of the two offices of cacique and governor in a single individual has prompted some misunderstanding as to the re-

[46] These statements are based on examination of the following documentation:
AGN, *Indios,* 1, exp. 79
Ibid., 2, exp. 518
Ibid., 2, exp. 627
Ibid., 3, exp. 693
Ibid., 4, la parte, exp. 120
AGN, *Tierras,* 24, exp. 6
Ibid., 34, exp. 1
Ibid., 3343, exp. 12
AGN, *Civil,* 516.

[47] Gibson, "The Aztec Aristocracy in Colonial Mexico," *Comparative Studies in Society and History,* Vol. II (1960), 169–96.

spective roles and functions of these offices. The office of cacique may be defined as a position of status and privilege based on hereditary right (see Chap. VI) as contrasted with the governorship, which was an elective office with functions of an executive and/or administrative character. Combination of the two offices obviously gave the hereditary native rulers additional prestige and influence, and enabled them to exercise a measure of control over their communities which, in the course of time, prompted increasing concern in the higher ranks of Spanish colonial administration. This may explain, at least in some measure, a marked trend toward separation of the offices of cacique and governor reflected in documents of the seventeenth century.

Codex Nuttall

6.

Royal Succession in the Mixteca Alta

Royal succession in the Mixteca Alta, both before and after the Spanish Conquest, was guided by a number of traditional principles. Processes of legitimate acquisition of royal title and privilege were carefully regulated and widely understood among the Mixtecs. Perception of the full range of practice and principle requires examination both of a particular kingdom at close range and of activities in several of the more important communities of the Mixteca Alta. Attention is focused on Yanhuitlán as a typical and well-documented example of the kingdom-*cacicazgo* in the sixteenth century, but for a fuller understanding of the complexities of royal succession, materials from Teposcolula, Tilantongo, Tejupan, Tlaxiaco, Chachoapan-Tamazola, Tlazultepec, Teozacoalco, Mitlatongo, and other communities will be considered.

During the post-Conquest Period frequent conflicts arose over *cacicazgos*. Many of these found their way to the Spanish courts and now constitute a valuable segment of the legal documentation preserved in Mexican and Spanish archives. Careful collation and examination of this material reveals the principal features of the royal institution in the Mixteca Alta.

Mixtec ruling families, acutely aware of linear continuity, made every effort to preserve the ancient tradition of succession in a direct line by carefully recording and remembering their genealogies and by vigorously defending their ancient rights. Subsequent to the Conquest a Mixtec ruler might seek to confirm traditional privilege for himself and his descendents through a series of legal confrontations, petitions, and official orders. This customary action and the fortunate preservation of the record make it possible to describe in detail the kingdom-*cacicazgo* of Yanhuitlán.

Succession at Yanhuitlán

Namahu and Cauaco were the native rulers of Yanhuitlán at the time of the Conquest.[1] At present, we do not know who preceded them. We can find no connection between either of these individuals and the Lord Three Monkey whom Herrera states was killed by the Mexicans in 1506,[2] nor is there a clear picture of the relationship between a Lord Nine House mentioned prominently in the *Códice de Yanhuitlán*[3] to either Namahu or Cauaco. The only good documentary evidence for the existence of Nine House comes from a 1582 record which states that a Nahui Calci was once lord of all the Mixteca.[4] Here, considerable interpretation is required. Nahui (Nahuatl: four) could be a shortened and incorrect version of Chicnahui (Nahuatl: nine); Calci could very easily be Calli (Nahuatl: house) or the reverential form Caltzin.

The Inquisition records of 1544–45[5] and the 1563 letter of Caballero to Valderrama[6] both mention that a Calci was a former ruler of Yanhuitlán. The latter source states that a Francisco Calci who had been ruler of Yanhuitlán left the title to his son, Don Domingo de Guzmán, who was cacique until his nephew, Don Gabriel de Guzmán, succeeded in 1558. This interpretation of the royal succession is very much in disagreement with the records of litigation.[7]

Caso translates Namahu as Eight Death and Cauaco as One Flower. A Lord Eight Death, "Tiger-Fire Serpent," appears in the *Codex Bodley* (19–11) as the husband of Lady One Flower, "Tiger Quechquemitl." They ruled a place shown as Feather Carpet-Jawbone-Arrow Beak in the *Codex*. Caso believes this to be Yanhuitlán.

1 AGN, *Civil*, 516.

2 Herrera, *Historia*, déc. 3, lib. 3, cap. 13.

3 JM and MH.

4 AGI, *Escribanía de Cámara*, 162.

5 AGN, *Inquisición*, 37, exps. 7, 9.

6 Scholes and Adams, *Cartas*, 297–302.

7 AGN, *Civil*, 516; AGN, *Tierras*, 400, exp. 1; *ibid.*, 985–86; AGI, *Escribanía de Cámara*, 162.

According to Caso, Lord Eight Death was son of the third king of the Fourth Dynasty of Tilantongo, a person called "Ten Rain," "Tlaloc-Sun." Caso equates Ten Rain of the *Codex Bodley* with Xico, listed in the 1580 litigation as the father of Namahu.[8] The brother of Eight Death, a man named "Yacqua," or "Four Deer," was ruler of Tilantongo at the Spanish Conquest. Eight Death (Namahu) and Four Deer (Yac Qua) are the last people to appear on the obverse of *Codex Bodley,* and Caso[9] states that these individuals were still alive in 1533. According to currently available sources, Namahu, probably a younger son, left Tilantongo in pre-Conquest times and became cacique of Yanhuitlán at the time of his marriage to Cauaco who was in line for the title as a direct descendent of the rulers of Yanhuitlán.

Namahu and Cauaco ruled Yanhuitlán at the time of the Conquest but were not baptized. Cauaco survived her husband and continued to be *cacica* of Yanhuitlán until her death, about 1530. Witnesses stated in 1580 that they had known both Namahu and Cauaco and that they remembered Cauaco as being alive about fifty years prior to 1580.[10] In a law suit brought in the 1530's by the first encomendero of Yanhuitlán, Francisco de las Casas, there is reference to the "*Señora* of Yanhuitlán" who had been visited by Juan Pelaez de Berrio, *alcalde mayor* of Antequera (Oaxaca de Juárez) in 1529.[11] Although not mentioned by name, the "*Señora*" most probably was Cauaco.

Namahu and Cauaco, married in accordance with native law, had five legitimate children. The oldest was María de Cocuahu.[12] María de Cocuahu (Two House) is shown in *Codex Bodley* (19) as being the daughter of the rulers of Feather Carpet-Jawbone-Arrow Beak, said to be the glyph for Yanhuitlán.[13] There were four other children. Three of them became rulers at Coixtlahuaca, Tezoatlán, and Tiltepec. It is not yet clear whether these individuals succeeded by direct succession or by

[8] AGN, *Civil,* 516.

[9] Caso, "*Los Señores de Yanhuitlán,*" *Actas y Memorias, 35° congreso internacional de americanistas,* I (Mexico, 1962), 437–48.

[10] AGN, *Civil,* 516.

[11] AGI, *Justicia,* leg. 117, no. 1.

[12] AGN, *Civil,* 516.

[13] Caso, "*Los Señores de Yanhuitlán,*" *Actas y Memorias, 35° congreso internacional de americanistas,* I (Mexico, 1962), 437–48.

marriage. We can identify only one of them, a man who in 1580 was called "Dradahuy."[14] In a document pertaining to 1544–45, however, he was called "Domingo de Guzmán," cacique of Tiltepec.[15] A fourth son was also called "Domingo de Guzmán," but he is clearly a different person. The second Domingo was the cacique-regent of Yanhuitlán and is identified by Caso as Seven Monkey, "Tiger-Torch."[16]

At the death of Cauaco, her daughter *Doña* María succeeded as ruler of Yanhuitlán. *Doña* María married Diego Nuqh, or Six Motion,[17] cacique of Chachoapan-Tamazola, around 1530. María and Diego ruled peacefully and were respected and recognized as caciques of Yanhuitlán and Tamazola-Chachoapan for a period of ten to twelve years. The couple spent most of their married life in Tamazola where their two sons were born. As was customary in the Mixteca Alta, the older son, Don Matias de Velasco, was reared in the town which he was to inherit, in this case Tamazola. Don Gabriel de Guzmán, the younger son, was taken to be reared in Yanhuitlán.[18] More detailed information on how Gabriel was cared for in Yanhuitlán is not present in the documentation.

Probably in the early 1540's María died. Since a half brother to Gabriel and Matías appeared prominently at Tecomatlán, an *estancia* of Yanhuitlán, around 1580,[19] it is assumed that Diego Nuqh survived María, remarried, and produced a third son, Diego de Guzmán. Don Gabriel was too young to assume the title of cacique at Yanhuitlán at the death of his mother, so the leading *principales* of the region designated Don Domingo de Guzmán, brother of *Doña* María, to serve as cacique-regent until Gabriel reach a responsible age. It was during his regency that Don Domingo was brought before the Inquisition for alleged practice of idolatry, human sacrifice, and polygyny.[20] Statements in the inquisitorial proceedings of 1544–45 indicate that Domingo (born in 1510) had been converted by the first wave of Dominican missionaries coming into the area in 1529. According to the testimony of the witnesses, however, Don Domingo, Don Francisco, and Don Juan, governors (?)

14 AGN, *Civil*, 516.

15 AGN, *Inquisición*, 37, exp. 9.

16 Caso, "*Los Señores de Yanhuitlán*," *Actas y Memorias, 35° congreso internacional de americanistas*, I (Mexico, 1962), 437–48.

17 *Ibid.*, I (Mexico, 1962), 437–48.

18 AGN, *Civil*, 516.

19 AGI, *Escribanía de Cámara*, 162.

20 AGN, *Inquisición*, 37, exp. 9.

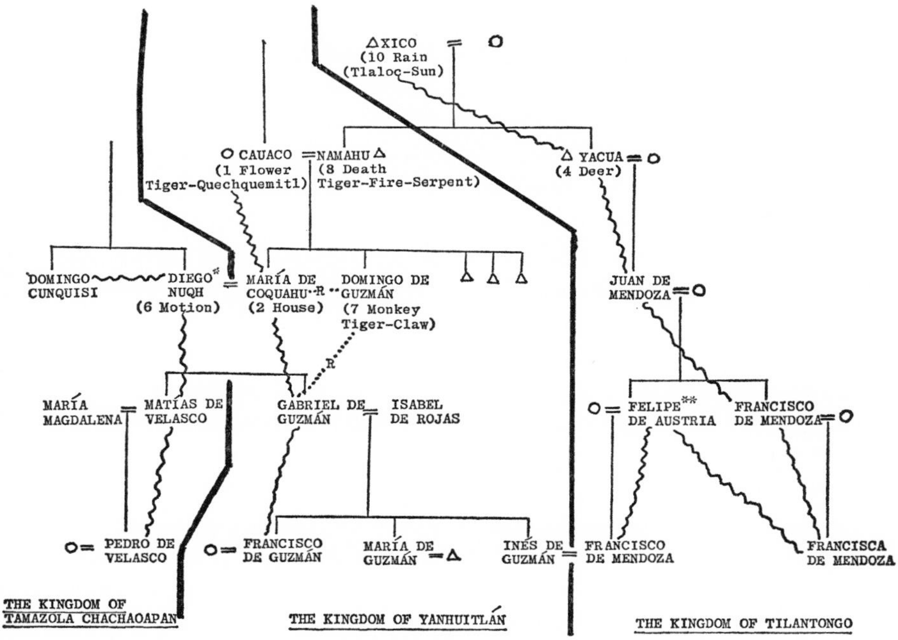

* Apparently remarried after the death of María de Coquahu.

** Remarried after the death of first wife, Inés de Osorio of Teposcolula.

Fig. 3. *The Order of Succession in Three Kingdoms of the Mixteca Alta, 1500–1600*

of Yanhuitlán, after having been baptized as Christians, reverted to paganism with sufficient enthusiasm to be brought to the attention of the missionary clergy. Domingo vigorously denied and challenged the testimony that was delivered against him. His claims must have established a reasonable doubt as to his guilt, for there is no record of his conviction or sentence. He was, however, forced to spend more than a year in prison in Mexico City as an accused person.

Domingo ruled peacefully and was recognized as cacique-regent until 1558. During this period he also occupied the position of governor of Yanhuitlán. This was to establish a precedent for the two caciques who were to succeed him during the sixteenth century. As stated previously, the two offices were separate and distinct, but the governorship insured the cacique of important additional powers and greatly affected the performance and nature of the role of the native ruler in colonial times. Domingo died on or shortly after September 22, 1558, at which time he executed his last will and testament. He apparently died without children.[21]

As had been intended by his parents, as provided by custom, and as designated in the will of Don Domingo, Don Gabriel succeeded to the title of cacique of Yanhuitlán as the "son of *Doña* María Cocuahu and the grandson of Namahu and Cauaco."[22] Don Gabriel was approximately twenty-two years of age at the death of Domingo and was of sufficient age to assume the title. Gabriel followed his uncle as governor, probably through election by the *principales* who gathered at the making of Domingo's will. Gabriel was confirmed both in the office of governor and as cacique in a viceregal order of December 17, 1559.[23]

Don Gabriel ruled as cacique and governor until 1591. He was an exemplary Christian, spoke Spanish, wore the clothing of a Spaniard, was known "throughout New Spain," and was said to be as honest, righteous, and intelligent a man as any Spaniard.[24] During the thirty-three years of his reign, Gabriel rose to great power and wealth and was clearly the most influential man in his community in all phases of native life. As will be seen in the next chapter, he left a great estate to his heirs at his death. Before the end of his life he had also acquired for his heirs the *cacicazgos* of Achiutla and Tlaxiaco through his marriage to Isabel de Rojas, daughter and heiress of the cacique of Achiutla.[25] Gabriel outlived his wife, but continued to act as ruler of his wife's domain until his own death. Before the marriage of Gabriel and Isabel, as had occurred at the marriage of Gabriel's own parents, it was agreed among the *principales* and parties to the union that the couple would send one of their children to be lord of Achiutla, but it is not clear which child this was to be. It is probable that the second child in line, male or female, was to inherit the Achiutla title. While the record indicates that Don Francisco, son and heir of Don Gabriel at Yanhuitlán, "consented" to allow

21 AGN, *Civil*, 516; see Appendix A–1.

22 AGN, *Civil*, 516; AGN, *Tierras*, 985.

23 *Ibid.*, 985; JM and MH, 36.

24 AGI, *Escribanía de Cámara*, 162; see Appendix A–4.

25 AGN, *Civil*, 516; AGN, *Tierras*, 400, exp. 1.

Codex Nuttall

his sister to occupy title at Achiutla,[26] it is likely that it was agreed at the time of the marriage of Don Gabriel to *Doña* Isabel that succession would take place in this manner. At any rate, Gabriel's daughter, *Doña* María de Guzmán and her husband, Miguel de Guzmán, eventually became caciques of Achiutla. Don Gabriel had gained possession of titles both through entitlement by direct descent from pre-Conquest rulers and through marriage to a *cacica,* the only legal means by which one could acquire a *cacicazgo* in sixteenth-century New Spain.

Don Gabriel was confirmed in his title by the viceroy on at least three separate occasions: upon succession in 1558; in awards of salary and services in 1567; and on August 3, 1581.[27] The first confirmation in 1558 marked Gabriel's succussion to the title following the death of his uncle, Don Domingo de Guzmán. At this time there was a contest over title between Gonzalo de las Casas (not to be confused with the encomendero of the same name), of the Yanhuitlán subject *estancia* of Izquisuchitlán, and Don Gabriel. The matter was presented for investigation, and the viceroy, Don Luis de Velasco, decided in favor of Gabriel.

Later, in 1581, a viceregal order confirmed Gabriel in his title on the basis of certain information which had been placed in the hands of the viceroy. This undoubtedly refers to the *probanza* (proof) of 1580 which has been preserved as *Civil* 516 in the Archivo General de la Nación, México, and which contains various orders, assessments, a memoria, an

26 *Ibid.*, 400, exp. 1.

27 *Ibid.*, 400, exp. 1; *ibid.*, 985; AGN, *Civil*, 516; JM and MH, 36.

interrogatory, and the testimony of sixteen witnesses in substantiation of Gabriel's claim to the *cacicazgo*.

While on his deathbed in August, 1591, Don Gabriel dictated his will. By its terms, the *cacicazgo* of Yanhuitlán was left to his only son, Francisco de Guzmán.[28] The will provided that if Francisco died without issue, the *cacicazgo* was to pass first to Gabriel's oldest daughter, María de Guzmán, and then to her children. If María died without issue, the *cacicazgo* was to pass to Gabriel's daughter, Inés, and then to her children, heirs, or successors by "*linea recta*." Thus Don Gabriel took measures to insure legitimate inheritance of the *cacicazgo* by means of direct succession, a tradition that had been observed in Yanhuitlán for more than five hundred years.[29] Gabriel stated in the closing portion of his will that he had done this to avoid the litigation and differences which might arise.[30] Gabriel had seen his own position threatened on at least three occasions, in 1558,[31] in 1580[32] and in 1582,[33] and was aware of the lawsuits which had arisen in other communities over *cacicazgo* proprietorship. Steps had been taken to insure that the *cacicazgo* remained in the hands of his descendents and that the dynasty be preserved.

On September 13, 1591, Don Francisco de Guzmán was given formal possession of the *cacicazgo* of Yanhuitlán. The viceroy again, however, required an investigation to determine if Francisco was cacique by *linea recta* and the individual most eligible to succeed Don Gabriel through the bloodline. A hearing was held in which Don Francisco's claim was substantiated by testimony and by documentation. The *alcade mayor* of Yanhuitlán gave a favorable opinion, and on November 16, 1591, Don Francisco de Guzmán was confirmed by viceregal decree in the title which he held until 1629, when it passed to his nephew, Don Baltasar Velasco y Guzmán.

Legitimacy

In matters of succession, the legitimacy of an individual's claim was

28 AGN, *Tierras*, 400, exp. 1; JM and MH, 34–36.
29 AGI, *Escribanía de Cámara*, 162.
30 AGN, *Tierras*, 400, exp. 1.
31 *Ibid.*, 985.
32 AGN, *Civil*, 516.
33 AGI, *Escribanía de Cámara*, 162.

dependent upon three conditions: (a) the recognized and legitimate marriage of the parents of the child; (b) the child had to be recognized by the general public as the offspring of his parents, and the parents were to accept and rear the child as their own; (c) both parents were required to be of ruler-cacique rank and caste.

These were ancient requirements that persisted throughout the sixteenth century. Before the Conquest a legal marriage involved the appearance of the bride and groom before the priests and nobles of the Mixteca at a traditional ceremony. From the decade of the 1530's it was of course mandatory that marriage be formalized under the auspices of the Catholic Church if it were to be considered a legal union for the purposes of succession. The tenets of legitimacy prevailing in the Mixteca throughout the sixteenth century were set forth and confirmed by testimony in cases of cacique succession at Yanhuitlán,[34] Teposcolula,[35] Tejupan,[36] and Tlazultepec.[37] The dates of testimony run from 1566 to 1597, but in each case there is reference to the existence of the concept of legitimacy in ancient Mixtec society. This is mentioned by Herrera: "For succession to the *Señorío*, the *Señor* had to marry a woman of his own caste; the children of these inherited . . . . And if the principal wife had no children, the bastards could not inherit."[38] The same requirements of legitimacy prevailed in Mixtepec,[39] Tecomastlahuaca, Justlahuaca, Ayusuchquilacala, Putla of the Mixteca Baja,[40] and Tututepec of the Mixteca de la Costa.[41]

Caste and Marriage

Every person of royal lineage, caste, and rank was a potential ruler either by right of birth or by marriage. A very high proportion of those eligible, an estimated 85 per cent, eventually held a title. Of five children

[34] AGN, *Civil*, 516.

[35] AGN, *Tierras*, 24, exp. 6.

[36] *Ibid.*, 34, exp. 1.

[37] *Ibid.*, 59, exp. 2.

[38] Herrera, *Historia*, déc. 3, lib. 3, cap. 12.

[39] RMEH, II, 142–46.

[40] *Ibid.*, II, no. 5, 135–46.

[41] AGN, *Tierras*, 29, exp. 1; *ibid.*, 46, exp. 2; AGN, *Vínculos*, 272; Burgoa, *Geográfica descripción*, I, 335; Berlin, *Fragmentos*.

born to Namahu and Cauaco of Yanhuitlán, all eventually held titles.[42] Both of the children of María de Cocuahu and Diego Nuqh, Gabriel de Guzmán and Matías de Velasco, held legitimate titles.[43] Diego de Orozco of Soyaltepec had five children, and all held titles.[44]

The proportion of cacique-rank individuals holding titles would be substantially reduced for the pre-Conquest and pre-epidemic era when life expectancy was greater than during the colonial period. Probably over a period of years the "surplus" became members of the nobility. There are occasional references around 1580 that rulers sometimes provided land to siblings who were without *cacicazgos*.[45] Don Gabriel de Guzmán brought a half brother to live in the Yanhuitlán *estancia* of Tecomatlán, where he was regarded as a privileged noble. Eventually, this person, Diego de Guzmán, attempted to found a dynasty in Tecomatlán. His attempts were vigorously contested, but by the end of the seventeenth century his descendents had succeeded in gaining recognition as caciques from an increasingly more tolerant Spanish administration.[46] The more general rule, however, was that these "disenfranchized" individuals were, by accident of birth and failure to marry into a *cacicazgo*, relegated to a subservient position under a sibling ruler as lords of *sujetos* within the community kingdoms. In time they lost their ruling caste identity and became simply members of the hereditary nobility. Possibly in many cases, as at Tecomatlán, they attempted to establish new dynasties. This could conceivably account for the appearance of new kingdoms throughout Mixtec history. At times, dependencies might break away from the community centers and their rulers. This would be followed by attempts to achieve political autonomy. The situation at Yanhuitlán in the late sixteenth and seventeenth centuries may have reflected the persistence of an ancient process of community fission. This could be the result of growing economy or population within the dependency or might indicate a diminution of ruling power on the part of the caciques.

As has been stated, a kingdom-*cacicazgo* could be acquired by birth,

42 AGN, *Civil*, 516.

43 *Ibid.*, 516; AGN, *Tierras*, 3343, exp. 12.

44 AGN, *Civil*, 516; AGN, *Tierras*, 24, exp. 6; AGN, *General de parte*, 1, f. 200*v*.

45 AGI, *Escribanía de Cámara*, 162.

46 AGN, *Tierras*, 655, exp. 2.

that is, by direct inheritance, or by marriage to one of equal rank and caste who held, or stood to inherit, a kingdom. Cases at Teposcolula[47] and Tejupan,[48] however, established that if an heir apparent died before inheriting a title, the surviving spouse held no right of succession. Conceivably their children might have a claim to the title, but this eventuality has not been clarified in the existing records.

Consanguinity and marriage were involved in every kingdom-*cacicazgo* in the Mixteca Alta. In each instance the possessor of a title was married. Legal union can be seen as validation for any kingdom-*cacicazgo*, for without it lineal perpetuity of title would have been impossible. When two individuals married, they became in effect a "joint person" in the legal terminology current in sixteenth-century New Spain. A husband often appealed a case in the name of his wife where she had succeeded to the title by birthright and her husband had married in from outside. "Joint person" cases were entered by the cacique husbands of the *cacicas* at Teposcolula in 1566–69[49] and at Tlazultepec in 1597.[50] The children of each union, of course, had rights to all titles and possessions joined in their parents.

Direct Descent

The manner of succession in the Mixteca Alta was traditionally determined on the basis of direct descent, that is, descent in the most direct and legitimate fashion possible from former native rulers. This was a specific requirement in all cases of royal succession. Without exception in the sixteenth century, any person, male or female, seeking to exercise the role of ruler-cacique, had to be of ruling rank and caste. One acquired this condition only by being the son or daughter of a father and mother who were both of ruling rank and caste. One's bloodline had to contain an uninterrupted series of royal-caste ancestors. This was a closed social universe that could be legally penetrated only by birth. Detailed documentation from the Mixteca Alta verifies the traditional recognition of this prescription and its application throughout the sixteenth century.

47 *Ibid.*, 24, exp. 6.
48 *Ibid.*, 34, exp. 1.
49 *Ibid.*, 24, exp. 6.
50 *Ibid.*, 59, exp. 2.

YANHUITLÁN: There is repeated evidence that the principle of direct succession was an inflexible requirement from A.D. 1000 to 1629.[51] There is no indication that there was any deviation from this principle for six hundred years, and it is likely that there was an insistence upon direct succession in the institution of the *cacicazgo* until the nineteenth century.[52]

TEJUPAN: The principle of direct succession was preserved from pre-Conquest times until at least 1700.[53]

TEPOSCOLULA: Direct descent was observed in ruler-cacique succession through the sixteenth and seventeenth centuries.[54]

TILANTONGO: Caso has shown direct succession for Tilantongo from A.D. 692 to the mid-sixteenth century.[55] Reconstruction of the genealogy was made possible through a utilization of pictorial[56] and documentary[57] materials. Data not previously utilized has further established that direct succession was observed throughout the sixteenth century and that among title-holders at Tilantongo was a woman, Francisca de Mendoza (Appendices B–4, B–5; Fig. 3).

CHACHOAPAN-TAMAZOLA: Succession in a direct line was observed in the case of this compound *cacicazgo* throughout the sixteenth century.[58]

TLACOTEPEC (Tlazultepec): While there was an adherence to the principle of inheritance and entitlement by direct descent from the mid-sixteenth century to 1600, there is no certainty as to the historical depth of such an observance. Testimony delivered in the 1590's indicated that it was a traditional concept, and attempted usurpation was circumvented

[51] AGN, *Civil*, 516; AGN, *Tierras*, 400, exp. 1; *ibid.*, 220; *ibid.*, 985–86; *ibid.*, 1433; AGN, *General de Parte*, 2, exp. 1053; AGN, *Indios*, 6, 2a parte, exp. 3; *ibid.*, 6, 2a parte, exp. 212.

[52] Caso, "*Los Señores de Yanhuitlán*," *Actas y Memorias, 35° congreso internacional de americanistas*, I (Mexico, 1962), 437–48.

[53] AGN, *Tierras*, 34, exp. 1; PNE, IV, 53–57.

[54] AGN, *Tierras*, 24, exp. 6.

[55] Caso, "*El mapa de Teozacoalco*," *Cuadernos americanos*, Vol. VIII, pp. 145–81; Caso, "*Explicación del reverso del Codex Vindobonensis*," *Memoria de el Colegio Nacional*, Vol. V (1952), 9–46; Caso, *Interpretation of the Codex Bodley 2858*.

[56] *Códices Nuttall, Vienna,* and *Bodley*; "*El Mapa de Teozacoalco*," *Cuadernos americanos*, Vol. VIII, pp. 145–81.

[57] PNE, IV, 72–73; the *relación* accompanying Caso's "*El Mapa de Teozacoalco*," *Cuadernos americanos*, Vol. VIII, pp. 145–81.

[58] AGN, *Civil*, 516; AGN, *Tierras*, 3343, exp. 12; PNE, IV, 82–87.

Interior of the sixteenth-century church of Yanhuitlán.

INSTITUTO NACIONAL DE ANTROPOLOGÍA E HISTORIA

Yanhuitlán. The building complex at center may represent the ruins of the cacique's residence, constructed in the sixteenth century.

through repetitive testimony verifying the direct descent from previous rulers of the legitimate successor, Doña Juana de Rojas.[59]

OTHER COMMUNITIES: There is good evidence that the requirement of direct descent from pre-Conquest native rulers was observed in Atoyaquillo,[60] Tamazulapan,[61] the two Mitlatongos,[62] Teozacoalco,[63] and Tequecistepec.[64]

POSSIBLE EXCEPTIONS: It is possible that the ruling line at Teozacoalco died out around 1540 and that no claimants appeared from a collateral branch of the lineage. Viceroy Mendoza, on September 26, 1542, ordered an investigation to be made in Teozacoalco because there had been considerable disorder since the *caciazgo* had been without a cacique for three years. Mendoza directed that an "election" be held immediately, "according to use and custom."[65] A second directive, issued on December 15, 1542, approved the election of Don Luis, Indian *principal* of Teozacoalco, as "governor."[66] As noted in chapter five, there was considerable ambiguity in the use of the terms "cacique" and "*gobernador*" during the Mendoza regime. Considering the nature of the duties specified for Don Luis, I can only assume that this was an election of a governor and not a cacique. If he had been elected a cacique, a breakdown of the system of direct lineal inheritance and legitimate succession would be indicated. It is known that a son of the cacique of Tilantongo became cacique of Teozacoalco during the 1560's. Caso interprets the ascension of this individual, Felipe de Austria, to mark the beginning of the Fourth Dynasty at Teozacoalco.[67] This could have been a delayed response to the extinction of the former rulers around 1540. Judging from what is known of royal succession in the Mixteca Alta, I believe it is probable that Felipe was the most eligible surviving kinsman of the former cacique. Alterna-

[59] AGN, *Tierras*, 59, exp. 2; Ronald Spores, "The Genealogy of Tlazultepec: A Sixteenth Century Mixtec Manuscript," *Southwestern Journal of Anthropology*, Vol. XX (1964), 15–31.

[60] AGN, *Tierras*, 44.

[61] AGN, *Civil*, 726, exp. 7.

[62] PNE, IV, 77–82.

[63] Caso, "*El mapa de Teozacoalco*," *Cuadernos americanos*, Vol. VIII, pp. 145–81.

[64] AGN, *Indiferente General*.

[65] AGN, *Mercedes*, 1, exp. 351.

[66] *Ibid.*, 1, exp. 490.

[67] Caso, "*El mapa de Teozacoalco*," *Cuadernos americanos*, Vol. VIII, pp. 145–81.

tive interpretations do exist. Perhaps the Tilantongo family made good an often mentioned claim, that customarily in the instance of defunct ruling lineages the rulers of Tilantongo had right of title to a number of kingdom-*cacicazgos* in the Mixteca Alta.[68] It is also possible that an outright usurpation took place. If this had happened, it seems that complaints would have arisen in the community or from the rightful heir to the title. None has appeared in the public records. Finally, it is conceivable that an election was held among the *principales* of Teozacoalco and that Felipe de Austria was selected as cacique. Neither the written record nor *El Mapa de Teozacoalco* clarifies this point.

Attempts to usurp titles by the same Don Felipe de Austria at Teposcolula in 1566 and in Tejupan in 1572–74 were unsuccessful.[69] Extensive testimony in both cases established the inaccuracy of the claims made by Don Felipe, and traditional principles of direct descent and inheritance prevailed in support of the rightful heirs. Similar attempts at unlawful seizure were defeated at Tlazultepec (modern Tlacotepec) in 1597[70] and Yanhuitlán in 1558.[71]

Frequently during the Colonial period a dying cacique would take great care to mention an heir in a will drawn up in a Spanish legal format. Such a will, executed by Don Felipe de Saavedra, cacique of Tlaxiaco, appears in Appendix B–2. Where the intended heir was neither a son nor daughter, but instead a niece, nephew, cousin, or an affinal relative, he or she might be referred to as having been "adopted." As is clear from numerous pieces of testimony and from statements of official policy, such wills were not final. The right of an individual, regardless of the text of a will, had to be reckoned in the traditional manner. That is, his eligibility by reason of direct descent from former rulers, and his position as the closest surviving relative of the deceased ruler had to be established.

Don Gabriel, cacique of Yanhuitlán, made a will in 1591 naming his son, Francisco de Guzmán, as heir to the *cacicazgo* of Yanhuitlán.[72] Despite the existence of such a clause, the viceroy of Mexico required an official investigation to be made to establish whether Francisco was in-

68 AGN, *Tierras*, 24, exp. 6; *ibid.*, 34, exp. 1; PNE, IV, 77–78.

69 AGN, *Tierras*, 24, exp. 6; *ibid.*, 34, exp. 1.

70 *Ibid.*, 59, exp. 2.

71 *Ibid.*, 985; JM and MH, 36–37.

72 AGN, *Tierras*, 400, exp. 1; JM and MH, 34–36.

deed the legitimate heir or whether there was another person who might have a better claim.[73] It was not until after the investigation verified that traditional requirements regarding "direct-line" succession had been satisfied that final viceregal approval was issued.[74]

Individuals named in wills at Tlacotepec,[75] Tejupan,[76] and Teposcolula,[77] although enabled to gain temporary power, were soon denied title because they were unable to satisfy requirements of direct descent and legitimate succession. Anyone thus "adopted" had also to be proved fit for title according to traditional tenet. Every effort was exerted by Spanish officials to insure proper succession through the recognition of native custom and by its incorporation into colonial law.

Despite the possible breech of tradition at Teozacoalco and the very temporary success at usurpation in Teposcolula and Tejupan, there is little to prohibit acceptance of direct descent from former rulers as a fundamental and overriding principle of succession throughout the sixteenth century. No last testament could supercede a biological and sociological fact.

Female Succession

Females inherited, possessed in their own names, and passed on titles at Yanhuitlán,[78] Teposcolula,[79] Tejupan,[80] Tlacotepec,[81] Tilantongo,[82] and at Tlaxiaco.[83] The manner of succession in these cases is revealed in petitions, wills, and other legal statements and is thoroughly verified by extensive testimony.

Transverse Succession

During a couple's reign it would be necessary for them to indicate the order of succession among their children. As in other phases of the

73 AGN, *Indios*, 6, 2a parte, exp. 3.

74 *Ibid.*, 6, 2a parte, exp. 3.

75 AGN, *Tierras*, 59, exp. 2.

76 *Ibid.*, 34, exp. 1.

77 *Ibid.*, 24, exp. 6.

78 AGN, *Civil*, 516.

79 AGN, *Tierras*, 24, exp. 6.

80 *Ibid.*, 34, exp. 1.

81 *Ibid.*, 59, exp. 2.

82 AGN, *General de Parte*, 1, exps. 832, 1047.

83 AGN, *Tierras*, 3030, exp. 6; AGN, *Indios*, 1, exp. 157; Appendix B–2.

royal institution, certain customary patterns must have evolved for operation in this potentially disruptive area. It is doubtful that selection of heirs was ever left to chance but was instead generally prescribed.

Documentary data have established that it was customary, at the time of the marriage of two persons of cacique rank, for the nobles of the Mixteca to foregather at the place of the marriage. This was done to celebrate, validate, and approve the marriage contract, and also to make some important decisions regarding succession.

For example, when Don Diego Nuqh, cacique of Tamazola-Chachoapan, and *Doña* María Cocuahu, *cacica* of Yanhuitlán, were married in Achiutla, the nobility gathered there and consulted among themselves and with the families concerned. It was decided at that time that the first child of the couple would inherit Tamazola-Chachoapan, the *cacicazgo* of the father. The second child was to receive Yanhuitlán. This was said to be an ancient custom that had been observed at the time of royal marriages since time immemorial.[84] No reference in the documentary record was made to the possible sex of the children or to the order of succession if the first child was a female. The two offspring in this case were both male. The elder, Don Matías de Velasco, inherited Tamazola-Chachoapan, and the younger, Don Gabriel de Guzmán, succeeded at Yanhuitlán. Testimony offered in this case conveys the impression that decisions on succession were made strictly on the basis of priority of birth. There are, however, a number of complexities.

Alfonso Caso has indicated that "succession to the throne or cacicazgo was in a direct line from father to son, usually observing the rule of primogeniture."[85] This would imply that the oldest son received everything and that no allowance was made for a title in possession of the mother. On the basis of a review of the manner of succession confirmed at Yanhuitlán,[86] Caso was later able to state that it was customary in the Mixteca Alta for the first child to inherit the *cacicazgo* of the father and the second born to receive that of the mother.[87] Finally, Caso remarks that if a ruler had two towns, he could divide his estate between

[84] AGN, *Civil*, 516.

[85] Caso, *Interpretation of the Codex Bodley 2858*, 20.

[86] AGN, *Civil*, 516.

[87] Caso, "*Los Señores de Yanhuitlán*," in *Actas y Memorias, 35° congreso internacional de americanistas*, I (Mexico, 1962), 437–48.

two sons.[88] The matter of sibling gender in determining succession has been largely neglected by Caso, and for good reason. The picture is not at all clear.

Legendary tradition in the two Mitlatongos holds that the ancient founder of the ruling lineage had two sons.[89] The older son inherited from his father the community (pueblo and *cabecera*) of Santa Cruz Mitlatongo, and the younger received Santiago Mitlatongo as a separate pueblo and *cabecera*. Each ruled independently of the other. The concept of division of an estate between two sons is thus clearly suggested by local lore. At the time of the Spanish Conquest, two direct descendants of these native lords were ruling the Mitlatongos. Yaqhii (baptized Don Francisco de Mendoza) held Santa Cruz, and Nucoy (Diego de Rojas) was ruler-cacique of Santiago. The division of a royal estate between two sons or among children, regardless of gender, would seem an ancient, desirable, and persistent pattern in the Mixteca Alta.

As I have previously noted, a reigning cacique in the sixteenth century might specify, in his last will and testament, the heirs and/or lines of succession to his *cacicazgo*. Gabriel de Guzmán, cacique of Yanhuitlán by right of inheritance, had also acquired the *cacicazgo* of Achiutla by virtue of his marriage to *Doña* Isabel de Rojas. Available documentation does not record any agreement concerning succession to the two *cacicazgos* at the time of the marriage. Don Gabriel's will, executed in 1591, contains the following provisions: (a) that he is lord and cacique of the pueblo of Achiutla and that after his death Achiutla belongs to his son Don Francisco; (b) that at the time of the marriage of his daughter *Doña* María to Miguel de Guzmán, Don Gabriel had allowed his daughter to possess Achiutla and that she was to possess it until her death; (c) that after the death of María the *cacicazgo* of Achiutla was to go to her brother Don Francisco, but that in the meantime Francisco was to allow possession by his sister.[90] These provisions may have violated some tenet of traditional Mixtec law of succession. The wording of the will implied legitimate inheritance of the Achiutla title by Francisco and temporary or tolerated possession by the sister. Perhaps it was agreed at the time of the marriage of Don Gabriel to the mother of the children

88 Caso, *Interpretation of the Codex Bodley 2858*, 20.

89 PNE, IV, 77–82.

90 AGN, *Tierras*, 400, exp. 1.

that the oldest child was to receive Yanhuitlán and the second born, Achiutla.

We do not know the order of birth of the children, nor do we know the precise rules in effect at the time. Don Gabriel did set down the future order of succession as follows:

> I declare that if the said Don Francisco, my son, should die without offspring or heirs that *Doña* María de Guzmán, my daughter, shall have and inherit and succeed to the *cacicazgos* and *señoríos* of Yanhuitlán and Achiutla, and after her and her children, the said *Doña* Inés, my daughter, and after her, her children and heirs and successors by *linea recta* . . . . This is my decision in order to avoid the litigation and differences that may arise one after the other.[91]

Thus Don Gabriel's will recognized the right of succession of his son Francisco to the *cacicazgos* of Yanhuitlán and Achiutla, but with the provision that María should be *cacica* of Achiutla during her life. If Francisco died without heirs, María and her children were to inherit both Yanhuitlán and Achiutla, and if María had no children, succession should pass to another daughter, *Doña* Inés, and her heirs.

Francisco, who had no legitimate children, was succeeded in 1629 as cacique of Yanhuitlán and Achiutla by his nephew Don Baltasar de Velasco y Guzmán. María was apparently allowed to possess rights to Achiutla for some time, but it is not known for how long. Burgoa described *Doña* Inés, sister of Francisco and María, married to Don Francisco de Mendoza (Pimentel), cacique of Tilantongo, as the richest and most powerful *cacica* of the Mixteca in the early seventeenth century.[92]

In general, the pattern of *cacicazgo* growth throughout the century seems to be typified by the cyclic acquisition, aggregation, fusion, and concentration on the one hand and by forces of dispersal, division, and fission on the other. At marriage there was frequently the joining of two *cacicazgos* in the "joint person" of a cacique and his wife. Just as often, however, there was marriage between an individual of cacique rank, but without a *cacicazgo* of his own, to a woman of cacique rank who held or stood to inherit a *cacicazgo*. An example comes from Soyaltepec, where there were four or five children but only one inte-

91 *Ibid.*, 400, exp. 1.

92 Burgoa, *Geográfica descripción*, I, 371.

Codex Nuttall

grated *cacicazgo*. Here the children were "married off" to heirs of other *cacicazgos*. More frequently, however, both marrying members would have *cacicazgos*.[93] Regardless of which marriage partner inherited or owned a *cacicazgo*, it became necessary either at the time of marriage or at the death of one of the partners to determine the sequence of succession. The order of inheritance among one's children was an important matter for consideration.

Abdication

Diego de Mendoza, a son of Diego de Orozco of Soyaltepec, became cacique of Teposcolula and Tamazulapan by marriage, and enjoyed sufficient security in this position to be able to vacate his inherited title of cacique of Soyaltepec in 1575 in favor of a younger brother.[94] Other abdications are known in the case of infirmity, marriage into another *cacicazgo*, and as gestures of generosity on the part of the rightful heir in favor of the next person in line.

Don Agustín de Rojas of Tlacotepec made a conditional abdication in favor of his sister, *Doña* Catalina, some time during the last quarter of

93 AGN, *Civil*, 516.

94 AGN, *General de Parte*, 1, f. 200*v*; Appendix B–3.

the sixteenth century. After Agustín's death his daughter, *Doña* Juana de Rojas, was successful in re-establishing title to Tlacotepec in 1599. As already indicated, Francisco de Guzmán in a similar fashion ceded the *cacicazgo* of Achiutla to his sister, but there is no indication that he gave permanent title; he appears as cacique of Achiutla in 1592.[95]

The *cacica* of Tejupan chose to step down from power in 1572 in favor of a young and capable nephew, Gregorio de Lara.[96] By doing so, she made certain of proper legitimate succession. A number of witnesses verified that this was acceptable procedure under customary Mixtec law and precedent. The move was approved by Spanish reviewing officials.

Lineage Failure

In the majority of cases, the parents ruled the domain to which their child eventually gained title. Frequently however, a child of a royal couple of one community might succeed to a title held by a collateral relative. This occurred when there was a failure of a lineal branch to produce an heir. There were several such instances in the Mixteca Alta in the sixteenth century. This necessitated reversion to the grandparental or possibly the great-grandparental generation of rulers. From that point, the most eligible surviving member of the lineage would be traced. The fact that an individual possessed a title elsewhere was no barrier to securing an additional kingdom-*cacicazgo* if he happened to be the most eligible member of the lineage. The successful candidate might be the cousin of the former ruler, as occurred at Tlacotepec[97] and Tejupan.[98] At Tejupan, a nephew succeeded his aunt, and a title passed from the caciques of Teposcolula to their niece.[99]

The ruling title of Tilantongo during the middle and late sixteenth century passed from the father, Don Juan de Mendoza, to the eldest son, Don Francisco de Mendoza, to a granddaughter, *Doña* Francisca de Mendoza. At the death of Francisca in 1576 the title passed to Don Felipe de Austria, the second son of Don Juan de Mendoza.[100] An uncle,

[95] AGN, *Indios*, 6, *la parte*, exp. 369.

[96] AGN, *Tierras*, 24, exp. 1.

[97] *Ibid.*, 59, exp. 2.

[98] *Ibid.*, 34, exp. 1.

[99] *Ibid.*, 24, exp. 6.

[100] AGN, *General de Parte*, 1, exps. 832, 1047; Appendices B–4, B–5.

in this case, inherited title from his niece. This was the same Don Felipe de Austria who held the *cacicazgo* of Teozacoalco and attempted to gain the *cacicazgos* of Teposcolula and Tejupan by claiming entitlement through his deceased wife, the heiress apparent who had died before her parents, and by virtue of an ancient "right" of the Tilantongo ruling families to certain vacant titles. After Felipe, the title of cacique of Tilantongo went to his son Francisco de Mendoza. The latter married Inés, the daughter of Don Gabriel de Guzmán, cacique of Yanhuitlán. Don Gabriel de Guzmán and Felipe de Austria were said to be first cousins (*primos hermanos*) in litigation of 1582,[101] but this does not seem to have been the case. The relationship and manner of succession of the Yanhuitlán and Tilantongo families are shown in Figure 3.

In another case of lineage failure, an early post-Conquest ruler of Tamazola-Chachoapan, Domingo Cunquisi, died without issue.[102] Since the line could be carried no further, Domingo was succeeded by his brother, Diego Nuqh, who headed a new line of rulers (Fig. 3).

Regency

In case both members of a ruling couple died while their children were still minors and considered unable to assume office because of age, a regent would be appointed. There is only one good example of a regency in the Mixteca Alta. This is the previously considered case of Domingo de Guzmán, cacique-regent of Yanhuitlán.

During the regency Don Domingo closely supervised the activities of his nephew Gabriel de Guzmán, acted in his name and on his behalf, and educated the young heir to assume the role of cacique. It can only be assumed that if he had not died, Don Domingo would have relinquished complete right to the title to his nephew within a very short time. Gabriel was twenty-two years of age in 1558 when he assumed the title that he was to possess until his death in 1591.

While the transition from a reign to a regency is relatively clear, the manner of the passage of title from the regent back to a ruler is not readily discernable. It is probable that at the proper age the royal heir would assume the full responsibility for the title, and the regent would step from authority to become a respected and powerful adviser to the

101 AGI, *Escribanía de Cámara*, 162.

102 AGN, *Tierras*, 3343, exp. 12.

ruler. The single documented instance of regency in the Mixteca Alta is inconclusive on this point.

Principles of Succession Reviewed

While most of the rules of succession in the Mixteca Alta had their origins in native custom, some reflected acculturative influences derived from Europe. From around 1550, Spanish concepts of *mayorazgo* (entailed estates) and inheritance seem to have had considerable effect on systems of native succession.[103] In particular, transverse succession, the most indefinite feature of all that has been discussed, seems to have been substantially affected at the end of the sixteenth century by European primogeniture. Cases of succession during the second half of the century revealed that if there were a son, regardless of his age relative to a sister or sisters, he would inherit a *cacicazgo*. An older son would inherit before a younger son.

We know, however, that early in the century *Doña* María Cocuahu inherited the *cacicazgo* of Yanhuitlán *before* her brother, Don Domingo de Guzmán, and that the mother of the children, Cauaco, was mentioned frequently as "*Señora*" of the community without reference to the father Namahu. Domingo de Guzmán came to power only as a regent in favor of his nephew, Don Gabriel de Guzmán. *Doña* María received title *from her mother*, and inheritance in this fashion is stressed in later claims to the Yanhuitlán title. Probably two patterns of succession existed in ancient times. An effort may have been made to keep certain titles in the female line and others in the male line. But more important was the practice of awarding the kingdom of one parent, probably the father, to the eldest child and that of the mother to a younger child. The latter seems to have been the case in the succession of Don Gabriel de Guzmán to Yanhuitlán and of his older brother to Chachoapan-Tamazola. Yanhuitlán was the more valuable *cacicazgo*. If primogeniture had been a guiding theme in succession during the early decades of the Colonial Period, the older son would have inherited both Tamazola-Chachoapan and Yanhuitlán, or, if he were to receive favored treatment, Yanhuitlán instead of Tamazola-Chachoapan. Quite the reverse was true. The older son, Matías de Velasco, received the poorer patrimony of the father, and

[103] During the sixteenth century, *cacicazgos* were frequently called "*mayorazgos*."

the younger son, Gabriel de Guzmán, received the richer *cacicazgo* of the mother. It is difficult to derive an inflexible principle from the above, except that there was a tendency for a title residing in female hands to remain in female hands in succeeding generations (i.e., Cauaco to María Cocuahu), and for an older son to inherit title from his father and for the younger son to receive title from his mother. While we do not know the rules of priority between a female and her brothers, we do know that there were cases where a woman received title and her brothers were sent outside to marry *cacicas* of other communities. This is precisely what occurred at Yanhuitlán in the case of María Cocuahu and her brothers.

If primogeniture did prevail in the late sixteenth century, it was greatly tempered by native custom, for every effort was made to protect the rights of secondary heirs. This is most apparent in cases from Yanhuitlán, Tlacotepec, and Tilantongo. Marriage of course furnished a convenient escape, and the efforts of caciques to negotiate advantageous marriages for their children can be read between the documented lines.

Among the several conditions of succession that have been discussed, I believe that the following are the most important and that they were thoroughly rooted in ancient Mixtec tradition.

1. Direct succession by lineal descendents took precedence over that of collateral or affinal relatives. A son, daughter, or grandchild inherited title before a brother, sister, uncle, cousin, nephew, or niece. As required by the principle of direct succession, a title would move in a vertical line. Only if an heir could not be found in the vertical line would the title move in transverse fashion to a relative of the former ruler in a collateral line. Lineal descendants, regardless of generation, inherited prior to relatives in collateral lines.

2. The concept of royal caste dictated that a nonruling-class individual could not appear in the genealogy of a native ruler. Ruling-class men married only ruling-class women for procreation of heirs and perpetuation of the lineage. The offspring of a ruling-class person and a noble was only a noble, and he could not gain legitimate title. As defined by Berreman, the designation of caste applies specifically to the Mixtec ruling class: "Castes are ranked endogamous divisions of society in which membership is hereditary and permanent."[104] Caste was carefully

[104] Gerald D. Berreman, *Hindus of the Himalayas*, 198.

guarded among the rulers of the Mixteca Alta from ancient times until at least the end of the sixteenth century.

These two features permeated the entire structure of royal succession in the Mixteca Alta and conditioned and took precedence over all other rules of royal inheritance. Other principles of succession, i.e., recognition, legitimacy, marriage, inheritance, order of succession, regency and abdication as protective devices, and lineage failure, can be reduced in their dimensions to two overriding and determining factors: legitimate succession by direct descent and caste. Preservation of these two elements ensured the survival of the native institution in its traditional form. When concepts of direct descent and inheritance and caste were seriously weakened in the decades after 1600, the native institution of the community kingdom no longer existed in its traditional form. All other features of native rule necessarily were affected by these two elements.

Codex Nuttall

7.
The Content and Composition of the Kingdom-*Cacicazgo* of Yanhuitlán

THE SIXTEENTH-CENTURY Mixtec community should be distinguished from the *cacicazgo* of such a community. The community was a territorial, demographic, and administrative unit composed of a center (*cabecera*), lands devoted to farming and collecting, and, in most instances, one or more subsidiary settlements (*sujetos*). The *cacicazgo*, however, was institutional in nature rather than territorial. It consisted of the sum total of the duties, prerogatives, goods and properties, and the prestige, power, and influence derived from and pertaining to the title and position of a native ruler-cacique. Although these constituent elements of a *cacicazgo* were normally related to a single community, it must be noted that in some cases, like that of Yanhuitlán, caciques claimed, as part of their royal patrimony, goods and properties located within the territorial limits of another community.

Like other features of Mixtec culture, the *cacicazgo* was a changing, fluent, expanding, and contracting entity, and was marked by accretion and attrition, fluctuation, and shift in function. Much depended upon the strength and ingenuity of the ruler-cacique as an individual. His will to achieve his ends and his ability to manipulate people, property, and thought had a marked effect on the nature of his *cacicazgo*. The content of a *cacicazgo* was shaped and conditioned by the personality of the individual cacique in interaction with a massive *macehual* class that he led and sought to exploit, the local nobility which lent him support and through which he ruled, the rulers of other kingdoms, and the fortunes of marriage between holders of separate cacicazgos. After the Conquest, the Spanish administrative, legislative, and judicial systems and the new economic orientations played a vital part in providing a new dimension to the institution.

Recognition and Obedience

In 1580 legal proceedings were conducted in the name of Don Gabriel de Guzmán to substantiate the validity of his title as cacique of Yanhuitlán, his right to receive labor service and tribute from the Indians of his *cacicazgo*, and the legitimacy of his claims to specific pieces of land as part of his cacique patrimony.[1] Sixteen witnesses, most of them of advanced age, were summoned to give testimony in response to an interrogatory of twelve questions which set forth the points Don Gabriel wished to prove and establish. Several of the questions dealt with his direct descent from pre-Conquest and early post-Conquest rulers of the *cacicazgo*, the regency of his uncle during his minority, and his marriage to a woman of cacique rank. These questions and the pertinent testimony have been summarized in the preceding chapter. Other questions considered significant components of the *cacicazgo*.

Question 10 reads substantially as follows:

> Do [the witnesses] know that in the time of the infidelity of the Indians [i.e., in pagan pre-Conquest times] the natives of this pueblo and its *estancias* recognized their caciques and *señores* in every way and obeyed, served, and respected them in everything, provided personal services for them, worked fields for the sustenance of their houses, and gave them in tribute large quantities of clothing, precious stones, feathers from Guatemala, and fowl? Also, is it known that [the caciques] were given all that they asked, and that as *señores absolutos* of the said pueblo and its province, everything they ordered was obeyed up to the arrival of the Spaniards, at which time the caciques were given a fixed assessment of what they could receive, and for that reason the caciques now suffer great need?[2]

Testimony of the sixteen witnesses, recorded in the third person by the scribe—a customary procedure—contains little more than affirmative paraphrasing of this question. The response made by Domingo Lopez, seventy years of age, is representative of the testimony of the other witnesses:

[1] AGN, *Civil*, 516.

[2] *Ibid.*, 516.

> In answer to the tenth question, the witness stated that it is certain and well known, as declared in the question, that in the time of the infidelity of the Indians, the natives of this pueblo of Yanhuitlán and its subjects recognized their caciques and *señores* in every way and served and respected them in everything, providing them with personal services, working fields for the sustenance of their houses, and gave them great quantities of clothing, precious stones, precious feathers from Guatemala, fowl, and all that they asked and commanded as *señores absolutos* of the said pueblo and its province, until the arrival of the Spaniards. Since that time the *señores* and caciques have been presented with an assessment of what they could receive, and the present witness has seen that for this reason the caciques are in great need.[3]

Question 10 and replies of the witnesses clearly indicate that recognition of the caciques as "absolute lords" and unquestioning obedience to them on the part of the Indians constituted a fundamental feature of the pre-Conquest *cacicazgo*, or kingdom, of Yanhuitlán. The 1580 proceedings sought to establish undisputed recognition within the Yanhuitlán community, and to the satisfaction of Spanish authorities, of Don Gabriel as reigning cacique, but he surely must have realized that he did not have the sweeping power enjoyed by his pre-Conquest predecessors. It was obviously his purpose, however, to ensure and validate his superior and commanding position as cacique of Yanhuitlán. His authority and influence as cacique were enhanced, of course, by the fact that he also held the office of community governor, but the record of the 1580 proceedings is discreetly silent on this point.

Service, Tribute, and Salary

Question 10 of the 1580 interrogatory also mentions the labor services and tributes in kind which the pre-Conquest caciques of Yanhuitlán received from the natives of the *cacicazgo*. The labor obligation included personal services for the cacique's household and the cultivation of fields for his sustenance and support. The interrogatory specifically mentions clothing, precious stones, Guatemala feathers (probably quetzal plumage), and fowl as items of tribute. The total amount of cacique income derived from labor service and payments in kind cannot be determined,

[3] *Ibid.*, 516.

but the tenor of Question 10 and the supporting testimony suggest it depended upon the demands made by the "absolute" reigning lords. After the Conquest these sources of cacique income were progressively reduced, and Question 10 records a complaint, often heard in sixteenth-century documents for other areas, that the fixed assessments for service, tribute, and/or salaries for caciques formulated by Spanish officials had resulted in great hardship and need.

Labor service was of great importance to the cacique in New Spain. It helped him to maintain the highest position in the native social scale and was obviously of tremendous economic significance. Consequently, it is not surprising that post-Conquest reduction of this form of "income" should have prompted widespread protest. In 1580 Don Gabriel, cacique of Yanhuitlán, sought to substantiate the justice of his general complaint on this point by presentation of specific data which serve to illustrate a significant feature of pre-Conquest custom.

Question 11 of the 1580 interrogatory, which deals with this specific subject, reads:

> Do [the witnesses] know that, besides the recognition and services that the caciques had, they had in royal patrimony many barrios with Indians for exclusive household service, and that these [Indians] were taken from the caciques when the Spaniards arrived in this land and were included with the rest of the tributaries, even though they had always been known to be Indians of the patrimony of the said *cacicazgo*? Belonging to this group are those contained in the memorial I am presenting, and I ask that the contents be shown to the witnesses. In that time there was a great number of these people and with the pestilences and mortalities that have occurred there has been great diminution, and at present there are 309 *casados* in the fourteen barrios contained in the said memorial.[4]

The memorial mentioned in Question 11 is the following:

> Memorial of the barrios that belong and pertain to the cacicazgo and *señorío* of Yanhuitlán, and to Don Gabriel de Guzmán as such cacique, which he asks to be shown to the witnesses.
>
> First, the barrio of Itnuñute, that has thirty-four *casados*.
> The barrio of Chiyoniñe, that has fifteen and one-half *casados*.

[4] *Ibid.*, 516.

The community of Tejupan. Pre-Hispanic remains may be found on the hill in the background.

The church and friary at Teposcolula, built in the sixteenth century by the Dominicans.

The barrio of Yuqhcava, that has seventeen and one-half *casados*.
The barrio of Yuchandodzo, that has twenty-six and one-half *casados*.
The barrio of Yuchaychi, that has twenty-eight and one-half *casados*.
The barrio of Tinduchi, that has eight *casados*.
The barrio of Muyahui, that has twenty and one-half *casados*.
The barrio of Yodzoconuu, that has eighteen *casados*.
The barrio of Tiyusi, that has forty-two *casados*.
The barrio of Nusaa, that has thirty-two *casados*.
The barrio of Dzaynu, that has twenty-nine *casados*.
The barrio of Atucu, that has eighteen *casados*.
The barrio of Tiqueui, that has thirteen and one-half *casados*.
The barrio of Tiquaa, that has six *casados*.[5]

The Indian witnesses who testified during the 1580 hearings gave affirmative answers to Question 11. By way of illustration we quote the declaration made by Domingo de Guzmán (sixty-seven years of age):

> In answer to the eleventh question, this witness affirmed what is stated in the question because this witness was well acquainted with the said Numahu and Cauaco, grandparents of the said Don Gabriel, who in their time had in the patrimony of the said *señorío* many barrios with Indians for domestic service. But when the Spaniards came to this New Spain, they removed these from the said caciques, and from others, and registered them so that they would pay tribute like the rest of the people, notwithstanding the fact, as the witness had always seen, that the said barrios and the Indians belonging to them were known to belong to the said patrimony. And from these barrios come those contained in the memorial that has been read to this witness; there were many more people in the time of the said Namahu and Cauaco, and with the pestilences and mortalities there are now many less. However, the witness does not know how many people remain in the barrios. This is what is known of this question.[6]

On the basis of the excerpts from the 1580 proceedings, it may be assumed that the barrios of Yanhuitlán were pre-Hispanic in origin and represent a native concept. "Barrio" is of course a Spanish term, and there seems to exist no adequate corresponding term in either Nahuatl or Mixteco. The concept was native, but under the Spanish occupation there must have been significant alteration. Employing our rule of thumb

[5] *Ibid.*, 516.

[6] *Ibid.*, 516.

equation of four people per *casado*, or tributary unit, we arrive at the figure of 1,236 (4 x 309 *casados*) people residing in fourteen barrios that were said to be for the exclusive personal service of the cacique of Yanhuitlán in 1580. The number of such individuals probably exceeded 2,000 in pre-Conquest times. Whether they were slave or free or landless peasants is not presently known, but what is clear is that the native ruler of Yanhuitlán traditionally had at his disposal and as part of his royal patrimony several hundred individuals dedicated to his personal service. After the Conquest, Spanish officials failed to recognize this privilege of the caciques. Question 11 clearly suggests that it was the contention of Don Gabriel that the Indians of the fourteen barrios listed in his memorial should not be subject to the labor and tribute assessments imposed by the Spaniards on the rest of the pueblo population.

Similar claims for exemption from post-Conquest assessments of tribute and labor service were made by caciques for Indians serving as tenant farmers (*mayeques*, also called "*terrazgueros*") on lands of their *cacicazgo* patrimony. They sought to justify such exemption on the ground that the *mayeques* had not been subject to tribute in pre-Conquest times. These claims were resisted by royal officials and encomenderos for the obvious reason that tribute exemption for the *mayeques* would naturally reduce the number of tributary units in Crown and encomienda towns.

Records of litigation and other legal documents provide specific data (although scant in many instances) concerning the services, tributes, and/or salaries accorded to post-Conquest caciques. The earliest record of this kind for Yanhuitlán is dated December 26, 1548, and reads as follows:

> In the city of Mexico on October 26, 1548, the most illustrious Lord don Antonio de Mendoza, viceroy and governor for His Majesty in this New Spain, assessed the food and service that the Indians of Yanhuitlán are obliged to give Don Domingo, *gobernador* of the said pueblo, because of his office and for the time that he will possess it.
>
> First, they are to give the said *gobernador* every day a turkey and ten male Indian servants and ten female Indian servants.[7]

[7] The Jiménez Moreno quotation of this *tasación* (JM and MH, 36), as taken from AGN, *Tierras*, 985, differs from the AGN, *Tierras*, 400, exp. 1, version of the order. The

Codex Nuttall

Further, they are to provide every six months two *xiquipiles* of cacao *gordo.*

Further, they are to spin seven *cargas* of cotton every six months and weave it into mantas.

Further, they are to work a field of wheat of three hundred brazas, caring for it and harvesting the crop.

Further, they are to work four fields of maize, two fields measuring four hundred *brazas en cuadra*, another of three hundred, and another of six hundred.

And this is what they have to give, and nothing more, and he may not request or levy more under penalty of being deprived of the privilege and being punished.[8]

This assessment clearly states that it was made in favor of the governor of the pueblo of Yanhuitlán. Don Domingo was both cacique-regent and governor in 1548. Again we are confronted by an ambiguity in terminology pertaining to the offices of governor and cacique which often was characteristic of documents of the Mendoza vice-regency. The services specified in the order of 1548 are clearly those that would be accorded a cacique and certainly not to a community governor.

The services and tributes (cultivation of the wheat and maize fields

former reads "... *y dies Yndios de servicio*"; the latter reads "... *y diez indios y diez indias de servicio.*"

[8] AGN, *Tierras*, 400, exp. 1; *ibid.*, 985; JM and MH, 36.

may be equated as either service or tribute) specified in the decree of 1548 doubtless represented a substantial reduction from pre-Conquest times. Personal service in the household of the cacique was now restricted to twenty persons daily, probably recruited on some kind of rotation basis from the barrios listed later in this chapter. Specific limitations were placed on the size of the fields to be worked for the benefit of the cacique. Other payments were limited to specified quantities of fowl, cloth, and cacao; there is no mention of the feathers and precious stones named in Question 10 of the 1580 interrogatory.

The actual extent of the fields to be cultivated for the cacique is a matter of considerable interest. They included a field of 300 brazas for wheat production and four fields, measuring 300, 400, 400, and 600 brazas each, for maize. Assuming that these fields were measured as those recorded in other documents of the period, I feel certain that the dimensions of the Yanhuitlán fields were 300 x 300, 400 x 400, and 600 x 600 brazas respectively. The braza is approximately 5½ feet, and there are 43,560 square feet in an acre. Applying these equivalents to dimensions of the Yanhuitlán wheat and maize fields, I find that in 1548 the cacique of Yanhuitlán enjoyed the harvest from 63 acres of wheat land and from 535 acres of maize fields. This means that he was allowed labor service for the planting, cultivating, and harvesting of a total of 598 acres. I believe that these lands comprised part of the royal patrimony of the *cacicazgo*.

For almost two decades subsequent to 1548 no official record of services, including tribute in kind, owed by the Indians of Yanhuitlán to their cacique can be found. A report by Alonso Caballero, a Spaniard in Yanhuitlán, addressed to Licenciado Jerónimo Valderrama, visitor-general of New Spain, has been summarized in Chapter III. This report asserted that the Indians of Yanhuitlán community were providing a large amount of labor each year for their cacique, and if credence may be given to Caballero's statements, such service may well have exceeded the schedules set forth in the viceregal decree of 1548. An interesting feature of Caballero's report was his assertion that the Dominican friars were conniving with the cacique to permit excessive use of native labor in the construction of a large housing complex for the cacique.

After 1548 the first record of an official schedule of "service" for the cacique of Yanhuitlán is dated March 6, 1567. On this date the Marqués de Falces, viceroy of New Spain, authorized an annual salary of ₱400 (*pesos de oro común*) to Don Gabriel de Guzmán, cacique and governor. This salary, to be paid from funds in the community chest, evidently took the place of payments in kind, turkeys, cloth, and cacao, mentioned in the viceregal decree of 1548. The 1567 schedule also stated that the Indians of Yanhuitlán should make any necessary repairs to the cacique's houses, and that they "shall plant and harvest his lands and cultivated fields." The extent of these fields was left to the decision of the Spanish alcalde mayor of Yanhuitlán.[9]

The annual salary of ₱400 accorded to Don Gabriel exceeded that normally granted to other caciques and/or governors of Indian communities in the 1560's and 1570's, and doubtless reflected the large population and flourishing economy of Yanhuitlán at that time. In contrast with the viceregal decree of 1548, the 1567 schedule did not stipulate any fixed quota of labor service for the cacique's household.

In the autumn of 1567 the alcalde mayor of Yanhuitlán, Jerónimo Mercado Sotomayor, ordered a measurement of the fields in the possession of the cacique and called a hearing to determine the amount of land that had previously been cultivated for him. There is no assurance that all of the *cacicazgo* land was surveyed. According to the manuscript record of the inquiry, it was determined and verified that six parcels of land, comprising, on the basis of our calculations, a total of 351 acres, had been worked for the benefit of the cacique, Don Gabriel de Guzmán. This figure represents a sharp reduction from the estimate of 598 acres in 1548. By virtue of the discretionary authority given him by the viceregal decree of 1567, the alcalde mayor ordered that four fields, comprising 183 acres, should henceforth be cultivated for the cacique.[10]

The viceregal order of 1567 stipulated that the cacique's annual salary of ₱400 should be paid from the community chest of Yanhuitlán, that is, from the *sobras de tributos* and other community income, and also that the labor of Indians assigned for service in the cacique's household and for work in his fields should be paid from the same funds at the rate of twenty-five cacao beans daily. This approximated the current daily wage

[9] AGN, *Tierras*, 400, exp. 1.

[10] *Ibid.*, 400, exp. 1.

of a half real, or 1/16 of a peso, for unskilled labor in many parts of New Spain. The alcalde mayor ordered, however, that the Indians engaged in cultivation of fields for the cacique's benefit should receive for their labor one-half of the harvested products of those fields.[11] His orders, coupled with the sharp reduction in the amount of land to be worked for Don Gabriel, obviously involved a considerable loss of income for the latter.

In 1573, Don Gabriel filed a petition before Viceroy Enríquez stating that in accordance with "ancient custom" many *principales* attended him in his household and that he was requesting the maintenance of these persons with the service of twelve Indians and their wives "in addition to the assessment" (doubtless a reference to household service granted by the viceregal order of 1567). In reply to his petition Viceroy Enríquez ordered that the cacique be given the services of six Indians and their wives, who were to be paid twenty cacao beans and food daily from community funds. (See Appendix C–5.) This order was reaffirmed by a viceregal decree in 1581.

The data presented above rather clearly indicate that the pre-Conquest income of the cacique of Yanhuitlán derived from labor service and tribute was subjected to specific limitations after the Conquest, and that these sources of cacique revenue, including salary in lieu of tribute, were progressively reduced during the sixteenth century. Nevertheless, Don Gabriel de Guzmán, who served as cacique from 1558 to 1591, continued to enjoy the usufruct of extensive *cacicazgo* lands, to which were added new sources of income resulting from the coming of the Spaniards.

Lands and Goods

Many caciques of New Spain in sixteenth-century Mexico made claim to buildings, lands, and goods that were described as part of their *cacicazgos*, and for which they claimed title and use by virtue of legitimate descent from pre-Conquest native rulers. These properties, so they asserted, were separate from the common, or community, holdings of the pueblos and subsidiary settlements included within their *cacicazgos*. Legal proceedings relating to *cacicazgo* lands, i.e., the royal patrimony of caciques, also record documentation to show that these lands, in many cases, had been worked by tenant farmers (*mayeques*), marked off from

[11] *Ibid.*, 400, exp. 1.

other commoners (*macehuales*) of the *cacicazgo*. Decisions of the Spanish courts in the sixteenth century recognized many of these cacique claims to royal patrimonial lands. The fact that these properties could not be legally alienated by a cacique may serve to explain in part the application of the term *mayorazgo* (entailed estate) in documents to describe a *cacicazgo* during the colonial period. It is evident, however, that in the course of time the patrimonial properties of many *cacicazgos* were progressively reduced by processes of attrition, such as the rapid decline of native population, or by judicial processes. Finally, it should be noted that a cacique might acquire personal property in the form of land, livestock, and other goods apart from his *cacicazgo* property, which he could freely dispose of by sale or gift during his lifetime, or in his last will and testament.

It is difficult on the basis of documentation available at present to make any firm estimate of the amount of land that comprised the royal patrimony of the *cacicazgo* of Yanhuitlán in the sixteenth century. Earlier in this chapter, estimates were made of the extent of lands, presumably *cacicazgo* property, to be cultivated for the benefit of the cacique by virtue of a viceregal decree of 1548 and the decision of the alcalde mayor of Yanhuitlán in 1567. Although these estimates may indicate a decrease in the patrimonial lands of the *cacicazgo* between 1548 and 1567, it is uncertain whether the fields included in such estimates constituted all of the *cacicazgo* land holdings.

During the legal proceedings of 1580, Don Gabriel de Guzmán filed a long list of real estate to which he claimed title as part of the royal patrimony of his *cacicazgo*. This list reads as follows:

> Likewise, as goods of the *cacicazgo* there are the large houses, where the alcalde mayor formerly lived, with their surrounding outbuildings.
>
> Likewise, the new arched houses made for Don Gabriel de Guzmán.
>
> The lands and fields belonging to the *cacicazgo* of Yanhuitlán are the following, all of which are in the *cabecera* of this pueblo:
>
> First, a field called "Yodzooconuu."
> Another field called "Yuchadzaa."
> Another field called "Saayuqh."
> Another field called "Tiyahui."
> Another field called "Ticacuii."

Another field called "Yuchañama."
Another field called "Ñuchua."
Another field called "Yuchañuu."
Another field called "Yuchacoondodzo."
Another field called "Yuchatoto."
Another field called "Itnuanino."
Another field called "Tiuico."
Another field called "Yodzonasaa."
Another field called "Yuucucha."
Another field called "Yuchanjaha."
Another field called "Duhuadziyahi."
Another field called "Duhuayoo."
Another field called "Totocoo."
Another field called "Yodzoñunduqh."
Another field called "Dzinicoo."
Another field called "Tiquaha."
Another field called "Tiyoco."
Another field called "Yuchayahua."
Another field called "Atucu."
Another field called "Yuchacanu."
Another field called "Yuchatnunii."
Another field called "Yuchatahuiyoo."
Another field called "Chayoo."
Another field called "Tindodzo."
Another field called "Titee."
Another field called "Chadzoco."
Another field called "Yodzodzayecu."
Another field called "Totoquaha."
Another field called "Adzite."
Another field called "Dzanañaña."
Another field called "Satinduu."
Another field called "Yuchadzinjaqh."
Another field called "Jisiyuu."
Another field called "Yuchaniñe."
Another field called "Dacucuchi."
Another field called "Andeye."
Another field called "Yuuicanu."
Another field called "Duhuanuñu."
Another field called "Ñuyoo."

Another field called "Yuchandehe."
Another field called "Yuchayoho."

In the *estancia* of Anañe there are the following lands and field: A field called "Titechi."

In the *estancia* of Tnuñuu is a field called "Yodzodzañuma."

In the *estancia* of Tiyuqh there are four fields called "Yuchadzayaha, Dacuyucha, Duhuacani, and Atata."

In the *estancia* of Tiyaha there are seven fields, which are as follows: Diyeca, Yuchanitnaa, Yuuinjiyo, Cahiydzo, Yuuicava, Cavaquaha, Jauico.

In the *estancia* of Yucucata there are two fields, which are as follows: Yodzonouico, which is a large flat lowland, [and] Duhuandoo.

In the *estancia* of Yuchandeye there is a field called "Sahañuto."

In the *estancia* of Chinduhua there is a field called "Yuchanduu."

In the *estancia* of Ñutuui there are two pieces of land: One is called "Cauatedza Yehe"; the other is called "Yodzonutuui."

In the *estancia* of Yodzoñuhu there are two fields called "Cauatechi and Yodzoñuhu."

In another *estancia* called "Yuchañunduu" there are two fields named "Yuhuaticaha" and "Cauandoco."

In the pueblo of Apoala there are nine pieces of land named as follows: Chadzoco, Yodzocachi, Yodzotinono, Yuchañunduu, Saayucuneñe, Maayucha, Yucuhocodzana, Jisiyuu, Yuhuindaya.

In the pueblo of Patla Ixtlauaca (Yodocono) there are eighteen fields named as follows: Ithutacu, Yodzotanjaa, Yuuidzitoñaña, Yutnundate, Yodzotinani, Noquaa, Chiyondacu, Tindudzi, Totoquaha, Yuchacoyo, Tandohe, Achacu, Duhuatutnu, Ticuii, Yucuacoo, Yucuañahi, Chayoo, and Yuhuyaui.

In the pueblo of Etlatongo there are six pieces of land and fields called in the Mixtec language by the following names: Yuchañucuisi, Dzumandacu, Yodzocuhua, Dzumanuhu, Yuchacuiñe, and Itnutoto.

In the pueblo of Notzixtlán there is a field with the following name: Dzumañuquaha.[12]

An interesting feature of this document is the territorial distribution of the 102 fields (*sementeras*) listed therein. Forty-six are described as being located within the limits of the center (*cabecera*) of Yanhuitlán, and twenty-two in subject *estancias*. In addition, it includes thirty-four

[12] AGN, *Civil*, 516.

plots located in other communities, nine in Apoala, eighteen in Yodocono (Patlaixtlahuaca), six in Etlatongo, and one in Nochixtlán. Question 12 of the 1580 interrogatory and the replies of witnesses thereto affirmed Don Gabriel's title as cacique to all of these lands.[13]

Since the 1580 document does not specify the extent of the fields included therein, an estimate of the total acreage of these holdings cannot be made. But the long and detailed list of lands claimed in 1580 by Don Gabriel clearly suggests that the properties cultivated for the caciques in earlier years (1548–67) did not constitute the entire landed estate of the *cacicazgo*. It may be assumed that the 1580 list included part or all of the lands mentioned in the documents of 1548 and 1567, that is, lands to be worked for the cacique by Indians of the Yanhuitlán community. It should be noted again, however, that the 1580 list also included, as part of the *cacicazgo* patrimony, lands located within the territorial limits of other communities, and it seems unlikely that these plots would have been cultivated for the cacique by the Indians of Yanhuitlán. It is possible that the cacique lands in other communities and also some of those within the Yanhuitlán community were worked by tenant farmers (*mayeques*), but the documentation available at present does not provide definitive evidence on this point.

At the time of the succession of Francisco de Guzmán as cacique of Yanhuitlán in 1591, a memoria of lands pertaining to the *cacicazgo* was executed at the direction of Spanish officials.[14] This account differed considerably from that of 1580. Thirty-five plots of land were claimed in and around Yanhuitlán, and twelve in the *estancia* of Tecomatlán. In addition, the memoria listed thirty tracts in other communities: nine in Etlatongo, one in Tonaltepec, five in Tlaxila, fourteen in Apoala, and one in Tocondeye. No measurements for these lands were supplied.

A total of 102 plots were listed in 1580 and 77 in 1591. Taking into account only the number of plots listed, a 25 per cent loss in *cacicazgo* lands would be indicated during the years 1580–91. Such a procedure can be quite misleading, however. The manner of naming fields in 1580 may have differed from that in use in 1591. Fields named individually in 1580 may have been combined in 1591. There is no indication that any lands were alienated between the dates of these inventories.

[13] *Ibid.*, 516.

[14] AGN, *Tierras*, 400, exp. 1.

In 1576, four years before the first inventory, Don Gabriel de Guzmán had donated a large tract measuring 760 x 190 x 650 x 275 varas (a vara was approximately thirty-three inches) in the vicinity of Soyaltepec to the Dominican Order.[15] But there is some question as to whether this was *cacicazgo* property. When Don Gabriel made the donation stating that "these are my own milpas," he could have been indicating that there were lands that he owned privately and individually, lands which were not a part of the *cacicazgo* patrimony and which presumably could not be alienated. It is possible, therefore, that the 1580 inventory, despite its explicit reference to "lands and fields belonging to the *cacicazgo* of Yanhuitlán," may actually have included certain plots privately held by the cacique. If some of these had been disposed of prior to the 1591 inventory, this might explain in part the discrepancies between the two lists.

Although the size and type of the lands mentioned in the officially approved memoria of 1591 remain unknown, it seems evident that the *cacicazgo* of Yanhuitlán in the last years of the sixteenth century continued to constitute a very large holding. It is postulated, however, that during preceding decades, there was a decrease in *cacicazgo* lands. Whether this came about by illegal sale, donation, or claims by individuals or communities cannot be stated at present. Possibly no part of the royal patrimony, as distinct from lands privately owned by the cacique, was lost. Until better documentary sources are found, this question remains open.

In addition to the lands that comprised the major part of the properties of their *cacicazgos*, the caciques of Yanhuitlán possessed movable goods of substantial value inherited or acquired during their years of office. It is difficult to distinguish *cacicazgo* property from personal acquisitions in the case of movable merchandise.

At his death in 1591, Don Gabriel de Guzmán left in movable goods fifteen hundred sheep, three horses, quantities of worked gold and silver, precious stones, items of clothing, art and religious objects, knives, cups, and plates, and other items. In his last will and testament he directed that the bulk of this property was to be sold at auction and that the proceeds, after adjustment of his debts, were to be *divided equally among his heirs.*

[15] *Ibid.*, 200.

The sale of his goods, exclusive of the livestock, conducted after his death netted approximately ₱350.[16]

Gabriel de Guzmán had engaged in a variety of business enterprises, and at death he left his heirs with a tangled skein of pending transactions. Listed in his testament are total credits of ₱560 and debts of ₱635. His will also ordered the expenditure of sizeable sums of money on special Masses to be said after his death and for other funerary observances. On the basis of numerous entries in his will it appears that he had carried on a loan business, taking guns, jewels, and clothing as collateral. The auctioned merchandise could have included a number of unredeemed pledges among other personal items. An excerpt from the will of Gabriel de Guzmán detailing goods accumulated up to 1591 is contained in Appendix D–6.[17]

The long list of movable goods represents a fluid body of possessions, a component of the *cacicazgo*, changing in content through time. There is no earlier inventory of goods, and it is most certain that the material changed in complexion from cacique to cacique, year to year, and day to day. By the sudden disposal of a large share of the collection of movable goods and its conversion to cash in 1591, there was an abrupt alteration in the composition of the *cacicazgo*. It is likely that there was a sharp increase in the rate of acquisition of nonconsumable movable property during the reign of Don Gabriel. There was a great rise in the general economy of Yanhuitlán from about 1550 to 1570, and the cacique as the most important and influential native person in the community must have gained in affluence. The total complex of 1591 represents the result of accumulation and attrition on the body of merchandise which moved from a fully native inventory at the Conquest to one increasingly composed of European goods. Items represented in the *Codex Mendoza* or in the local tribute lists might be seen as the type of portable wealth of a Conquest-level cacique: feathers, costumes, vessels, jewelry, precious stones, dyestuff, gold dust, ceremonial paraphernalia, and a number of utility items. The will and auction of 1591 represent the opposite end of the continuum when Spanish merchandise constituted 90 to 95 per cent of the total inventory of possessions. The conversion of goods to money

[16] *Ibid.*, 400, exp. 1.

[17] *Ibid.*, 400, exp. 1; JM and MH, 34–36.

represents a further alteration in the material composition of the *cacicazgo*.

The Granting of Special Privilege after the Spanish Conquest

The cacique, standing at the very pinnacle of Indian society, was accorded privileges that no other person of native birth, or even most Spaniards, could ever expect. Considering the great respect which was traditionally accorded him and the influence which he exercised in other aspects of native life, it is not surprising that he played a considerable role in the political activity of the community. He was probably called upon to give his opinion in important matters, even though he might hold no official position in the formal hierarchy. Because of his lifelong term as ruler, he could be expected to have gained great power and influence over the elected officials and, as shown in an earlier chapter, had great authority in local appointments and elections. The fact that caciques were often elected as governors attests to the confidence of the *principales* and the natives in the ability or right of these lords to occupy the highest elective office in Indian government. While lands, political power, and services may have shown gradual diminution in the eighty years subsequent to the Conquest, the prestige of the cacique in some ways increased, and certain of his economic interests were protected by official means.

The granting of special privilege was a common practice in sixteenth-century New Spain. The post-Conquest caciques of Yanhuitlán had been granted not only the services, lands, goods, and salaries heretofore described, but, in addition, received many special privileges accorded only to the native nobility and caciques of New Spain.

From the time of the first Christian caciques of Yanhuitlán, María Cocuahu and Diego Nuqh, until the end of the reign of Don Francisco de Guzmán, all were granted the rank of don, a title reserved in the sixteenth century to the Spanish hidalgo class. Among the native population it was normally only the cacique or a person of noble lineage who was officially permitted to bear the title of don.

During the last quarter of the sixteenth century Don Gabriel de Guzmán was given a permit to raise or have in his possession fifteen hundred sheep, an enormous quantity of livestock to be owned by one person. He also possessed horses and other livestock, wore Spanish riding habit, and bore firearms, all of which were indicative of highest rank. These privileges could be gained only by specific viceregal order in the sixteenth century.[18] The granting of these privileges began during the regency of Don Domingo de Guzmán, but was not as extensive as in the case of Don Gabriel and Don Francisco. Through permission of the viceroy, Don Gabriel also engaged in the profitable merchandising of European as well as native goods in Yanhuitlán.[19] The latter privilege gave him an important source of income and afforded considerable economic advantage over other merchants in the community.

By virtue of his position as cacique, Don Gabriel during his reign was the recipient of more privileges, special grants, and immunities than any other non-Spaniard in Yanhuitlán. This can also be said to have held true for his predecessor, Don Domingo, and his successor, Don Francisco. Don Gabriel, however, was without question the most influential native person in Yanhuitlán during the Spanish sixteenth century. This realization leads us to a consideration of the role of ruler-cacique which will constitute Chapter VIII.

Codex Nuttall

18 AGN, *Tierras*, 400, exp. 1.
19 AGN, *Indios*, 3, exp. 540.

8.

The Changing Role of the Ruler-Cacique in Mixtec Culture

FROM THE DECADES just prior to the initial confrontation between Spaniard and Mixtec until the early decades of the seventeenth century, the ruler-cacique clearly occupied a pivotal position in native society. A series of individuals successively occupied that role during the sixteenth century, and each viewed the exercise of office in a different way. As the culture underwent change, so did the manner in which the role was perceived and performed undergo transformation. The gradual redirection and reformulation of Mixtec society served as the dynamic backdrop for shifting emphasis and function in the role of the community ruler.

The less detailed information, archaeological and documentary, presently available for the pre-Hispanic era necessitates rather broad generalization on the role of the ruler during this important period in Mixtec history. A larger corpus of documentation, printed and manuscript, for post-Conquest times makes it possible to formulate more specific statements concerning the position and influence of the cacique in that portion of the sixteenth century, when the traditional norms of Mixtec culture were subjected to modification and change by the impress of European modes of government, society, and thought. I have made an intensive study of unpublished documentary sources relating to Yanhuitlán, the most populous of the Mixtec communities during the contact period. Similar materials for other Mixtec communities have been less intensively examined for purposes of comparison, and on the basis of these investigations, I feel that the discussion of the role of the ruler-cacique in Yanhuitlán has a basic validity for the greater Mixteca Alta in the sixteenth century.

In the last section of this chapter I will present some general conclusions concerning cultural developments in the Mixteca Alta, recommendations for future study of this important area, and comment on methodological procedures, especially with reference to the value and use of documentary materials for the study of Mesoamerican cultures.

The Pre-Conquest Scene

In the preceding chapters I have postulated the existence in pre-Hispanic times of several regional lordships, or kingdoms, in the Mixteca Alta that may be identified and associated with major valley components. Reference has been made to vague statements in sixteenth-century sources to a great lord of all the Mixteca in pre-Conquest times, but most of the data presently available do not provide substantial proof for this concept. Moreover, it seems clear that the conquest of the Mixteca Alta by the Aztecs resulted only in the imposition of controls and procedures which would ensure prompt periodic payment of tribute to the lords of the Culhua-Mexica, but without the imposition of fundamental changes in the autonomy and internal government of the Mixtec regional lordships. If these conclusions are valid, they obviously imply pre-eminence for the pre-Conquest lords of the Mixteca Alta in their respective areas.

The Mixtec pictorial codices, insofar as their content has been analyzed by Alfonso Caso and other modern investigators, give a special emphasis to the genealogy, marriage, and descent of pre-Conquest rulers, and to events relating to the careers of some of these leaders of Mixtec society and culture. This would suggest that in pre-Hispanic times the native lords occupied positions of paramount influence and prestige, and that Mixtec history before the Spanish Conquest must be equated in large measure in terms of the activities of these cacique-chieftains. The pre-Conquest role and status of the native lords of the Mixteca, as suggested by the pictorial codices, are confirmed by data recorded in the Reyes grammar and the Alvarado dictionary of Mixteco, first published in 1593, which reflect the results of the language studies carried on by Dominican friars during early post-Conquest years. Reyes gives a long list of words describing parts of the body and activities of Mixtec lords,

Hand-carved door of the church in Teposcolula.

Low-relief pre-Hispanic sculpture in the plaza at Yucuita.

and also terms for addressing them, that differed from those employed for the commoners. The Alvarado dictionary records numerous words and phrases to designate the leaders of native society, e.g., *yya* ("*señor*"), *yya canu* ("*señor grande*"), *yya yevua* ("*principe*"), *yya yyo* ("*señor de siervos*"), etc. The dictionary also lists special descriptive terms for caciques: to cite a single case, for the tatooing of caciques as opposed to the tatooing of commoners which is signified by a different word.

Post-Conquest documentation contains references to the "absolute" authority of the ancient rulers of the Mixteca. The Inquisition hearings of 1544–45 in the *procesos* of the cacique-regent and two *principales* of Yanhuitlán record statements that the natives of the Mixteca Alta gave unhesitating obedience to their caciques, looked to them for guidance, and followed their wishes without question.[1] In Chapter VII, I have cited similar data drawn from the 1580 *probanza* of Don Gabriel de Guzmán, cacique of Yanhuitlán.

The function and status of the Mixtec ruler-cacique and his relationship to his subjects are also revealed in the following statement of Herrera:

> There were in the land many captains, knights, teachers, and lawgivers; they had sorcerers and physicians. And because everything was decided by the cacique, and since they were not in the habit of entering where he was, they had two *relatores*, who in their language were called mediators. They were located in a chamber of the palace where they heard those having business (with the cacique) and they conveyed these things to the *Señor* and returned with his responses. They were the advisors to the *Señor*, and they were old, wise, and experienced men who had first been priests in the temples. They sought to be affable and efficient, and they received gifts of jewelry and things to eat. He who gained permission to speak with the cacique entered barefoot without raising his eyes; and he who entered did not spit or cough, nor did he place his feet on the mat where the cacique was seated.[2]

Power and authority moved from the ruler through the nobility (*Principales*) to the barrios of the *cacicazgo* center (*cabecera*), to the subject dependencies, and to the individual citizen. Flowing in the opposite direction was the recognition of that power and authority and sub-

[1] AGN, *Inquisición*, 37, exps. 5–11.

[2] Herrera, *Historia*, déc. 3, lib. 3, cap. 12.

mission to it—obedience, respect, personal services, and tribute. These same concepts and procedures characterized the status and role of the post-Conquest native lords, but subject to progressive modification as the result of Spanish dominion.

The Role of the Ruler-Cacique in Yanhuitlán

I now wish to turn to an analysis of the role-complex of the cacique as it was performed by a series of title-holders and as it underwent modification during the sixteenth century. The discussion is posed within the context of a fluent culture, a stream of time, a succession of related individuals, and a category of activities.

From 1500 to 1600 the ruler-cacique of Yanhuitlán was the most important, most affluent, and most influential person in the life and activities of that community. As ruler, he guided the political, social, and religious life of his community. The measure of his authority and influence was modified during these hundred years, but at the end of the sixteenth century he was still the most powerful and respected personality in Yanhuitlán.

Although the *cacicazgo* of Yanhuitlán on the eve of Spanish Conquest comprised a part of the tributary empire of the Culhua-Mexica, its native rulers, like those of other *cacicazgos* of the Mixteca Alta, continued to enjoy "absolute" authority in the conduct and control of local affairs. Their power and influence were limited only by their sense of propriety and the tolerance of the nobility (*principales*) and their lesser subjects. The nobility found it advantageous to support and assist their leader, and as a group they did not seem to have questioned cacique authority; the commoners apparently gave unquestioning allegiance and obedience to their native lord. Spanish dominion imposed some limitations on the authority of the ruler-cacique of Yanhuitlán, but these checks, in the case of the first rulers of the Colonial Period, were less stringent than those regulating activities of caciques who came to power in the seventeenth and eighteenth centuries. It is evident from documentary testimony that Namahu and Cauaco, as well as María and Pedro, continued to enjoy unquestioned authority, that they performed their offices in an orderly fashion, and that they earned the respect and loyalty of their contemporaries who survived them. The Christian baptism of María and Pedro may have had considerable effect on their lives and the manner in which they performed their roles as supreme community rulers, particularly in regard to their traditional position as religious and ceremonial leaders. Unfortunately the available documentation relating to Namahu and Cauaco, and to Pedro and María, is not of sufficient refinement to permit further comment. It is possible, however, to discuss the roles of their successors in greater detail.

Don Domingo de Guzmán, who served as cacique-regent for his nephew Don Gabriel, represents the transition from pre-Conquest ruler to post-Conquest cacique of Yanhuitlán. Born in 1510, Don Domingo had been reared in the native tradition as a privileged member of society. He belonged to a small group at the top of the social and political structure. The power of this group to exert control over its domain was unquestioned. Even under threat of domination from Tenochtitlán, the structure of local society had remained intact. Tolerance of the *status quo* was a notable feature of the relationship of the Mexicans to the subjugated communities of the extensive tribute empire.

For the first twelve years of his life, Don Domingo participated fully in native Mixtec culture. He enjoyed a privileged status as the member of a large and powerful ruling family even though order of birth had placed him in the position of a royal prince who was never likely to inherit a royal title. His sister, María de Cocuahu, stood to succeed to the title at Yanhuitlán. The remaining siblings were to gain titles in other communities by normal succession or by marriage. So far as can be determined, he was the youngest member of a royal family, and his main hope for gaining title was by marriage to an heiress to a royal title. There is no indication that the woman whom he married succeeded to a title in her own right. Also, it is not likely that Domingo was trained for the role of cacique-regent of Yanhuitlán which he was later to assume.

Although born several years before the Conquest, Domingo was greatly affected by the imposition of the new cultural order. He was a vacillating convert to Christianity, a person who never fully adjusted to the strong new elements and forces that penetrated his culture. He could not be depended upon as a fully effective performer in the Spanish program of directed acculturation or as a reliable administrator or intermediary. By the late 1520's, he was confronted by a foreign culture and a new system of values. Spanish culture offered much that was desirable and worthy of assimilation, but certain elements were incompatible with an ancient pattern of life. He could neither dismiss his Mixtec heritage nor accept every tenet of the Spanish Colonial Period culture. Domingo did, however, effect the transition from the fully Mixtec rulers, Namahu, Cauaco, María de Cocuahu, and Pedro Nuqh, to his Hispano-Mixtec successors, Don Gabriel and Don Francisco de Guzmán. From the standpoint of the changes that were taking place in his culture, the regency of Don Domingo de Guzmán is most symbolic in that it signified the transition from the autochthonous life of Yanhuitlán to the more complex culture of the post-Conquest Period.

Don Gabriel de Guzmán, who assumed authority as cacique of Yanhuitlán in 1558 and held the office until his death in 1591, was perhaps the most remarkable Indian personality of the Mixteca Alta in the sixteenth century. He achieved an enviable reputation as a powerful and respected leader of native society, recognized both by his own people and by his Spanish superiors (see Appendix A–3). He presided over the richest and most populous of all the Mixtec *cacicazgos*, and held this position for thirty-three years. He was often requested to substantiate his claim and prove his entitlement to the office of ruler-cacique and his cacique patrimony, and it is because of these legal proceedings that we know so much about him.

Don Gabriel was deeply immersed in all manner of business enterprise, as shown by the award of special privileges to engage in commerce in Yanhuitlán and by the tangled skein of his financial affairs at the time of his death.[3] He was not above taking advantage of his position as cacique to further his personal ends, but he continued to retain the respect of those around him. He was the strongest and most resourceful of all the Yanhuitlán caciques for whom we have extensive documentation. Possibly only one other Mixtec ruler, Don Felipe de Austria of Teozacoalco and Tilantongo, compares to Don Gabriel in stature and in skill in manipulating the *cacicazgo* institution.

If any individual can be said to typify the Mixtec cacique of the sixteenth century, to stand as the archtype, that person would be Don Gabriel de Guzmán, who emerges as a true man of action and a leader

[3] AGN, *Tierras*, 400, exp. 1.

and manipulator of public opinion and affairs. Realizing his capacity for leadership, the missionary clergy assisted in his education, and Spanish governmental authorities accorded recognition of his hereditary position as leader of his community. As cacique, he stood in an intermediate position between Spaniard and Indian, and his conduct and character symbolize the new Hispano-Indian culture that was forming in his time. Although born after the Spanish Conquest, Don Gabriel was reared with complete awareness of his native cultural heritage and of his royal status. He did, however, ally himself with the Spaniards more than had any of his ancestors. He was one of the very few native rulers who was able to speak, write, and read Spanish to the point of being called "*ladino*."[4] He served as an effective agent for the transmission of Spanish colonial culture to the native population, and Spanish officials reciprocated by acknowledging his status and privileges and confirming him as ruler-cacique of Yanhuitlán.

Thus in the time of Don Gabriel a new dimension, the utilization of the *cacicazgo* as a device for directed acculturation, was added to this native institution. The office and influence of the ruler-cacique were effectively manipulated to promote the missionary program conducted by the Dominican friars. The Inquisition hearings of 1544–45 record considerable evidence of the continuing practice of native religion during the regency of Don Domingo de Guzmán, although the *procesos* formulated in the case of the cacique-regent and two Yanhuitlán *principales* lapsed without final judgment as to their guilt or innocence.[5] Available documentation indicates that Don Gabriel de Guzmán faithfully observed the tenets of Christianity and actively collaborated with the Dominican friars in the advancement of the missionary program and in

[4] AGI, *Escribanía de Cámara*, 162; AGN, *Tierras*, 400, exp. 1.

[5] In the 1530's, Fray Juan de Zumárraga, first bishop of Mexico City, serving as inquisitor, had investigated several cases in which baptized Indians were accused of continuing their practice of native religion. The most famous of these cases involved Don Carlos, cacique of Texcoco, who was found guilty and paid the supreme penalty of being burned at the stake. This case, which occurred in 1539, provoked serious criticism of the Bishop by officials in Spain. He was replaced as inquisitor by Licenciado Tello de Sandoval, a member of the Council of the Indies, who was sent to Mexico in the early 1540's to conduct a general visitation of the viceregal government of New Spain. (See Richard Greenleaf, *Zumárraga and the Mexican Inquisition, 1536–1543*.) The new inquisitor, who served as judge in the Yanhuitlán cases, may have deemed it expedient to terminate the proceedings without formal judgement.

the construction of the massive church and friary in Yanhuitlán. The 1563 report of Alonso Caballero, cited in preceding chapters, indicates that the friars in turn facilitated the building of a rather elaborate housing complex for the cacique by diverting Indian labor from church construction to this project.

Spanish officialdom also made use of native governmental organization, including the office of cacique-governor, for draining off the wealth of the *cacicazgo*. This represented a continuity from the days of the Aztec Empire. The Spaniards availed themselves of a previously existing tribute artery and elaborated it for the support of the Spanish encomendero and the Church. Although the viceregal government recognized the traditional right of the ruler-cacique to receive labor services and tribute from the people of his *cacicazgo*, this form of cacique income was considerably reduced during the "reign" of Don Gabriel. Losses sustained by the cacique in this respect were offset, at least in part, by his private business enterprises, fostered to some extent by special privileges granted by the viceregal officials.

Don Gabriel symbolizes the new order of caciques in the Mixteca, who, while maintaining an intimate tie to the past which justified and validated their position in the social hierarchy, made conscious efforts to embrace a new system of values and a new way of life. These were the Christian caciques. No longer was there marked tension between the old morality and religion and the new ethico-religious concepts that had rendered Don Domingo de Guzmán incapable of serving as a completely effective agent in the transition from the ancient way of life to that of the post-Conquest Period. Early Colonial culture included much that was old, but required a reorientation that Don Domingo could not or did not wish to make.

As the outstanding representative of the new order of caciques, Don Gabriel played a major role in the process of cultural continuity and change in the Mixteca Alta. But he also realized that forces of attrition were threatening the traditional *cacicazgo* institution. Consequently, he sought by means of the legal proceedings of 1580, to obtain official recognition of his cacique status and his cacique patrimony.[6] And by his last will and testament, dictated in 1591, he took action to ensure legiti-

[6] AGN, *Civil*, 516.

Codex Nuttall

mate succession to his *cacicazgo* and for preservation of the institution that had expanded in function during his reign but which had probably contracted in terms of lands, movable goods, and services.

Don Francisco de Guzmán was a man much like his father Don Gabriel. He was fully a Christian; in the style of his ancestors, he played a leading role in religious observances and ceremony, and, as his father had done, he acted as an intermediary in the mission activities of the Dominican Order. He was wealthy in the goods and property of the *cacicazgo*, and he continued to enjoy the privileges and incomes of that institution. Francisco spoke Spanish, and he was frequently called upon in an official capacity to investigate disputes in other communities. Although he somehow lacked the enthusiasm and ambition of his father, he nevertheless enjoyed an equal amount of respect. Forces that had threatened the *cacicazgo* of Yanhuitlán during the later years of the reign of Gabriel seem to have been held in check during Francisco's time. There is little mention of him in the litigation of the early seventeenth century prior to 1629, when he was succeeded as cacique of Yanhuitlán by his nephew Baltasar de Velasco y Guzmán. The important changes and reorientations in the role of ruler-cacique had taken place before Francisco inherited the title in 1591, and during his reign the *cacicazgo* attained the highest degree of stability since pre-Conquest times.

The Mixtec Achievement

Retrospective evaluation of the long-range development of culture in the Mixteca Alta prompts the question whether the Mixtec pattern at the time of the Spanish Conquest had fulfilled its potential. In view of the limited technology and the inclination of the Mixtecs to farm only level valley or terrace lands, it seems doubtful that the Mixteca Alta could have supported a higher level of cultural development than it had in 1520. Furthermore, it seems unlikely that the area could have maintained a larger population in pre-Conquest times than it did in the peak years of the mid-sixteenth century, assuming of course that the decades of 1550–70 were characterized by an increase of population after the devastating epidemics of the 1540's. The land, the technology, the political structure, and the economic orientation (agriculture with a heavy supplementation of hunting and gathering) of the Mixteca Alta probably would have never permitted the rise of a great urban civilization.

The demands on available land seem to have been as great in pre-Conquest times as at present. Dahlgren, in fact has suggested that population pressures in the Mixteca forced or contributed heavily to post-Classic Mixtec invasions of the valley of Oaxaca.[7] Perhaps 80 per cent of the Mixteca Alta is composed of sharply sloping to rugged mountain land. The remaining 20 per cent is for the most part formed by narrow and irregular valleys. Several of these valleys, Yanhuitlán, Tamazulapan-Tejupan, and Tlaxiaco, are relatively open. Even these are punctuated by declivities, hills, and rocky fingers of mountain land protruding from the bordering ranges, which make it difficult to lay out and work farm plots and render much of the land unsuitable for Mixtec agriculture.

The valley of Yanhuitlán, the largest, reaches roughly from Yanhuitlán in the northwest to Jaltepec in the southwest, the over-all length being some twenty kilometers. The greatest width of the valley floor is perhaps five to eight kilometers. This is the greatest expanse of open land in the entire Mixteca Alta. The Mixtecs were farmers who hunted and gathered to supplement their diet. Agriculture was intensive and irrigation was practiced where feasible. Mountain land was not used except in rare instances. The Mixtecs lived in the valleys and worked the

[7] Dahlgren, *La Mixteca.*

valleys. They did not dwell to any extent in the mountain fastness preferred by some of their Zapotec and Mixe contemporaries to the east. Nor did they attempt to farm the high slopes. These were lands given over to religious shrines and hunting preserves and, after the Spanish Conquest, grazing lands. People tended to congregate in the valleys. The most densely populated areas were the valleys of Yanhuitlán, Tamazulapan, Tlaxiaco, Coixtlahuaca and the valley system of Teposcolula. Sosola, Almoloyas, Apoala, Tilantongo, Mitlatongo, and Achiutla were situated in more mountainous regions with only very limited valley lands, and the population in these areas was correspondingly small and more dispersed.

In both the valley and mountain towns there was a need to resort to the construction of artificial terraces in the lower arroyos and between the ridges extending down into the valleys. These furnished level plots which could be irrigated by controlling run-off in the natural channels of water flow. Extensive terrace systems may now be seen in the vicinity of Nochixtlán and in several other localities in the Mixteca Alta.

The land, then, imposed restrictions and influenced to considerable degree the course of Mixtec cultural development. There were no great open plains where an agricultural group might flourish and develop an urban civilization. A people attracted to valley agriculture was hampered in their development by the terrain which they chose as their homeland. The growth and expansion of Mixtec culture knew limitations that could be overcome only by a change in values and a shift in technology. Perhaps this could account for the differing achievements of the Mixtecs and such groups as those residing in highland and coastal Peru. The ancient Peruvians existed in somewhat analogous environments of limited potential but were able through a superior technology and suitable value orientations to develop an advanced urban civilization.[8] Divergences in Mixtec and Peruvian patterns are clearly apparent. The Peruvians—at least in Postclassic times—were able to build a political institution capable of binding together a vast area, even a series of semi-

[8] See W. C. Bennett, "The Andean Highlands: An Introduction," in J. H. Steward (ed.), *Handbook of South American Indians*, II, BAE *Bulletin No. 143*; Wendell C. Bennett, "The Archeology of the Central Andes," *ibid.*, II; John H. Rowe, "Inca Culture at the Time of the Spanish Conquest," *ibid.*, II; George Kubler, "The Quechua in the Colonial World," *ibid.*, II.

discrete valleys, into a common political and economic entity. Mixtec society was not of that caliber. While there are repeated references to a great lord ruling the Mixteca in the years before the Spanish Conquest, no further evidence can be adduced to verify the existence of such a grand scheme of government or, if it existed, to describe its operation. It probably did not exist. What existed instead was a large number of valley or regional societies, comprising a number of autonomous communities. Each was ruled by an autocratic ruler assisted by a body of noble retainers, advisers, and assistants. While these rulers were undoubtedly closely related, there is no evidence of their unified control by a central figure. The idea that the center of political authority for all or most of the Mixteca might rest in the rulers of Tilantongo does not hold up under scrutiny. The House of Tilantongo represented "the most honored" of the Mixtec lineages, and to emphasize a consanguineal tie with the rulers of Tilantongo served to reinforce and validate claims to royal title and privilege in other communities, but such claims did not in this instance carry political implications.

During the period from A.D. 1100 up to the time of the Spanish Conquest, either no one ruler could muster adequate support to establish himself as a great leader capable of binding these several socio-political and economic entities into a single state or "empire," or it simply did not occur that such a condition of life might be desirable. For the present, every resource, historical, archaeological, and ethnological, points to the existence of the many autonomous community kingdoms, coexisting and disputing but independent, and their persistence in time from the pre-Conquest years until the end of the sixteenth century. I would, therefore, contend that Mixtec society before the Conquest can be viewed in terms of these local kingdoms grouped into several semidiscrete valley or regional subcultures. I have chosen to refer to these cultural divisions, which also have validity for the post-Conquest Period, as the regional components of Mixtec culture. The fact that all of these were united by common cultural themes and a vast web of royal kinship makes the distinction among them no less meaningful.

Retrospect and Prospect

The present work represents an attempt to collect, organize, and utilize several types of source materials and through them to observe a developing culture and one of its major institutions during the most dynamic and complex century in Mixtec history. Rather than simply describe two configurations, one before the Conquest and one after, I have sought to depict a culture in its fluid state. I have found this to be a most difficult task, but the shortcomings of the present study should not deter further efforts in this direction. Methodologically speaking, anthropologists have far to go in their efforts to deal with the dynamics of culture, but as they more adequately grasp the historical dimension of cultural analysis, they can work toward a time when they can speak of cultures as flexible and fluid entities extended over periods of years, decades, or centuries. The respectable but time-worn technique of dissecting a cultural continuum into a sequence of discrete phases is not appropriate for the description and analysis of cultures as ongoing behavioral complexes. At present archaeologists deal very inadequately with such phenomena. Anthropology, if it is to advance our understanding of the processes of cultural growth and development, must seek to establish and improve methods whereby culture can be depicted in its naturally fluent condition.

Many of the conclusions appearing in the foregoing pages have been drawn on less than ideal evidence. This is particularly true for archaeological inferences. When the protohistoric and historic periods have been discussed, however, the evidence has been substantial, and conclusions rest on a firm foundation of reliable ethnographic fact. The cultural configurations that have been established are derived from archaeological reports, historical documents and chronicles, field investigations, and from the interpretations of specialists. This approach has been based on the assumption that the integration of the resources and findings of archaeology, linguistics, history, and ethnology provides a sound methodology for the study of cultural continuity and change.

In Chapter II intensive investigation of specific areas of the Mixteca Alta was proposed as a necessary preliminary for acquisition of a fundamental knowledge of Mixtec archaeology. Subsequent to these studies archaeologists should be able to trace and define general trends from Preclassic to Postclassic times with considerable accuracy. The continuing study of the pictorial codices by Caso and Smith will elucidate the chronology of pre-Conquest Mixtec history, significant features of ancient Mixtec culture, and the fortunes of the several dynastic lineages.

Linguists have given attention to the structure of the Mixtec language and its affiliations with other Mesoamerican tongues. The value of these studies cannot be denied, but I believe that documents like the Reyes grammar and the Alvarado dictionary of Mixteco have not been adequately exploited as resources for the study and analysis of Mixtec culture. Whatever faults or deficiencies these missionary works may have from the standpoint of the modern science of linguistics, patient examination of their content will produce a rich harvest of cultural data. Consequently, it may be pertinent to direct attention to some observations made by the Americanist Daniel Brinton in 1885. It was Brinton's contention that many of the colonial vocabularies of Mesoamerica merit comparison with European dictionaries of the same period, and that study of native American languages can be used, "like the reflection of a microscope," to reveal the family and social life, the customs and laws, the superstitions and religion, "and the secret and hidden mysteries of aboriginal man."[9]

I have emphasized the value of the historical document which may be reduced to raw ethnographic data and incorporated into a reconstruction of a specific but fluent socio-cultural continuum. The better and more abundant the documentation, the better archaeologists may follow and describe the development of individual cultures over extended periods of time. Without documentation archaeologists must base their reconstructions on what they may discern from archaeology and modern comparative ethnology. The record of the former is incomplete, and as concerns the latter, trying to infer the past from the present, even in the conservative rural societies of Mexico, is a risky procedure and is likely to produce a marked distortion of past reality. Where archaeologists have specific documentation from the sixteenth century forward, as in Mexico, they are doing less than their best if they fail to utilize the available record to the utmost in attempting to discover what actually happened.

Several significant features of Mixtec culture have been observed as they were conditioned by temporal and historical factors. These range in magnitude from a total cultural tradition (Mixtec culture) or the

[9] Scholes, "Franciscan Missionary Scholars in Colonial Central America," *The Americas*, Vol. VIII (1952), 391–416.

generalized features of native government in Mexico to the population profile, religious practices, economy, socio-political organization, and communal structure of a specific locality like Yanhuitlán, Oaxaca, and the content and function of Yanhuitlán's ruling institution and its changing complex of goods, privileges, services, and properties. An attempt has been made to consider a specific role, that of cacique-ruler, over a period of one hundred years and to make certain judgments as to the personalities and modes of performance of the individual occupants of that role-complex.

It is now possible to more adequately realize the potentialities and limitations of the historical document as an ethnographic device. It can be specific in its content; it allows the anthropologist to follow the history and cultural development of a society, and in the case of colonial Mexico, a single community or even a particular role can be observed; the document records what would inevitably be lost. The reliability of written records can be scrutinized by careful collation and comparison with other forms of evidence, and the raw data, that is, the documentation, can be subjected to repeated examination and re-evaluation. Judicious use of documentation requires such an approach.

The writers of sixteenth-century documents were not trained ethnologists, and they could not foresee the interests of twentieth-century anthropologists. Consequently there are limitations to the use of such records, particularly in the study of social and community organization. Unfortunately there are no treatises on the Mixtecs that are comparable to those of Sahagún for the Aztecs and Landa for the Mayans. Available documents often record hints and suggestions on many aspects of Mixtec life, but it is sometimes quite difficult to find sufficient material to complete the picture of a particular cultural element. Despite these limitations, unpublished archival documentation contains more specific cultural data than one might suspect. For the anthropologist the major obstacle to the use of this documentation is the laborious process of gleaning information that was considered useful to Spanish administrators from a mass of verbiage and legal formulary and converting it to pertinent ethnographic data. This task calls for considerable patience, but the effort will pay substantial dividends.

The final word has been written on none of the subjects treated in this book. An effort has been made to present a description of a little-known culture and an analysis of some of its more significant institutions as they appeared in the sixteenth century. This book is designed to serve as a stepping stone to further study. It is hoped that the definition of problems and procedures will serve to stimulate new inquiry into the cultural development of the Mixtec people and that similar studies will be made of other cultures of Oaxaca and Mexico. It is my intention to undertake further investigations to supplement and test the findings set forth on these pages, and similar efforts by other Americanists are eagerly anticipated.

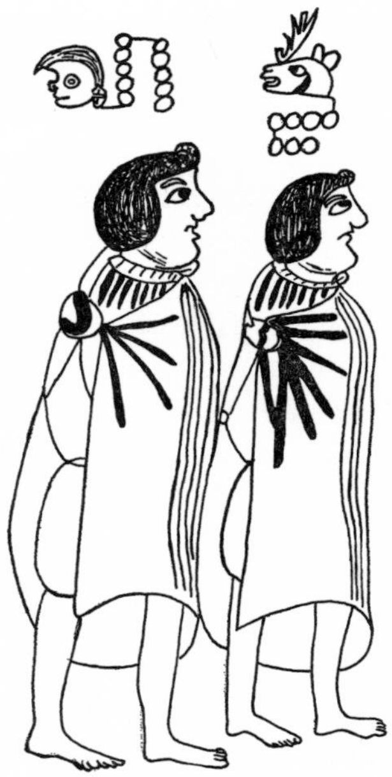

Códice de Yanhuitlán

APPENDIX A
Reproductions of Sixteenth-Century Documents

Appendix A–1

Certified Copies of the last will and testament of Don Domingo de Guzmán, cacique-regent of Yanhuitlán, and viceregal approval of the succession of Don Gabriel de Guzmán, 1558 (AGN, *Civil*, 516).

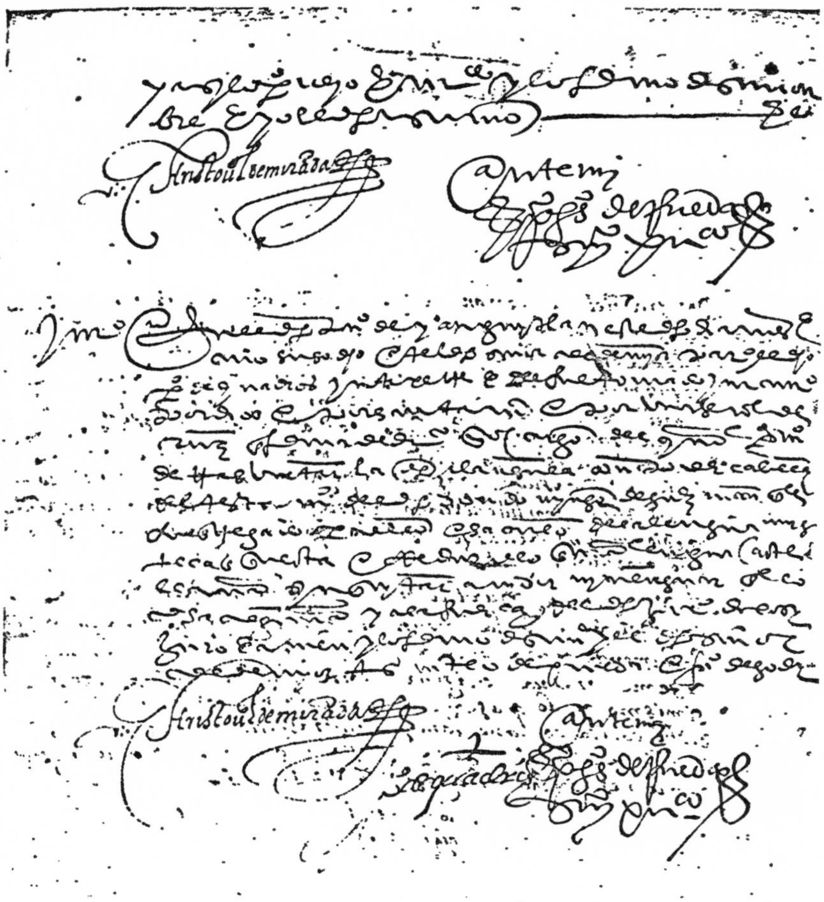

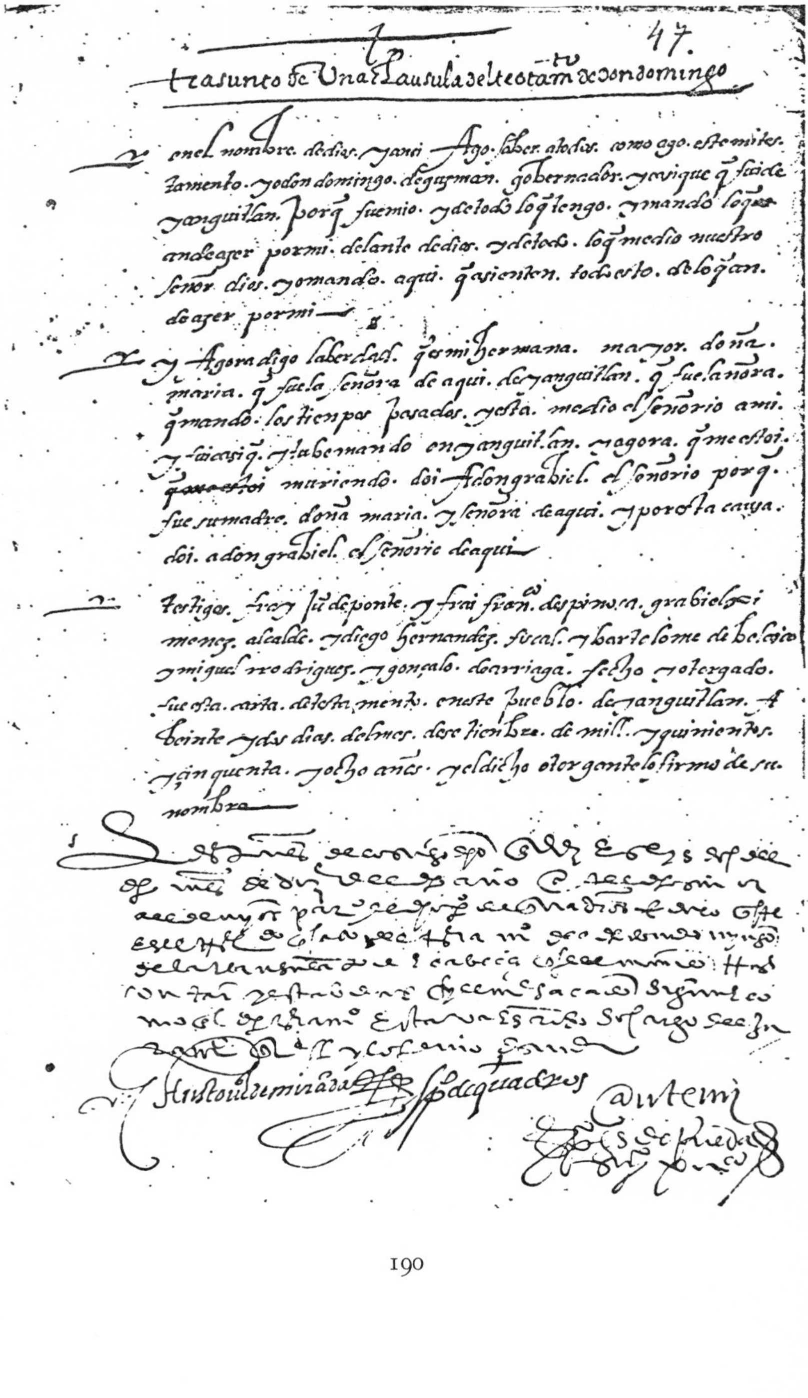

47.

trasunto de una clausula del testamento de don domingo

en el nombre de dios y amen. ago saber a todos como yo esto mi testamento yo don domingo de guzman gobernador y cacique q fui de yanguitlan porq fue mio y de todo lo q tengo y mando lo q ande hazer por mi delante de dios y de todos lo q medio nuestro señor dios y mando aqui q asienten todo esto de lo q an de hazer por mi

y agora digo la verdad q es mi hermana mayor doña maria q fue la señora de aqui de yanguitlan q fue la señora q mando los tienpos pasados y esta medio el señorio a mi y asi q y la be mandado en yanguitlan y agora q me estoi muriendo doi a don grabiel el señorio porq fue su madre doña maria y señora de aqui y por esta causa doi a don grabiel el señorio de aqui

testigos fray ju de ponte y frai fran despinosa grabiel ximenez alcalde y diego hernandez fiscal y bartolome de belasco y miguel rrodrigues y gonçalo de arriaga fecho y otorgado fue esta carta de testamento en este pueblo de yanguitlan a beinte y dos dias del mes de setienbre de mill y quinientos y cinquenta y ocho años y el dicho otorgante lo firmo de su nombre

[illegible]

Cristoval de miranda … de quadros

Ante mi … de Pineda …

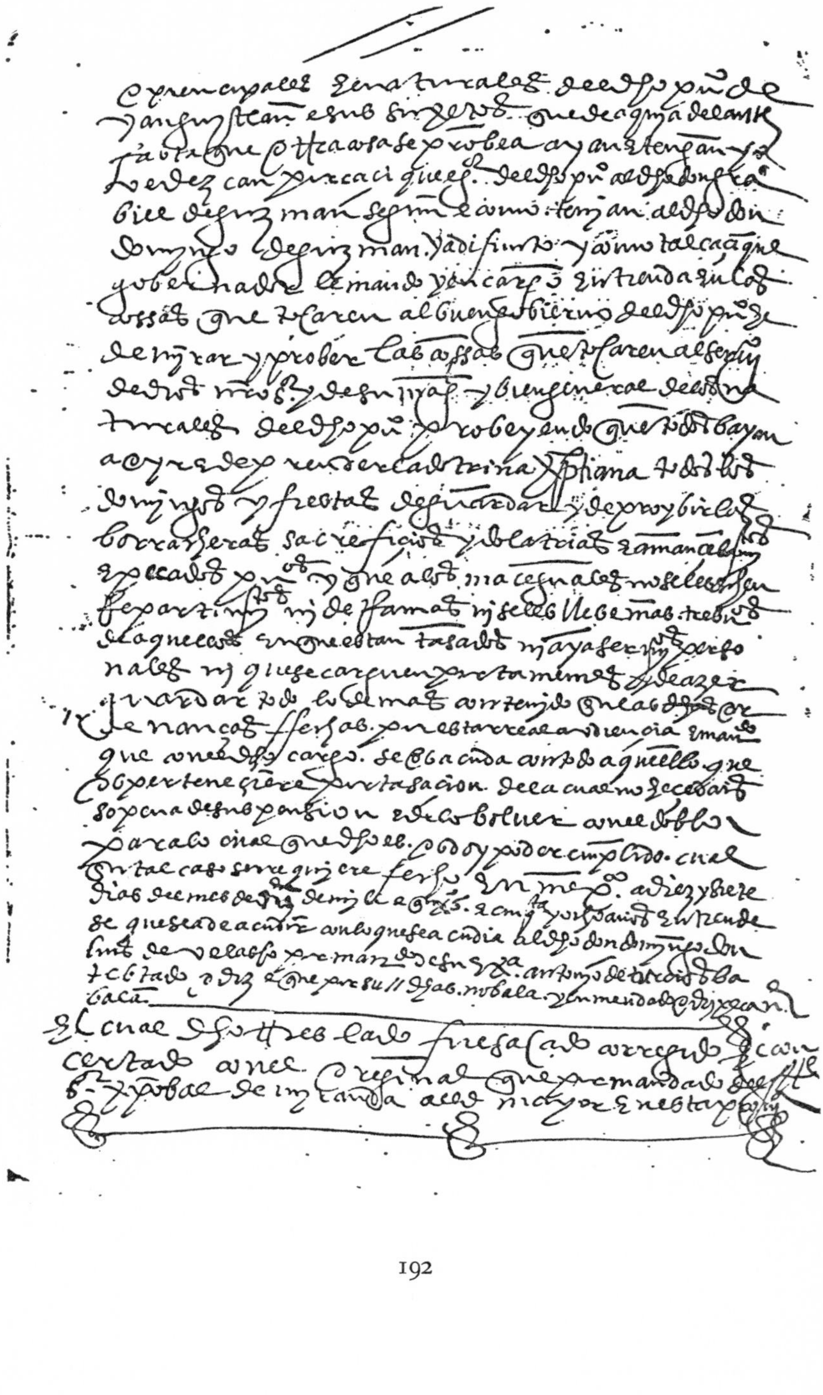

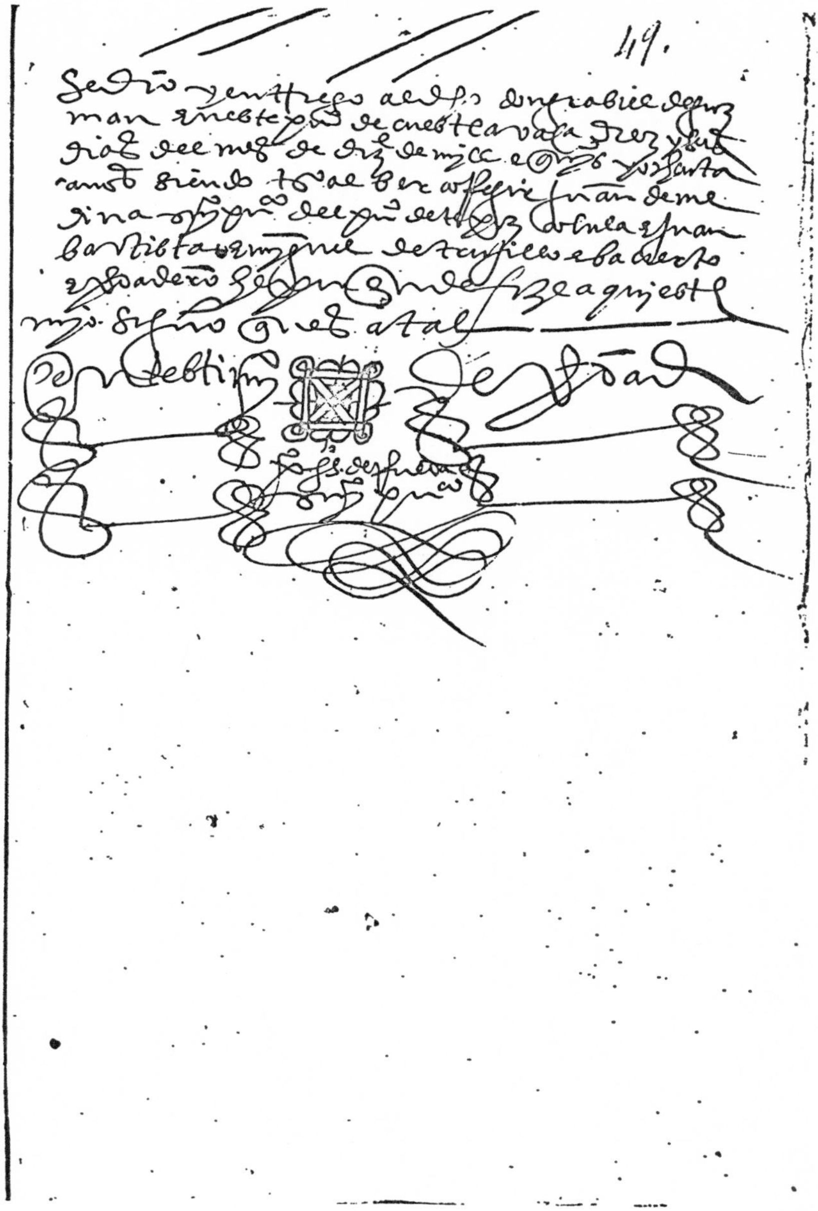

Appendix A–2

The *Sujetos* and Barrios of Yanhuitlán, 1565 (AGI, *Escribanía de Cámara*, 162).

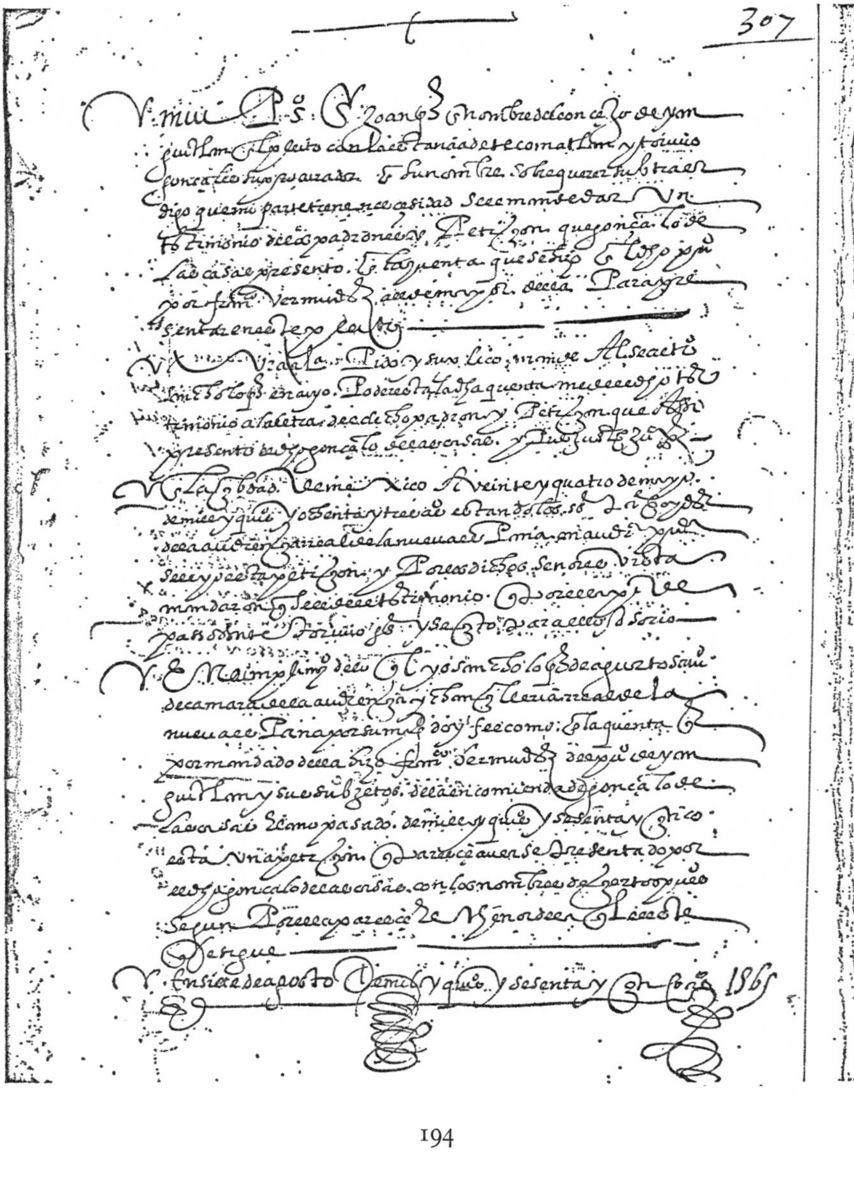

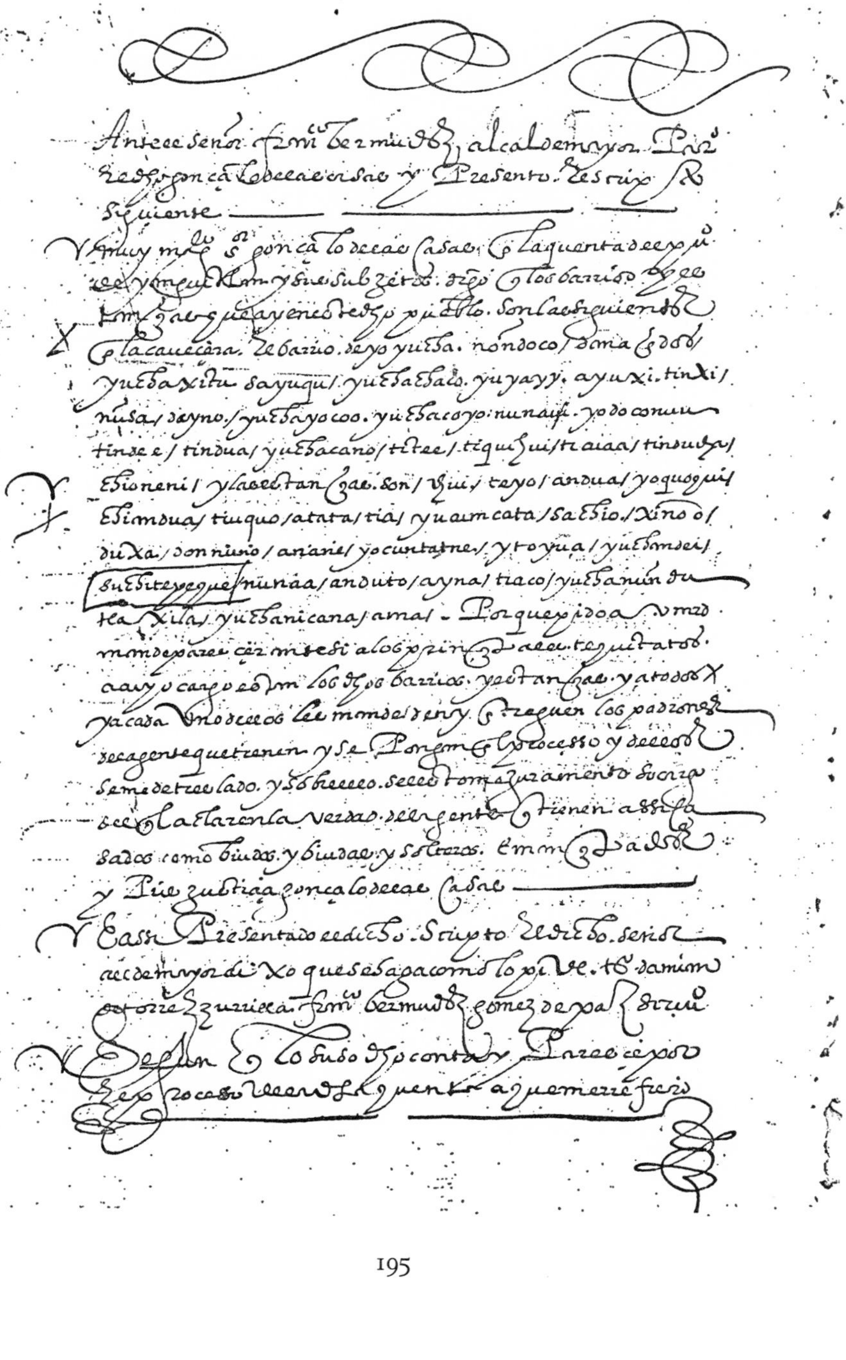

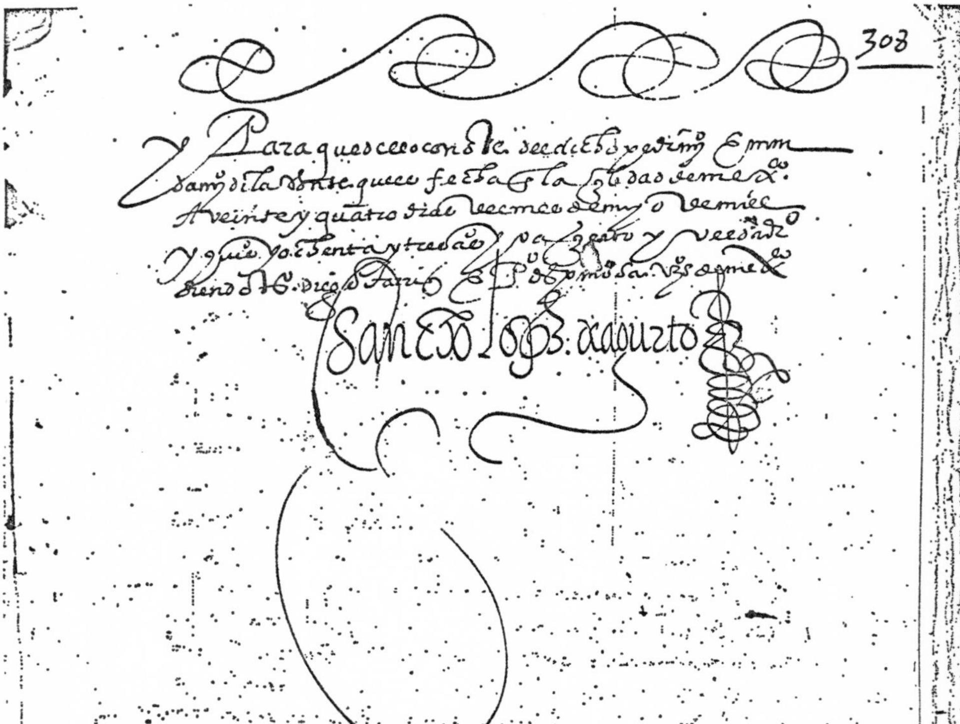
308

Sancho lopez de agurto

Appendix A–3

Interrogatory Concerning the Character of Don Gabriel de Guzmán, Cacique of Yanhuitlán, and the Responses of Fray Melchor Montano, Fray Alonso de Alvarado, Fray Martín de Mondragón, and Miguel García Renzino, 1582 (AGI, *Escribanía de Cámara*, 162).

256

Muy Poderoso señor Por las Preguntas siguientes
sean examinados los testigos que se presentaren por parte de los
yndios governador y principales del pueblo de yanguitlan
en el pleyto con los yndios de la estancia y sujeto de tecomatlan
acerca de la sesion que la dicha estancia pretende de los [illegible]
estancia de la chayabonos

1 Primeramente si conocen a las partes y si tienen noticia de la causa
sobre que es este pleyto

4 Yten si saben que don antonio de belasco casique del pueblo de malinalte
peque es suegro de don diego de gusman parte contraria y principal
de la dicha estancia de tecomatlan por yntercesion y medio del qual
los yndios del pueblo de malinaltepeque testificaron y dixeron
sus dichos en esta causa en favor de los de tecomatlan y para que
el dicho don antonio de belasco los negocio persuadio y mando
que dijesen sus dichos en favor del dicho don diego su [illegible] y de
los de el dicho su pueblo y estancia de manera y con rigor que siguiese
que los yndios le es tan obedientes y le tienen miedo entienden
los testigos que no osaran ni osaron hazer otra cosa sino en su favor
de los de tecomatlan digan lo que saben y como

4 Yten si saben que don gaspar casique del pueblo de mitlaltongo
es hermano legitimo y natural de padre y madre del dicho don
diego de gusman y asimismo mando y persuadio a los yndios
que del dicho pueblo testificaron en esta causa antes y al tiempo
que dixesen sus dichos que testificasen en favor de la dicha estancia
de tecomatlan y del dicho su hermano y es todo de tal manera que
creen y entienden los testigos que los dichos yndios no osaron ni osaran
hazer otra cosa aunque no supieron ni saben lo que les pre
guntaron digan los testigos todo lo que acerca de esto saben y entienden

4 Yten si saben que los yndios de los dichos dos pueblos de malinaltepeque
y mitlaltongo respeto de los dichos sus casiques estan y estaban

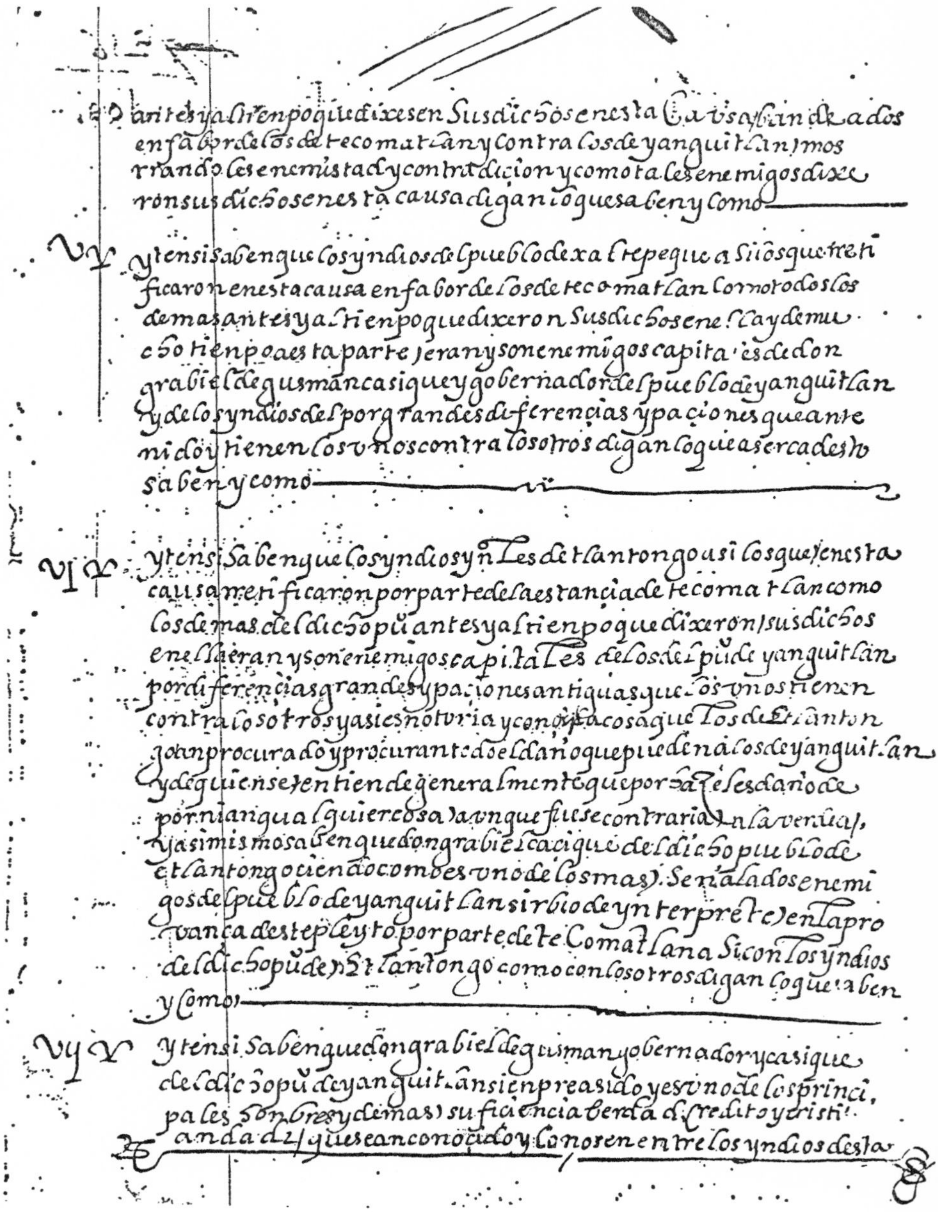
antes y al tienpo que dixesen sus dichos en esta causa y abian dado
en fabor de los de tecomatlan y contra los de yanguitlan mos
trando les enemistad y contradicion y como tales enemigos dixe
ron sus dichos en esta causa digan lo que saben y como

V X. yten si saben que los yndios del pueblo de xaltepeque a si los que testi
ficaron en esta causa en fabor de los de tecomatlan como todos los
demas antes y al tienpo que dixeron sus dichos en ella y de mu
cho tienpo a esta parte heran y son enemigos capitales de don
grabiel de gusman casique y gobernador del pueblo de yanguitlan
y de los yndios del por grandes diferencias y paciones que an te
nido y tienen los unos contra los otros digan lo que a cerca desto
saben y como

VI X. yten si saben que los yndios y naturales de tlantongo asi los que en esta
causa testificaron por parte de la estancia de tecomatlan como
los demas del dicho pu. antes y al tienpo que dixeron sus dichos
en ella eran y son enemigos capitales de los del pu. de yanguitlan
por diferencias grandes y paciones antiguas que los unos tienen
contra los otros y asi es notoria y conocida cosa que los de tlanton
go han procurado y procuran todo el daño que pueden a los de yanguitlan
y de quien se entiende generalmente que por hazer les daño de
pornian qualquier cosa aunque fuese contraria a la verdad,
y asimismo saben que don grabiel casique del dicho pueblo de
tlantongo siendo como es uno de los mas señalados enemi
gos del pueblo de yanguitlan sirbio de ynterprete en la pro
vança deste pleyto por parte de tecomatlan asi con los yndios
del dicho pu. de tlantongo como con los otros digan lo que saben
y como

VII X. yten si saben que don grabiel de gusman governador y casique
del dicho pu. de yanguitlan siempre a sido y es uno de los princi
pales honbres y de mas suficiencia berdad credito y cristi
andad y que es an conocido y conoren entre los yndios desta

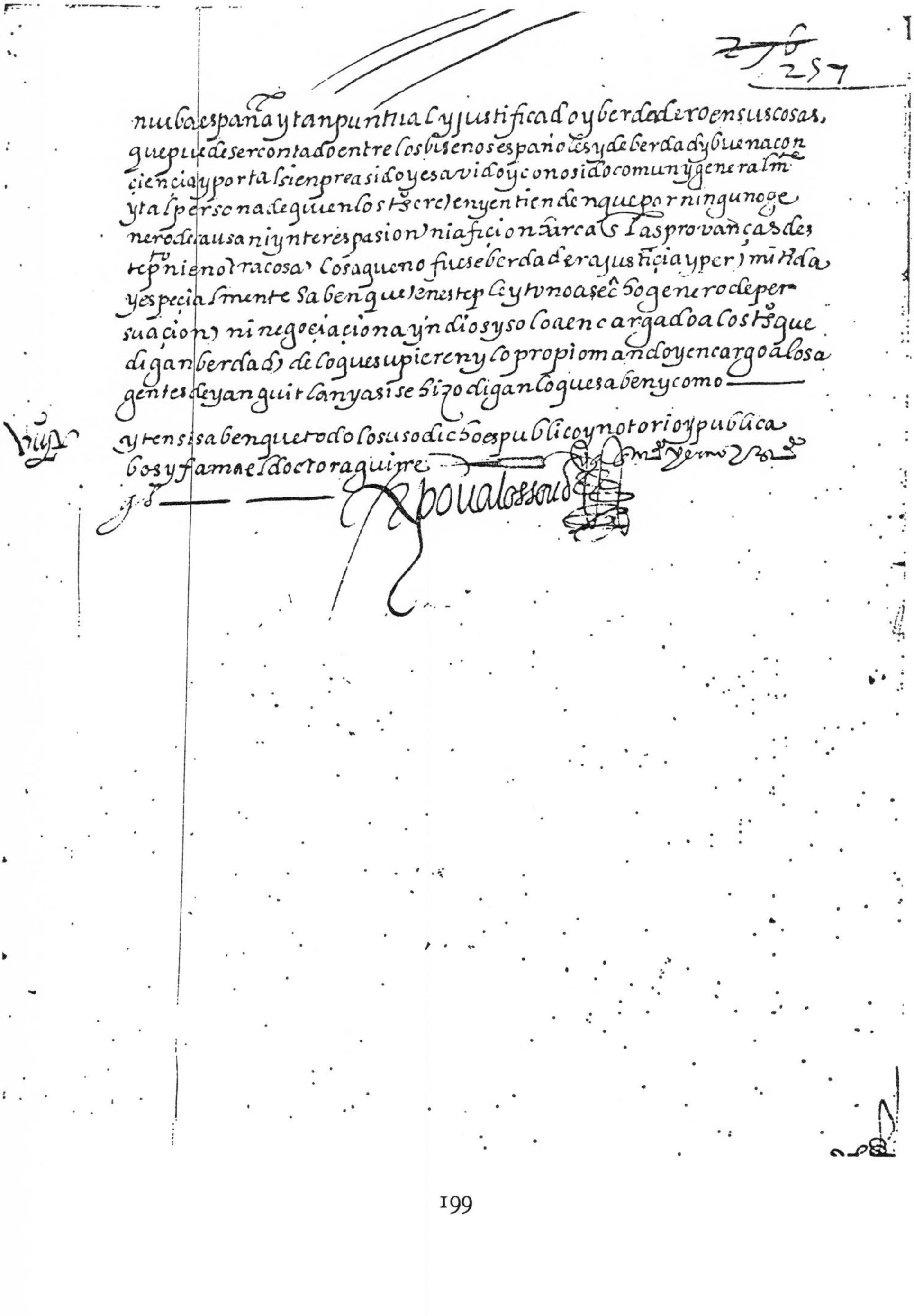

nueba españa y tan puntual y justificado y berdadero en sus cosas,
que puede ser contado entre los buenos españoles y de berdad y buena con
ciencia y por tal siempre a sido y es avido y conosido comun y generalm[ent]e
y tal persona de quien los s[eño]res creen y entienden que por ninguno ge
nero de causa ni ynteres pasion ni aficion acerca de las provanças des
te pleito ni en otra cosa dixera cosa que no fuese berdadera justicia y permitida
y especialmente saben que en este pleito y en el ... no a se echo genero de per
suacion ni negociacion a yndios y solo a encargado a los t[estig]os que
digan berdad de lo que supieren y lo propio mando y encargo a los a
gentes de yanguitlan y asi se hizo digan lo que saben y como
y tienen si saben que todo lo susodicho es publico y notorio y publica
boz y fama el doctor aguirre

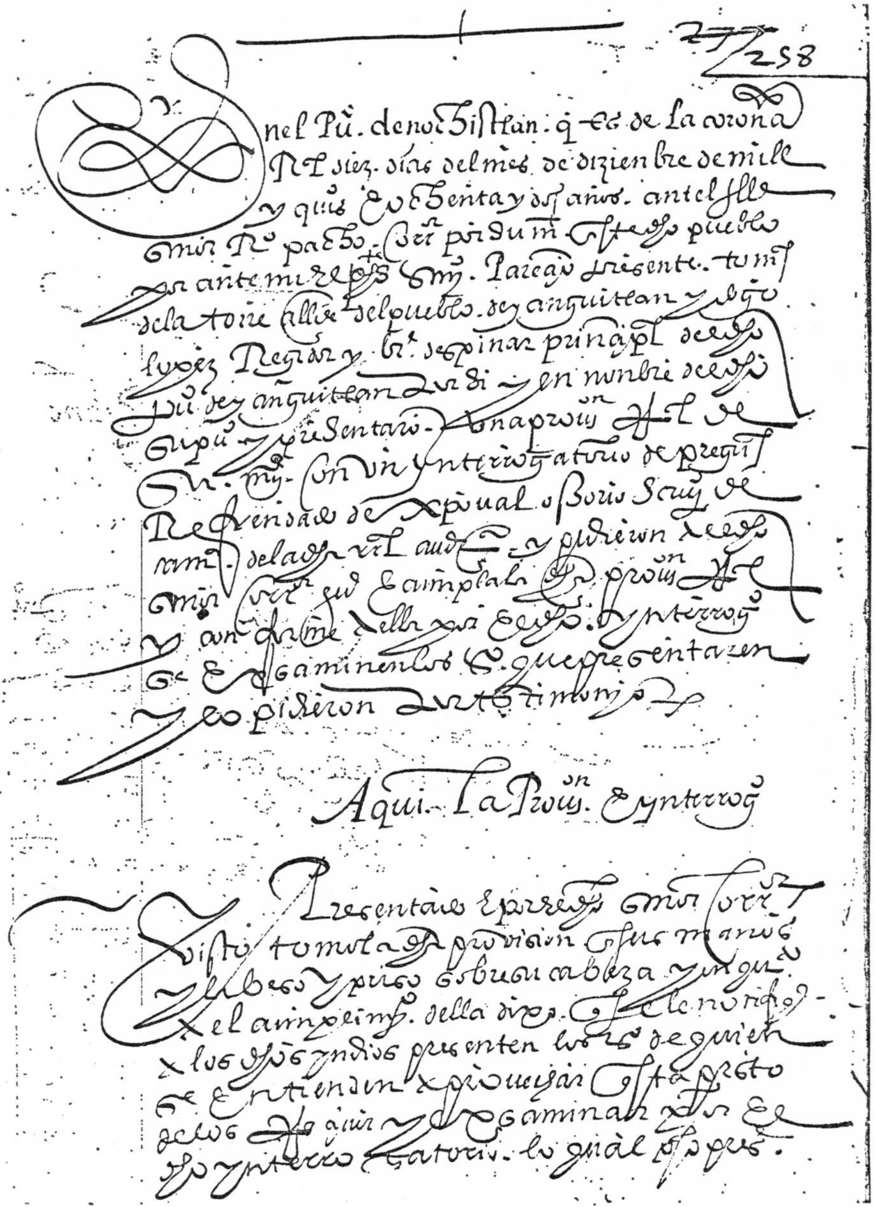

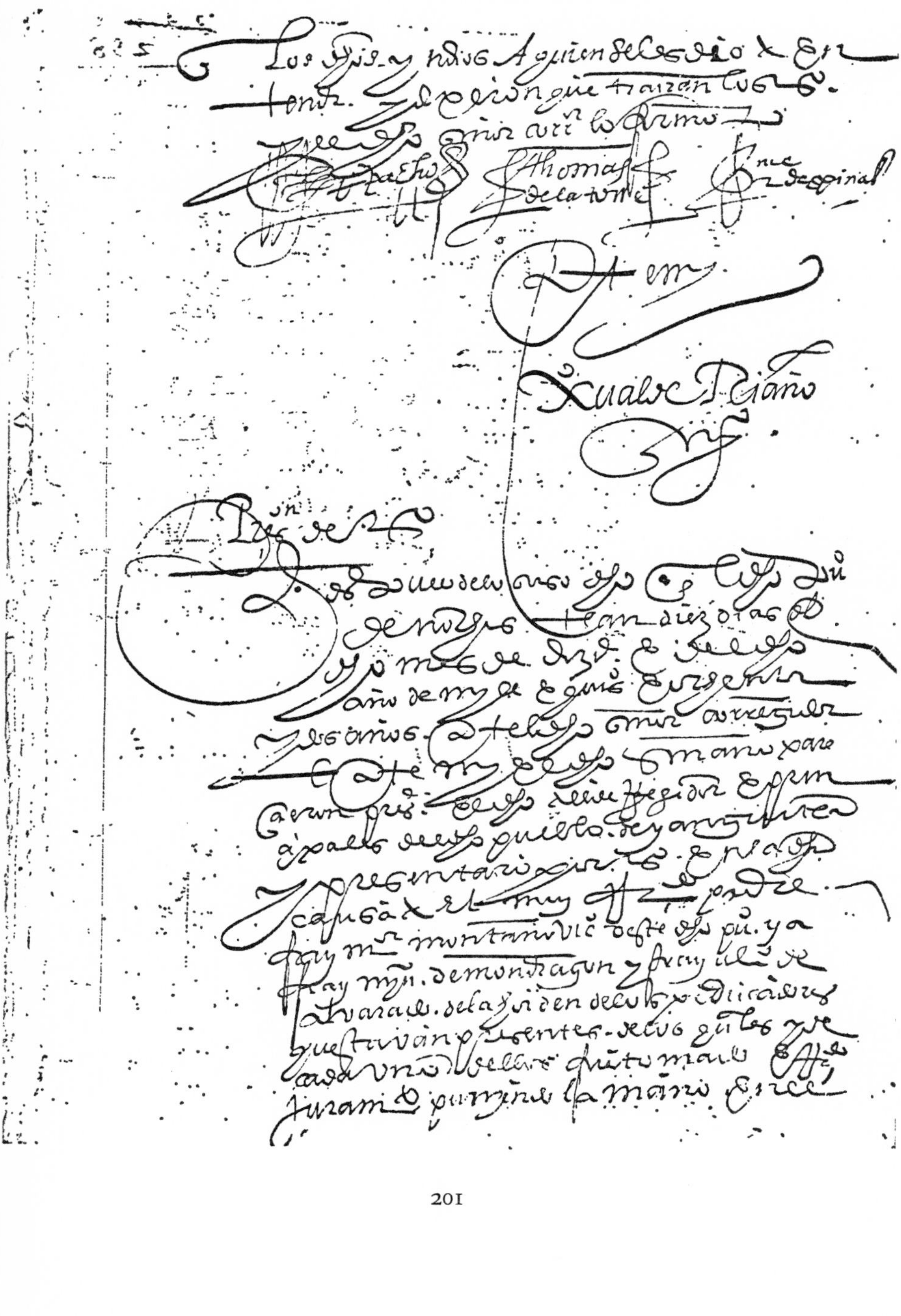

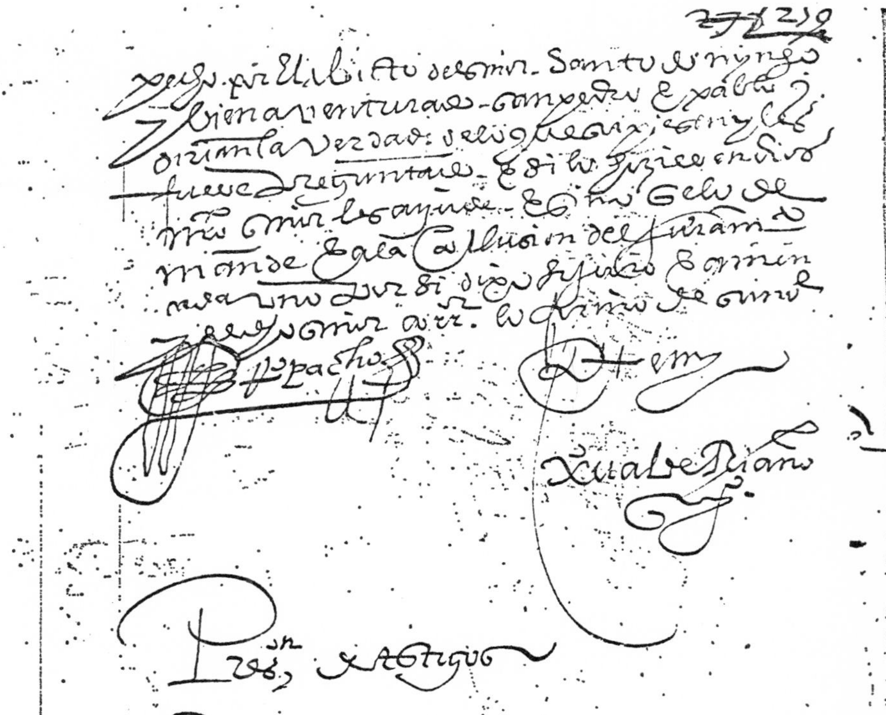

[illegible]

su madre. E por las palabras de los
santos quatro evangelios
y de una señal de cruz [illegible]
[illegible] sobre que pusieron
sus manos derechas que dirian verdad de lo
que supiesen y les fuese preguntado
y si ansi lo hiziesen Dios nuestro señor
les ayude e si no el lo demande. E a la
conclusion del juramento dixeron si juro
amen [illegible]
[illegible] de su nombre

[illegible]

[illegible]

Xual de Triano

Lo que los dichos dixeron y
depusieron siendo preguntados
por la primera e ultima e tercera preguntas
del interrogatorio para que fueron
presentados es lo siguiente

[illegible]

[illegible]

Xual de Triano

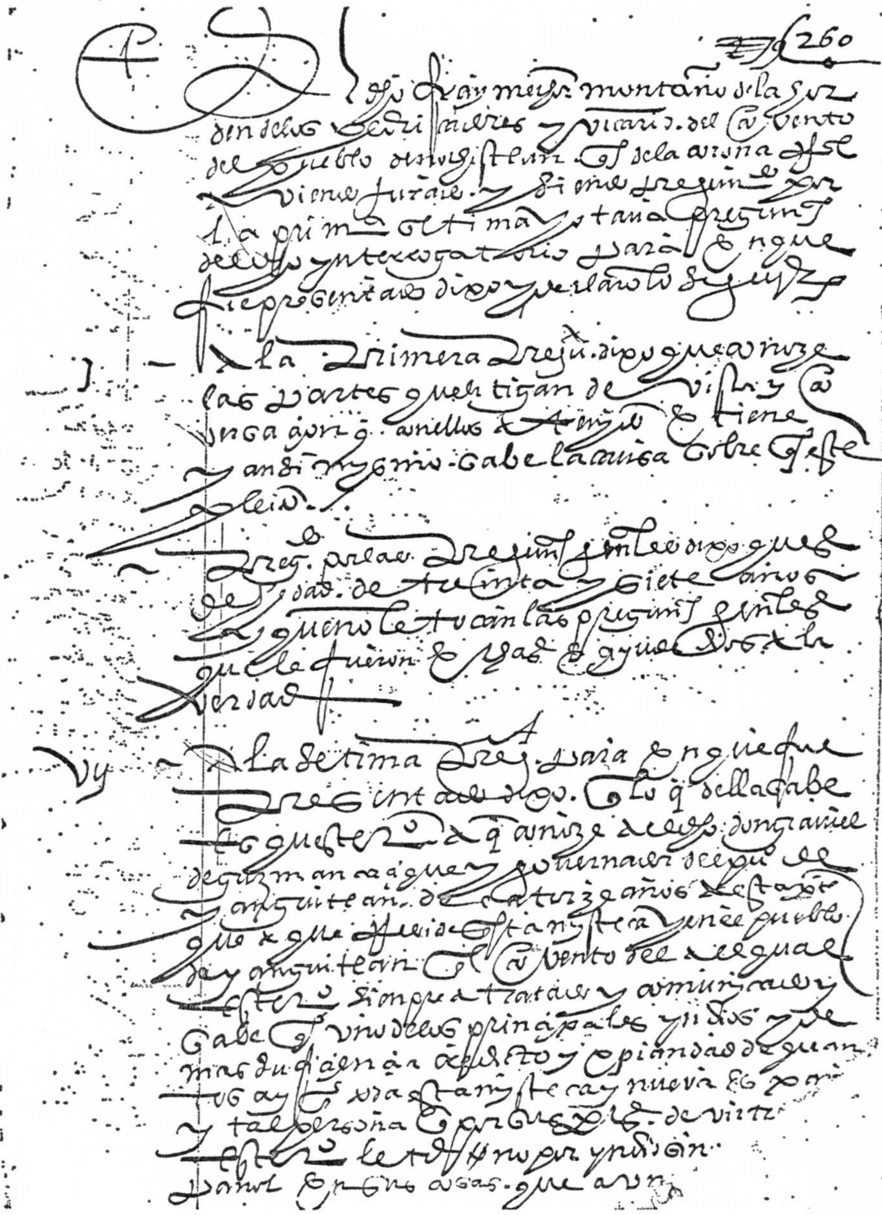

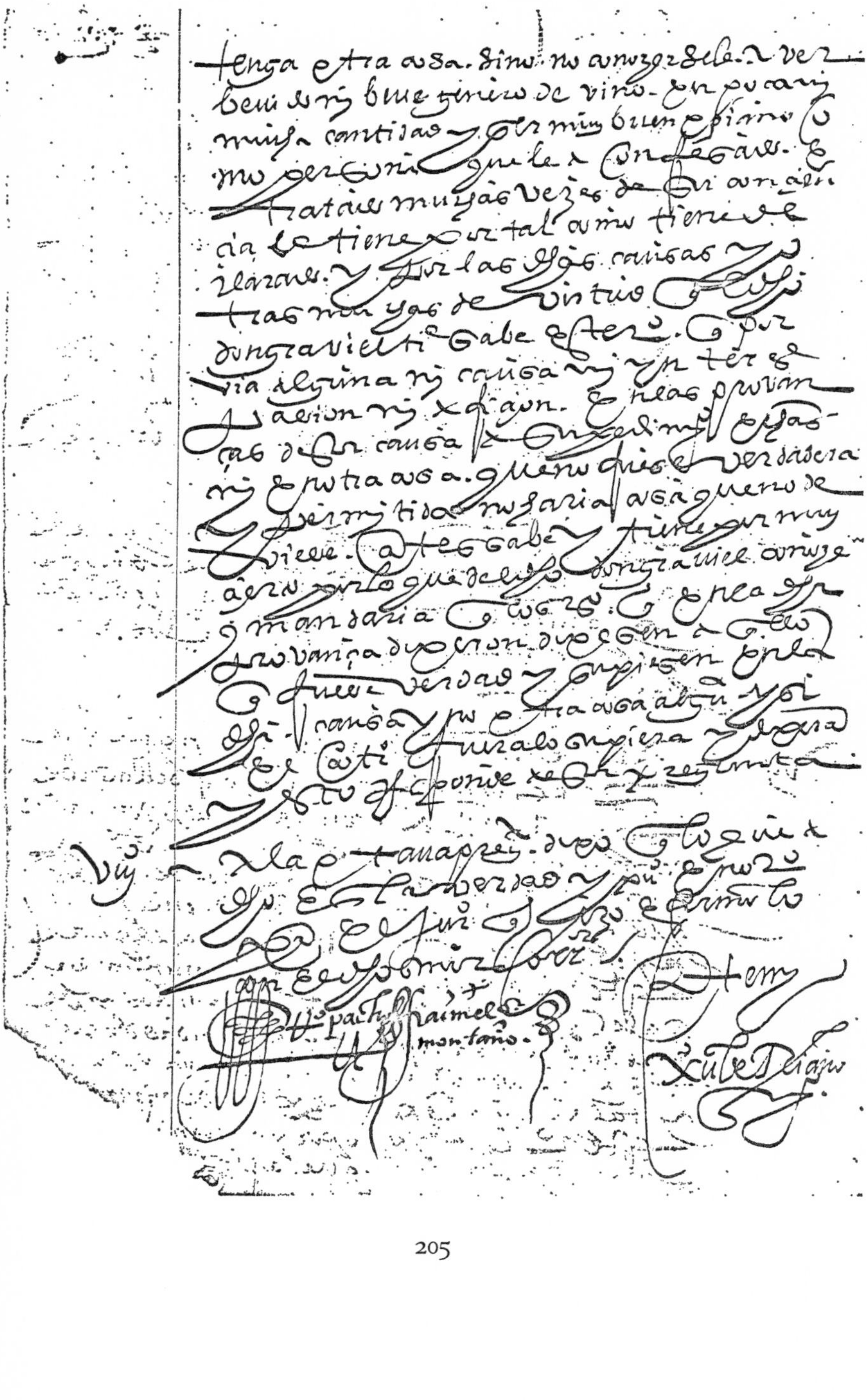

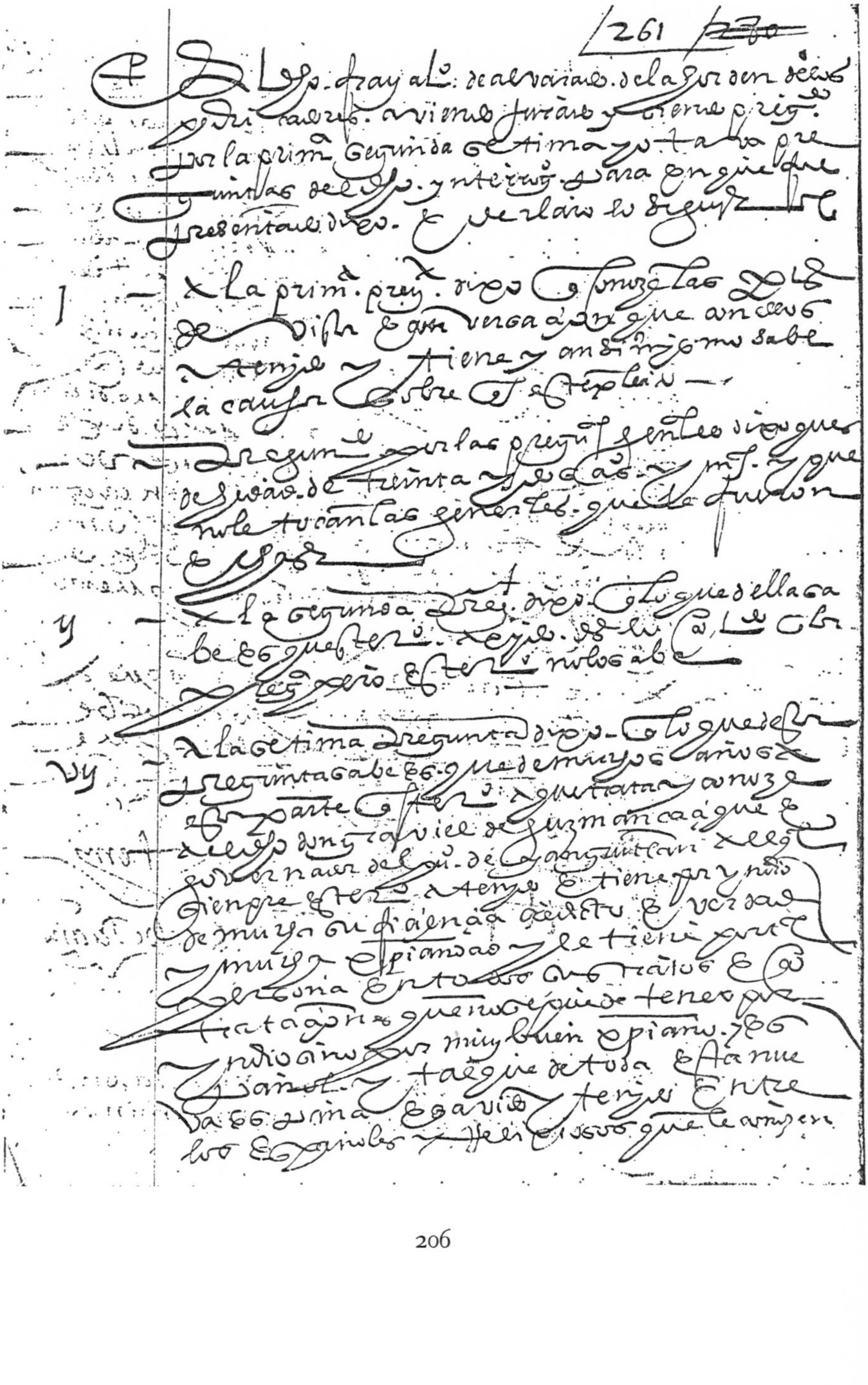

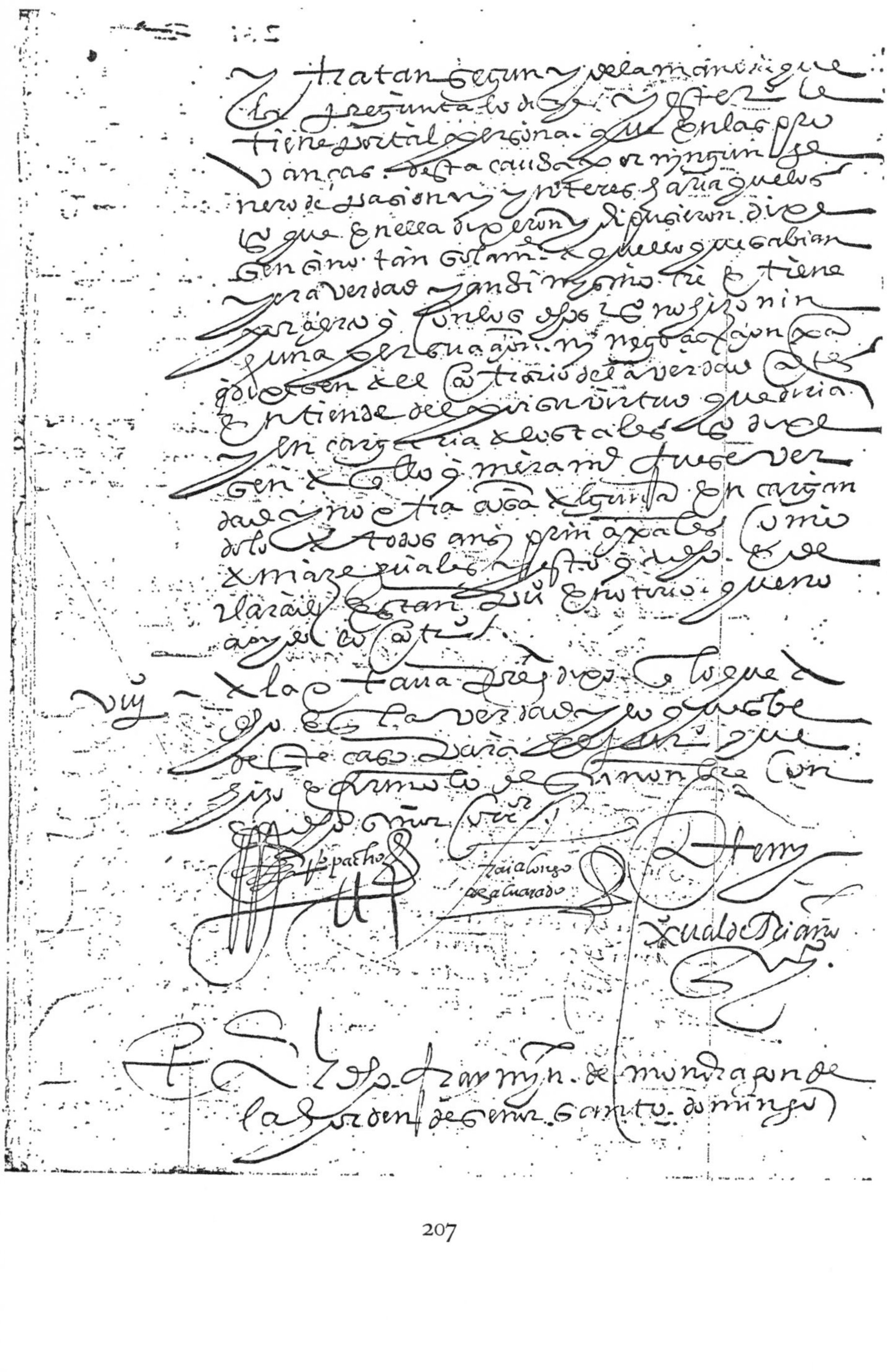

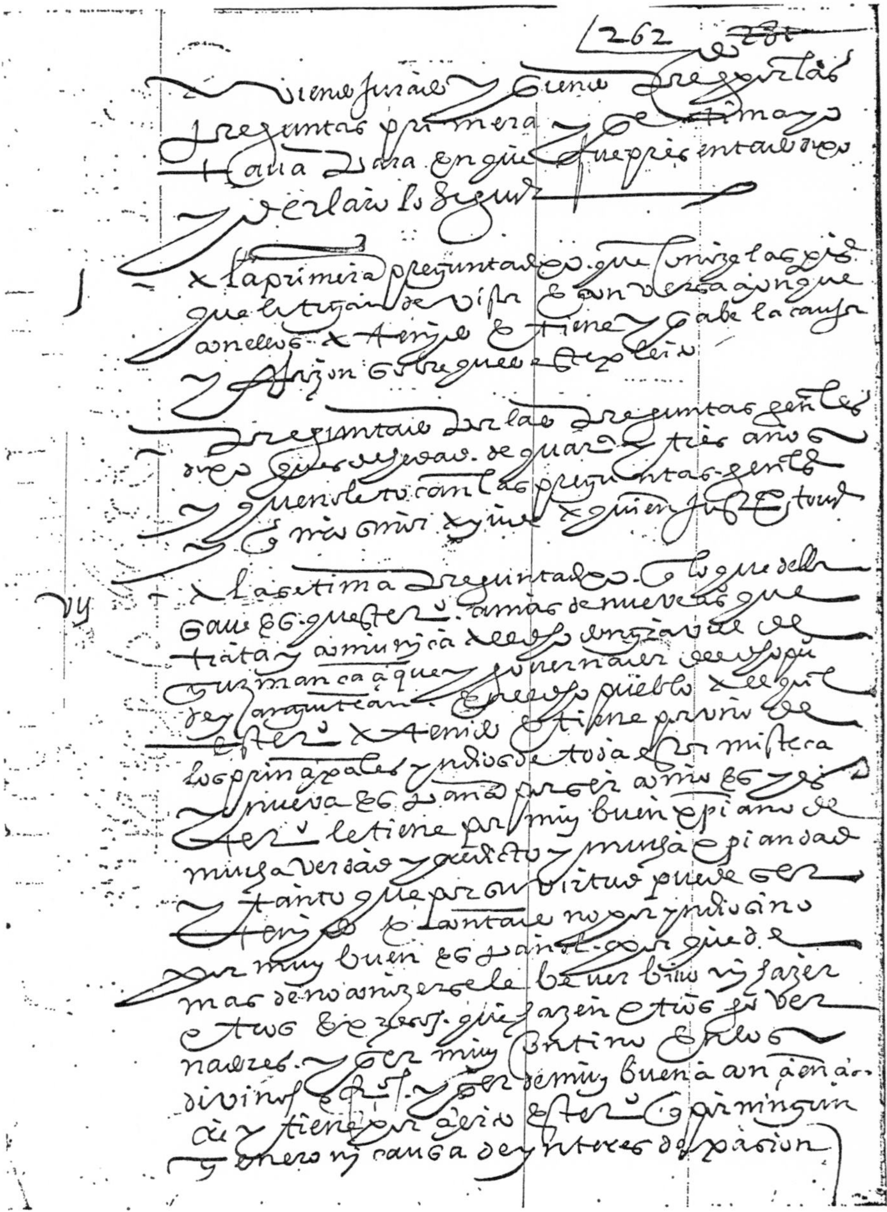

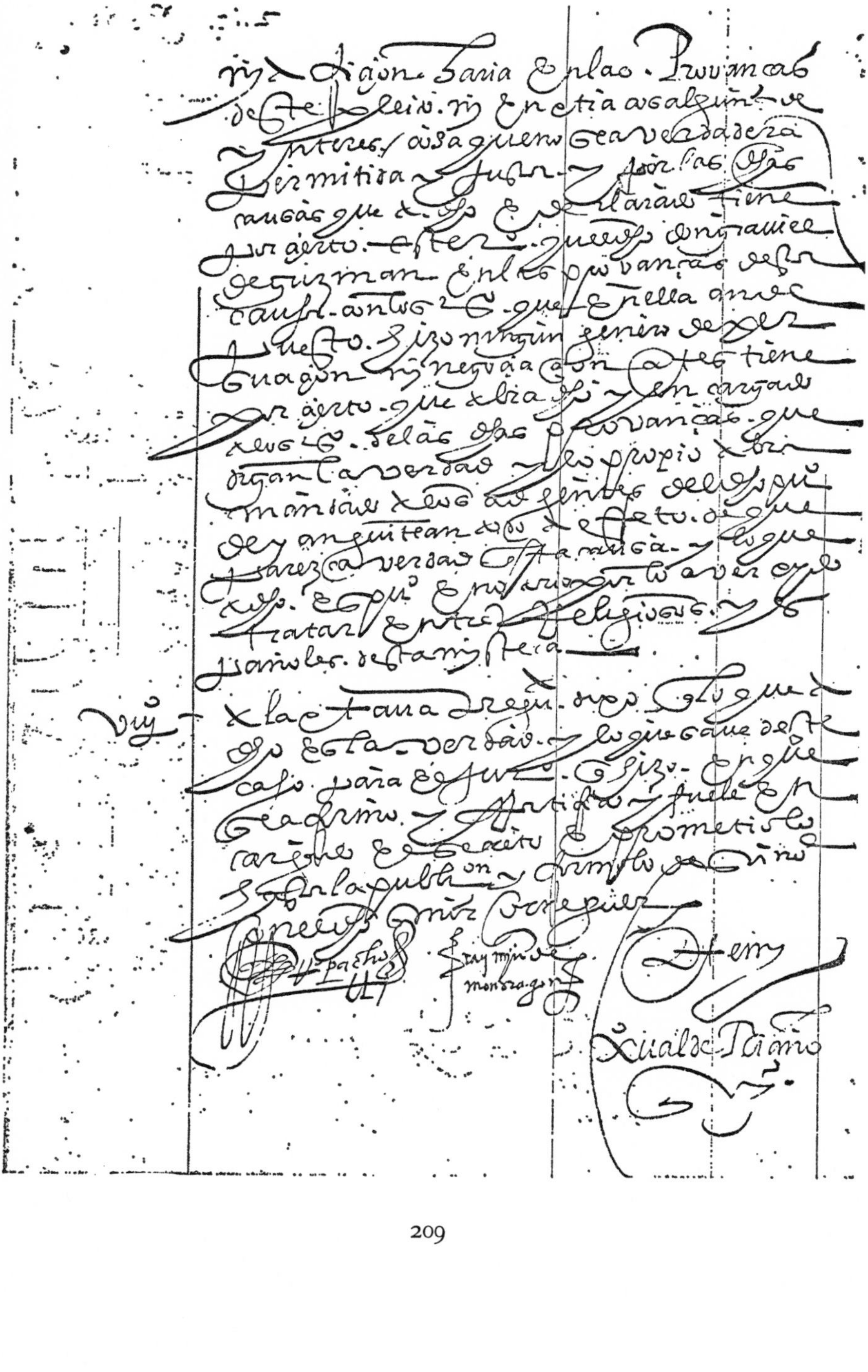

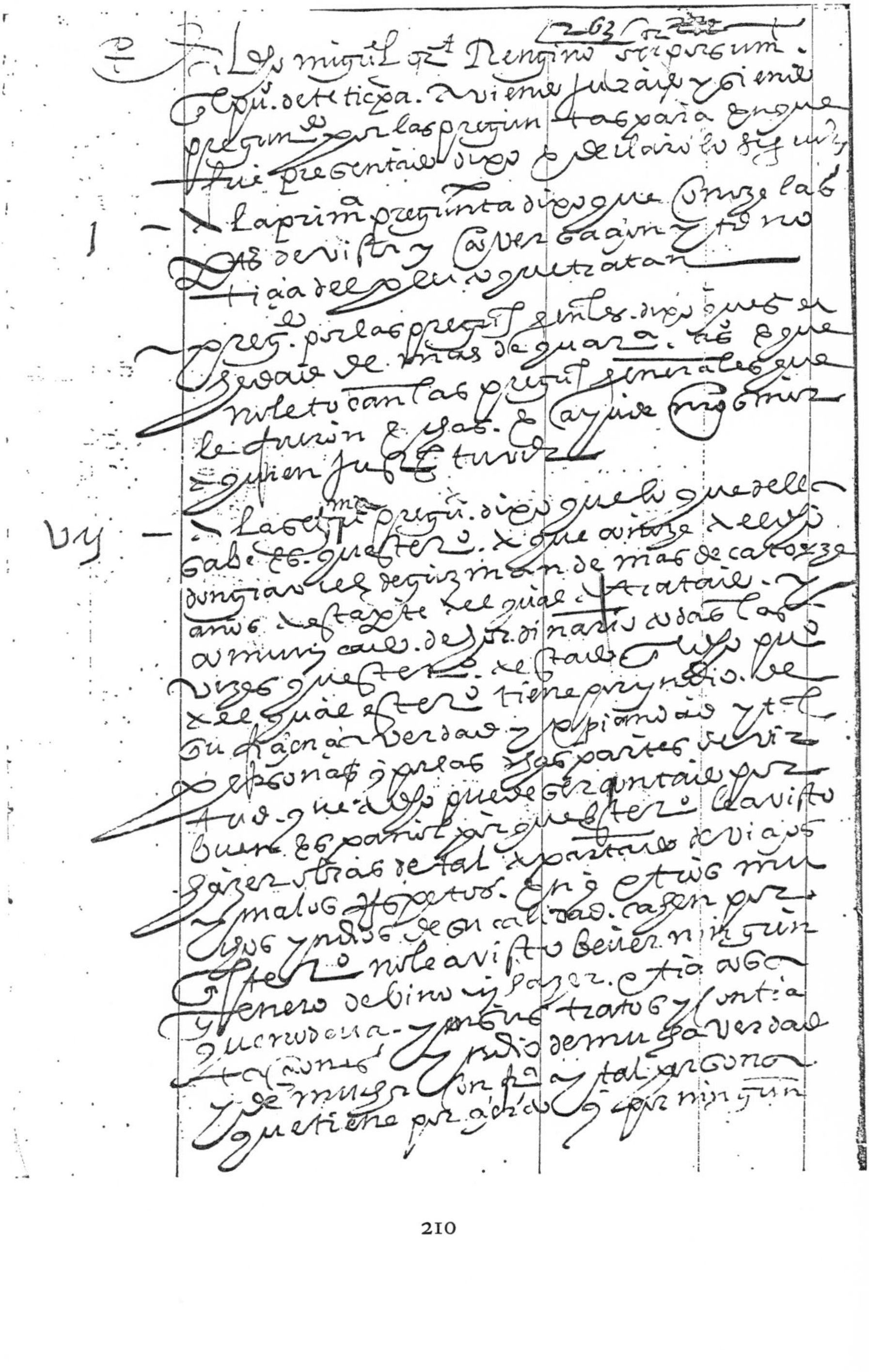

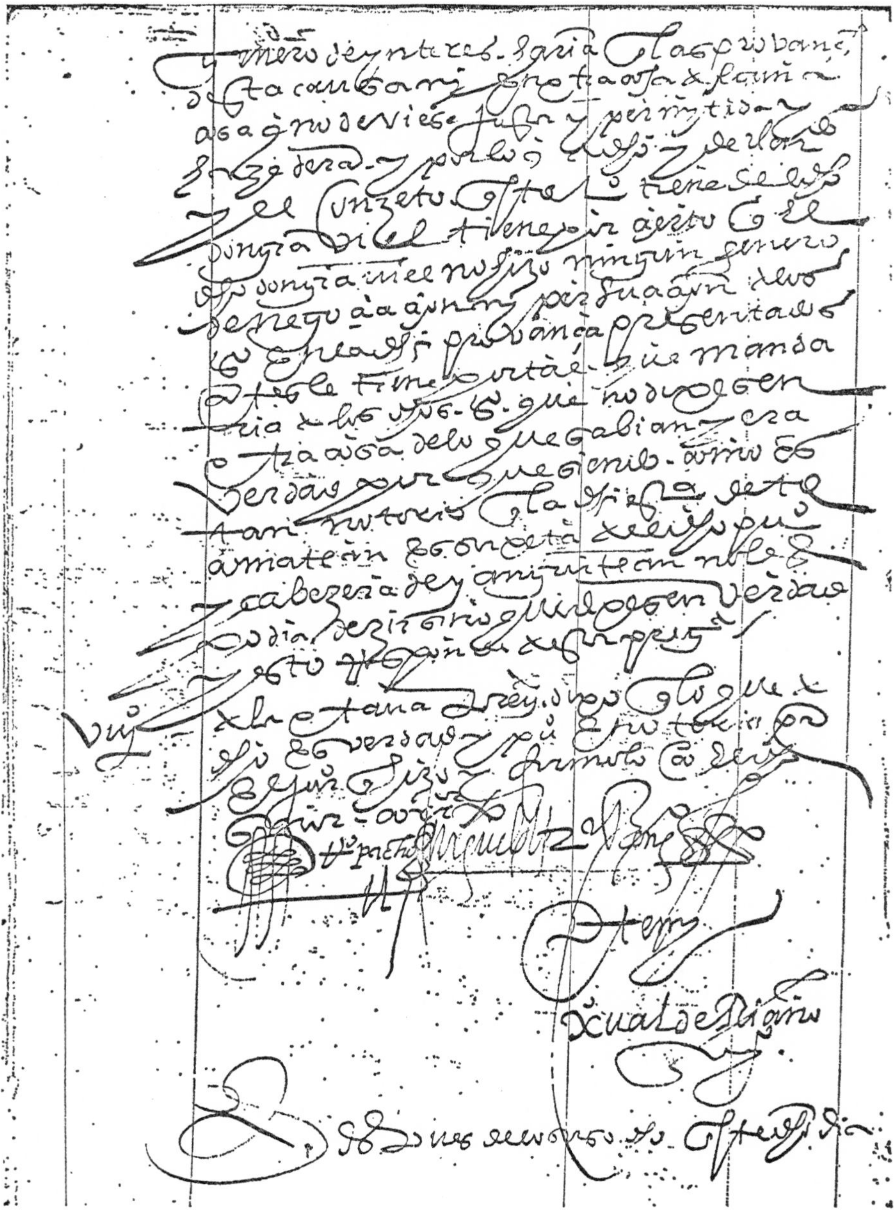

Appendix A–4

Testimony Given in 1582 by Domingo Hernández, an Indian Noble of Tilantongo (AGI, *Escribanía de Cámara*, 162).

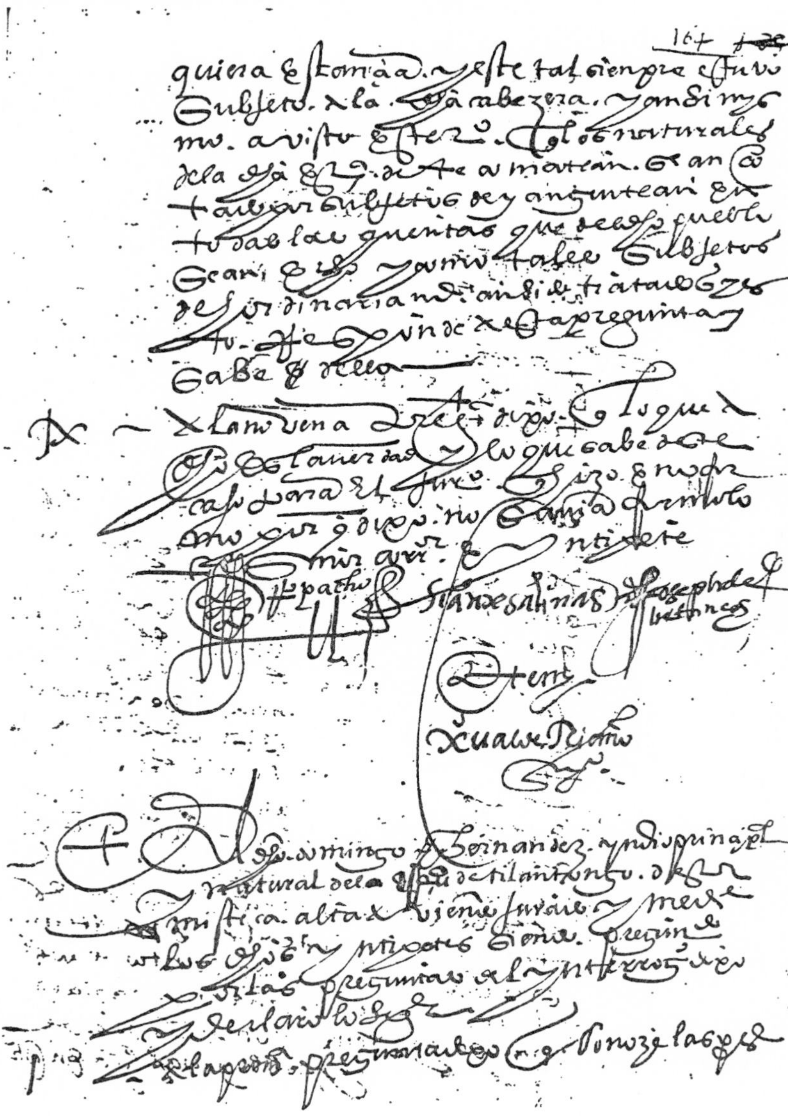

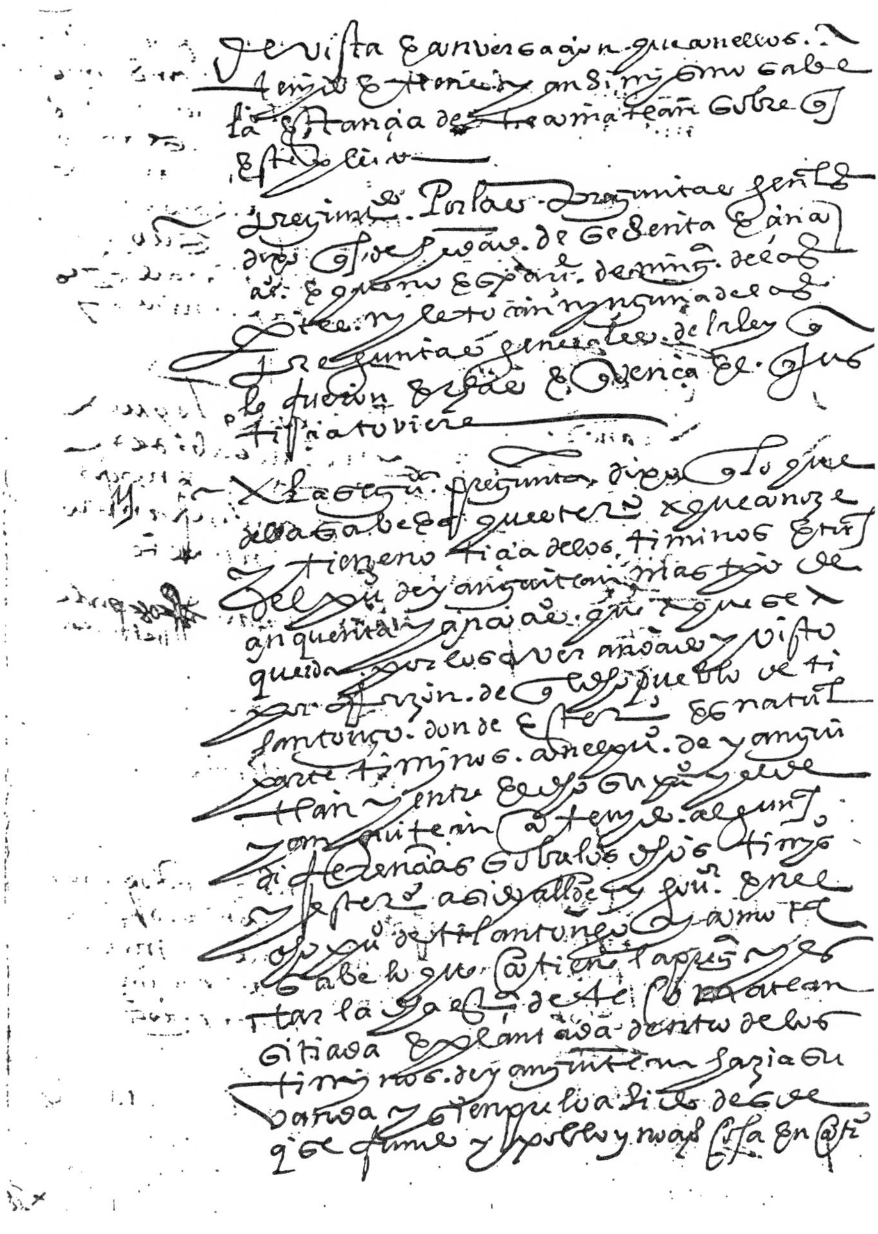

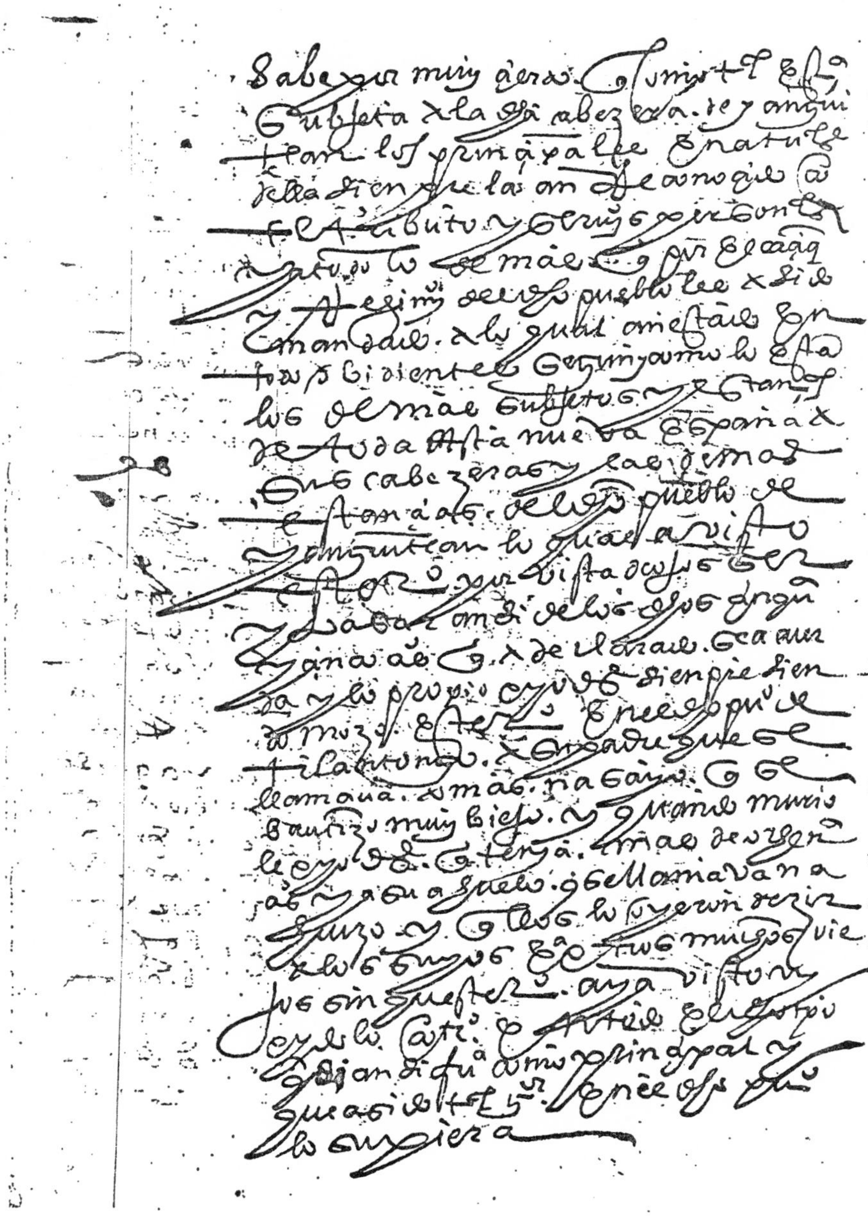

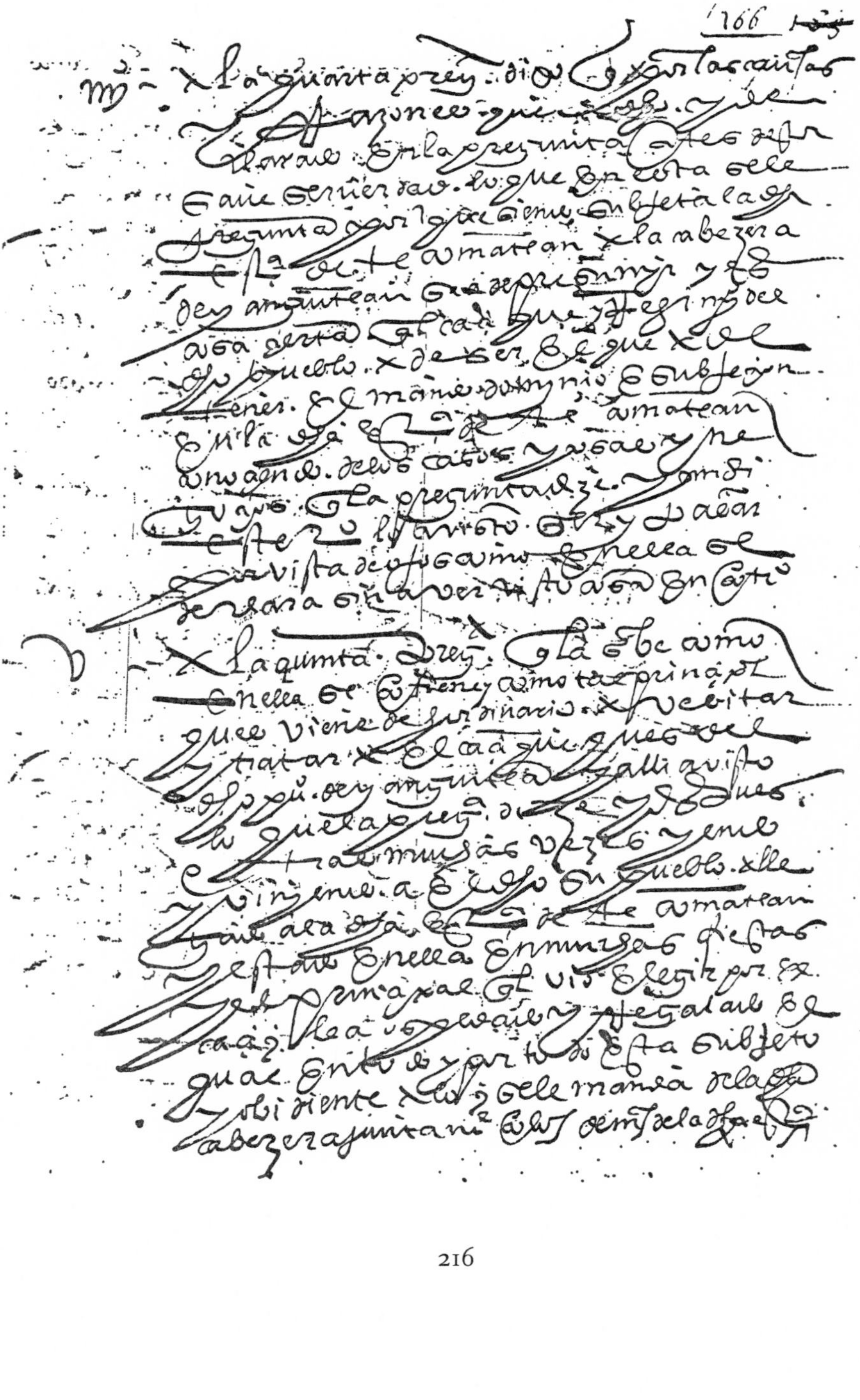

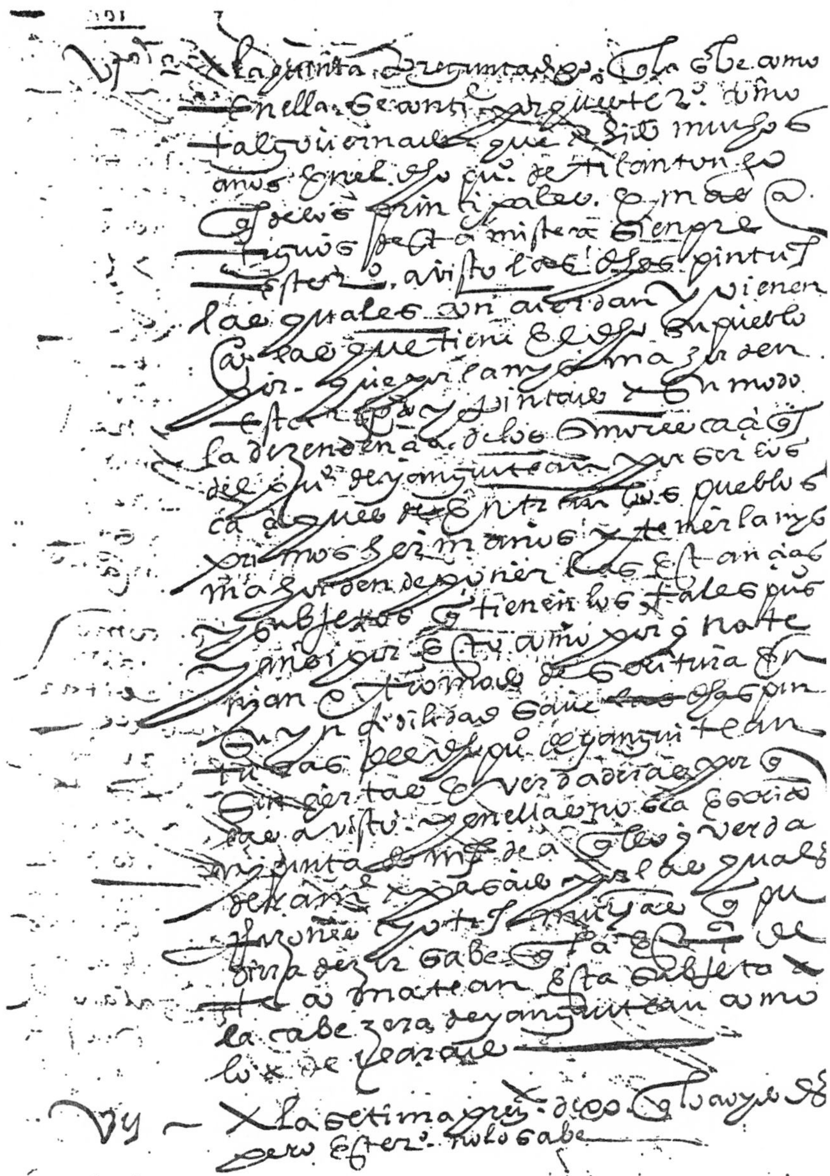

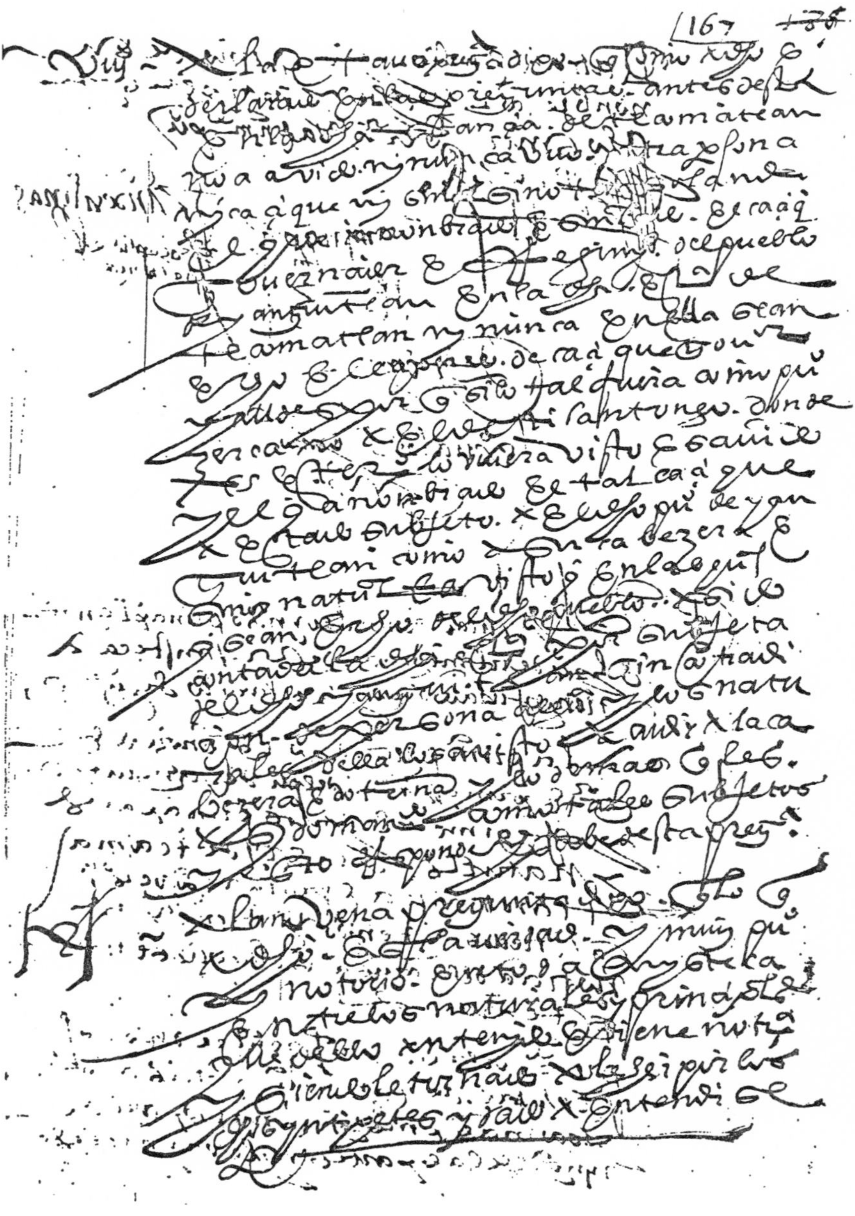

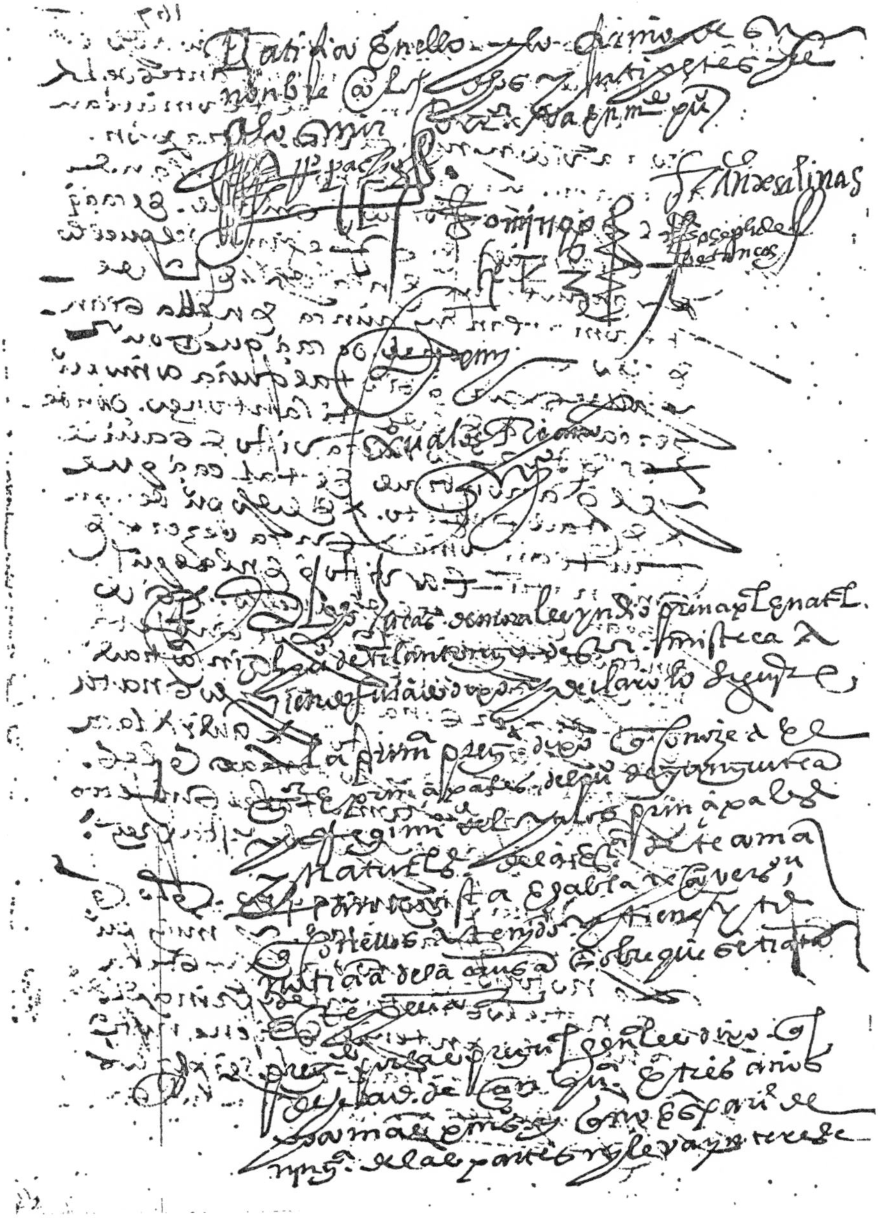

Appendix A–5

A Map of the Valley of Yanhuitlán-Nochixtlán, 1599 (AGN, *Tierras,* 1520, exp. 2).

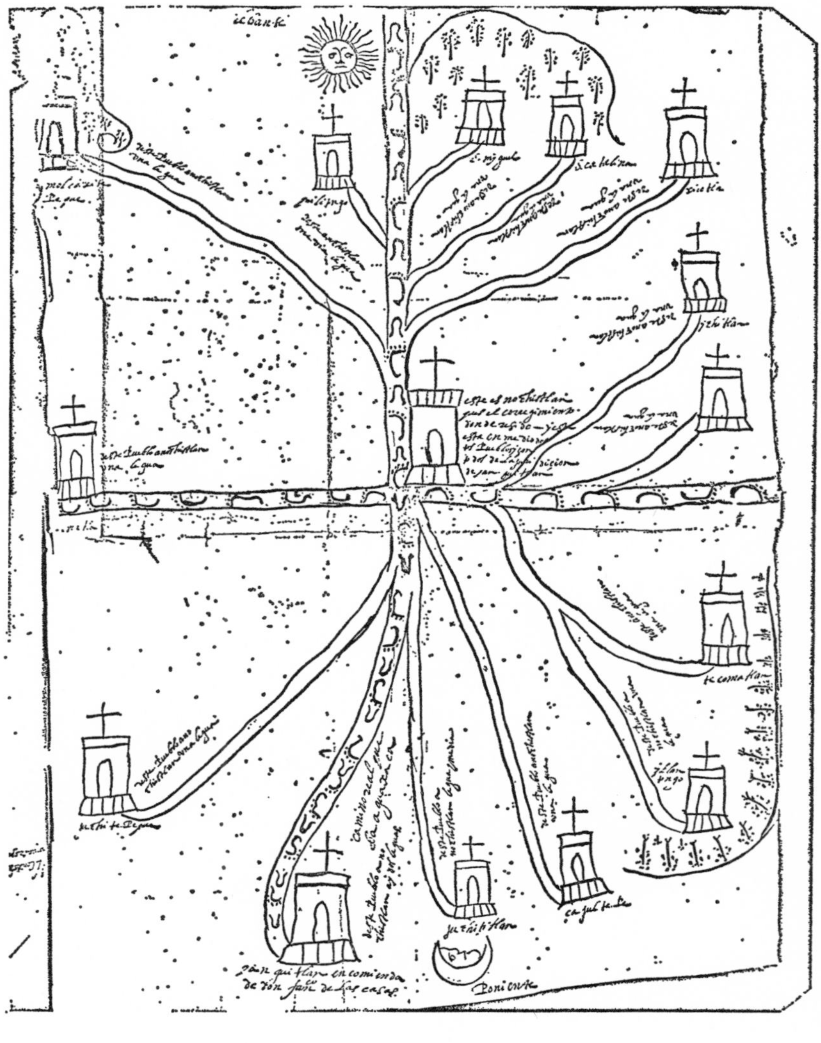

APPENDIX B

Edited Copies of Spanish Documents

Appendix B–1

Viceregal Decree Pertaining to Lands of the *Cacicazgo* of Tilantongo Located in the Community of Atoyaquillo, January 14, 1564 (AGN, *Mercedes*, 7, 253*v*).

Yo don Luis de Velasco, etc. Por cuanto don Francisco de Mendoza, cacique y gobernador del pueblo de Tilantongo, me hizo relación que ya me constaba el pleito que se trata en esta Real Audiencia en grado de apelación entre él y don Diego, Cacique del pueblo de Tiltepeque, sobre ciertas tierras que él tiene y posee de su patrimonio en el pueblo de Atoyaquillo en las cuales tiene sus terrazgueros y casas principales de morada; y que estando en posesión de todo ello algunos naturales del dicho pueblo de Atoyaquillo so color del dicho pleito impiden a los dichos terrazgueros que no reparen las dichas casas, y que las de Tilantongo no entren en el dicho pueblo de Atoyaquillo, impidiéndoles su libertad, ni que el dicho don Francisco tenga en sus propias tierras dos principales que tengan cargo de sus terrazgueros y beneficiar sus tierras, antes se entran en ellas los de Atoyaquillo en lo cual reciben agravio; y me pidió que acerca de ello mandase proveer del remedio necesario para evitar nuevas diferencias y por mi visto, atento a lo susodicho, por la presente mando que en el inter que en esta Real Audiencia se determina lo que sea justicia se determina lo que sea justicia en el negocio que de suso se hace mención, no se haga novedad alguna de lo determinado y proveído por Alonso de Canseco, alcalde mayor de la provincia de Teposcolula, atento que está en grado de apelación de lo que determinó

Francisco de Villagra por mi comisión; conforme a lo cual el dicho don Francisco, gobernador de Tilantongo, no excediendo de lo que le pertenece, pueda tener en sus tierras las personas que le pareciere para tener cargo de sus terrazgueros y reparar las casas que tiene de su patrimonio en el dicho pueblo de Atoyaquillo, sin que las otras partes se lo impidan ni se entremetan a labrar tierras ni corta árboles en lo que fuere suyo hasta que como dicho es se determine la causa so perder el derecho, lo cual se entienda sin perjuicio del derecho de las partes. Y otrosi mando que los del dicho pueblo de Atoyaquillo no impidan a los del pueblo de Tilantongo el entrar en el dicho pueblo, tianguis y mercados de él, ni los de Tilantongo a los de Atoyaquillo por razón de la . . . . (manchado el original) de guerra, so pena que serán castigados porque no han de impedirse sus libertades porque difieran sus gobernadores sobre las dichas tierras. Fecho en México, 14 de enero de 1564 años. Don Luis de Velasco. Por mandado de Su Señoría, Antonio de Turcios.

Appendix B–2

Last Will and Testament of Felipe de Saavedra, Cacique of Tlaxiaco, November 5, 1573 (AGN, *Tierras*, 3030, exp. 6).

Jesús, María y Joseph

Hoy cinco de noviembre del año de mil quinientos y setenta y tres años, del nacimiento del hijo de Dios en el mundo, en el año que en su idioma contarían los años *cuiva coeequaa*; ahora se acaba mi vida, yo don Phelipe de Saavedra, cacique de Tlaxiaco, que creo real y verdaderamente en las tres personas, Padre, Hijo y Espíritu Santo, tres personas distintas y un solo Dios verdadero de la Santísima Trinidad, quien me dio el cuerpo y alma, creo que es hijo de Dios Jesucristo, se hizo hombre en el mundo, creo en todo aquello que cree nuestra santa madre iglesia católica, todos los cristianos, los que guardian los mandamientos de Dios; yo don Phelipe de Saavedra, estoy muy malo, y es la justicia que Dios me envió, ofrezco mi cuerpo que Dios me dio a la tierra de donde fue criado. Y por eso es mi voluntad hacer mi testamento para mi alma y por mi hija doña María de Saavedra, cacica de este pueblo. Primero ofrezco mi alma y mi cuerpo a Dios Nuestro Señor que la crío y la infundío en mi cuerpo en este mundo, y primero ofrezco mi alma a Dios Nuestro Señor y así para servir el santísimo beático y el santo sacramento de la extremaunción;

y si me muero, pido que me entierren donde está enterrada doña Juana. Y así le doy a mi hija este pueblo y cabecera de Tlaxiaco y de Achiutla, que es mi pueblo y por ser buen pueblo, y así lo dijo mi madre doña Inés, cuando murió esto ví que mandó; y que si Dios es servido que viva mi hija doña María y que se case con el hijo de mi hermana doña Isabel, que coja esta cabecera y la de Achiutla, y así ahora que tenga el santo rosario, y juntamente que vea y atienda a todos mis principales, que hagan lo mismo, éstos y los de Achiutla. Y así si me muero digo sea enterrado mi cuerpo donde dije, donde está doña Juana; allí ofrecerán las santas oraciones por mi alma todos los años. Yo don Phelipe doy lo que es mío, una sonaja de plata y quince cascabeles de plata y asimismo doy a un natural que se llama Melchor López y Mateo, los dos éstos y los del glorioso San Antón Mduhuaasico, se lo dejo para que queden a mis hijos los de dichos de San Antón, que son tierras de Tlaxiaco donde están, y tierras del Paraje nombrado Yutasocosahui que son mis tierras como su cacique. Y todos los principales de esta cabecera de Tlaxiaco, todo esto mando se haga como ordeno. Aqui se acaba mi testamento, hoy cinco de noviembre de mil quinientos setenta y tres. Lo vieron hacer los testigos don Gonzalo Hernández, gobernador, y don Francisco Vázquez, don Cristóbal de la Cueva, Juan López, alcalde, y Pedro Gómez.

Appendix B–3

Abdication of Title to the Cacicazgo of Soyaltepec, February 4, 1575 (AGN, *General de Parte*, 1, f. 200*v*).

En el pueblo de Yanguitlan, cuatro días del mes de febrero de mil quinientos y setenta y cinco anos, ante el ilustre señor don Pedro Ladrón de Guevara, alcalde mayor por Su Majestad, mediante Fernando Vázquez Durán, intérprete del juzgado del dicho señor alcalde, de que yo el escribano yuso escrito doy fe, pareció don Diego de Mendoza, persona que asimismo entiende y habla la lengua castellana, hijo legítimo de don Diego de Orozco y doña María de Zárate su legítima mujer, caciques y señores en el pueblo de Zoyaltepeque, y governador y cacique que es del pueblo de Tamazolapa; y dijo que por cuanto él tiene de hacer cierta escritura en favor de don Bartolomé de Orozco su hermano, que pedia y pidió al dicho señor alcalde mayor le mande dar y dé licencia, poder y facultad para poder hacer y otorgar la dicha escritura, y pidió justicia.

Don Pedro Ladrón, don Diego de Mendoza, Hernán Vázquez Durán. Ante mí Antonio de Luxán, escribano de Su Majestad.

Y por el dicho señor alcalde mayor visto lo pedido por el dicho don Diego, dijo que le daba y dio la dicha licencia, poder y facultad cual de derecho en tal caso se requiere para poder hacer la dicha escritura con las fuerzas, vínculos y firmezas que sean necesarias, según y como lo pide; y asi lo mandó, y firmólo de su nombre. Don Pedro Ladrón. Ante mí Antonio de Luxán, escribano de Su Majestad.

Y por ende, por virtud de la dicha licencia al dicho don Diego de Mendoza dada y concedida, dijo que de su grado y buena voluntad sin premia ni fuerza que le sea hecho en pública ni en secreta; y que por cuanto él es hijo legítimo de don Diego de Orozco y de doña María de Zárate su legítima mujer, a quien podría suceder el cacicazgo y señorío del pueblo de Zoyaltepeque, como hijo mayor del dicho don Diego su padre; y porque él tiene el cacicazgo y señorío del pueblo de Tamazulapa y de Tepozcolula y vive y reside en los dichos pueblos, en los cuales goza de los dichos cacicazgos, y no puede asistir en el dicho pueblo de Zoyaltepeque a gozar del dicho cacicazgo; y conforme a la dicha su costumbre y faltando el hijo mayor, yéndose a casar y vivir en otro pueblo y cacicazgo, sucede segundo hijo, que por aquella vía y forma que de derecho major lugar haya él cedía y traspasaba y renunciaba y renunció el aución que a él tiene y le pertenece y puede pertenecer en cualquier manera a don Bartolomé de Orozco su hermano legítimo para que suceda en el dicho cacicazgo (de Zoyaltepeque) con todo lo a él anexo y perteneciente según y como el dicho su padre lo tiene, y si era necesario le hacía y hizo donación del dicho cacicazgo y tierras y terrazgueros a él pertenecientes y de lo que dicho es, que por fin y muerte de los dichos sus padres le puede pertenecer en cualquier manera. La cual dicha renunciación y donación le hacía y hizo al dicho su hermano por ser pobre, y que se pueda casar honradamente y por la dicha costumbre antigua que entre ellos ha habido y hay, para que sea suyo y lo goce él y sus herederos y sucesores y de aquel o aquellos que de él tuviere voz, causa o razón en cualquier manera; y traspasó en el dicho don Bartolomé de Orozco con todo el derecho y aución, y se desistió y apartó de la propiedad y señorío y otras acciones reales y personales que por cualquier razón le pertenezcan y puede pertenecer al dicho cacicazgo y señorío, y desde luego lo renunció y traspasó en el dicho su hermano, como dicho es, y le dio poder y facultad para que él por su propia autoridad pueda tomar la posesión de él; y renunció las leyes que dicen que no valgan la donación inmensa y general de todos sus bienes, por lo cual venga en pobreza, cuanto mas que él tiene y confiesa tener otros muchos bienes de que muy congruamente se puede sustentar. Y prometió y se obligó a no la revocar ni ir ni venir contra esta dicha donación y renunciación por escritura pública ni por testamento ni por codicilio ni de otra manera tácita o expressamente en tiempo alguno, antes quiere y es su voluntad que la sea firme para siempre jamás. Y para lo así guardar y cumplir, obligó su persona y bienes habidos y por haber, y dio poder cumplido a cualesquier justicias de Su Majestad para que a ello le compelan y apremien a lo guardar y cumplir bien así y tan cumplidamente, como so lo que dicho es fuese sentencia definitiva, pasada en cosa juzgada; y renunció la apelación y suplicación y cualesquier leyes, fueros y derechos que en su favor sean, y la lay en que dice que general renunciación de leyes *fecha non vala*; y pidió al dicho señor alcalde mayor apruebe y confirme esta dicha escritura y mande que se guarde y compla. Y por el dicho señor alcalde mayor visto lo pedido por el dicho don Diego de Mendoza, dijo que le había y hubo por desistido del dicho derecho y aución del dicho derecho y aucion del dicho cacicazgo, y aprobaba y aprobó la dicha donación, y mandó que se guarde y cumpla como si fuese sentencia pasada en cosa juzgada. Y firmólo de su nombre el dicho señor alcalde mayor y el dicho otorgante y intérpretes, estando por testigos Bartolomé de la Rocha, Bartolomé de Cazorla y Antonio Lucas, españoles, estantes en este dicho pueblo, y don Gabriel de Guzmán, cacique y gobernador, y don Carlos de Guzmán y Tomás de la Torre, alcaldes de este dicho pueblo, y Jusepe de Betanzos, Gonzalo López, y Diego de Silva, principales del pueblo de Achiutla. Don Diego de Mendoza, Hernán Vázques Durán. Don Pedro Ladrón. Ante mí Antonio de Luxán, escribano de Su Majestad. Por ende yo el dicho escribano lo escribí y hice aquí este mi signo a tal en testimonio de verdad, Antonio de Luxán, escribano de Su Majestad.

Appendix B–4

Viceregal Decree Pertaining to Cacique Succession in Tilantongo, March 29, 1576 (AGN, *General de Parte*, 1, f. 154).

Don Martín Enríquez, etc. Hago saber a vos don Carlos de Zúñiga, alcalde mayor del pueblo de Tepozcolula, en cuya jurisdicción cae el pueblo de Tilantongo, que por parte de don Felipe, cacique que se dice ser del dicho pueblo de Tilantongo, me ha sido hecha relación que don Francisco de Mendoza, su hermano, difunto, fue el cacique de él y natural del dicho pueblo, el cual dejó una hija legítima que sucedió en el dicho cacicazgo y ésta murió sin dejar hijo ni hija que le sucediese, de cuya causa le pertenece a él, el usufructo del dicho cacicazgo como su hermano mayor legítimo. Y me pidió se lo mandase adjudicar, dándole título de él para que se le acudiese con el patrimonio del dicho cacicazgo, o con lo que al presente fuese justo según la disposición del tiempo. Y porque quiero ser informado de lo que de yuso se hará mención, por la presente osmando que citando el concejo del dicho pueblo de Tilantongo, brevemente sepáis y averiguéis el derecho que el dicho don Felipe tiene al dicho cacicazgo, y por qué causa, razón y descendencia le pertenece; y si algún otro pretensor saliere a ello admitáis la información que diere; y juntamente con lo demás me informéis de ello para que se provea lo que convenga, con la razón de lo que se daba al dicho don Francisco, cacique, y a su hija, y lo que agora se da al cacique que es, y de la gente que habrá en el dicho pueblo, y lo que se distribuye de las sobras y procedido de la comunidad y en quién y lo que se podrá dar para la sustentación de él que verdaderamente fuere cacique. Hecho en México a 29 días del mes de marzo de 1576 años. Don Martín Enríquez. Por mandado de Su Excelencia, Sancho López de Recalde.

Appendix B–5

Viceregal Decree Pertaining to Cacique Succession in Tilantongo, June 6, 1576 (AGN, *General de Parte*, 1, f. 197).

Don Martín Enríquez, etc. Por cuanto don Felipe de Santiago, cacique del pueblo de Tilantongo, me hizo relación que don Francisco de Mendoza, su hermano mayor difunto, fue el cacique natural, y por su muerte sucedió en el dicho cacicazgo una hija legítima suya nombrada doña Francisca, y que por ser ésta muerta, sin dejar hijo ni hija, le pertenecía a él, el dicho cacicazgo como a hermano del dicho cacique con todo lo anexo y perteneciente a él; y me pidió se lo mandase adjudicar. Y por mí se cometió a don Carlos de Zúñiga, alcalde mayor de la provincia de Tepozcolula, que averiguase si le pertenecía el dicho cacicazgo al dicho don Felipe, y por qué causa, y lo que se daba a su hermano y sobrina y de dónde, y otras cosas necesarias a la justificación de la causa. Y el dicho alcalde mayor hizo la dicha averiguación por donde costa que el dicho don Felipe de Santiago es derecho sucesor del dicho cacicazgo, sin otro pretensor; y que a la dicha doña Francisca, última cacica se le daban por tasación mía doscientos pesos de oro común, con que de ellos diese cincuenta pesos al gobernador que fuese, y asimismo se le diesen las sementeras y indios de servicio, leña y cacao que se daba al dicho don Francisco su padre. Atento a lo cual, por la presente mando que de aquí adelante hasta que otra cosa se provea y mande, se acuda al dicho don Felipe de Santiago como a tal cacique del dicho pueblo con todo lo contenido en la tasación que llevaba la dicha doña Francisca su sobrina, hija del dicho don Francisco de Mendoza su hermano, con la condición de dar de los dichos doscientos pesos de tepuzque se le dan cincuenta pesos de salario al que es o fuere gobernador, y cuando él lo fuere, los lleve por tal. Hecho en México a 6 días del mes de junio de 1576 años. Don Martín Enríquez. Por mandado de Su Excelencia, Sancho López de Recalde.

APPENDIX C
English Translations of Spanish Documentary Materials

Appendix C–1

Native Burial Practices as Revealed in the Inquisitorial *Procesos* of 1544–46 (AGN, *Inquisición*, 37, exp. 10).

In the said pueblo of Yanhuitlán, on April 14, 1546, the said Lord Judge Commissary, for investigation of that which was stated by Diego, native of Etlantongo, that Don Juan ordered an Indian girl killed and buried in the house of one Juan on the occasion of the death of his mother-in-law, went to the residence houses of the said Juan *indio* where, together with the said Juan *gobernador* and in the presence of myself, the said notary, and the said witnesses named below, in a chamber of the said dwellings he ordered the opening of a grave where the said Don Juan had ordered the said girl to be buried. And it was opened and they removed from it certain skull bones and other bones of the body that appeared to be those of a boy or girl together with certain *piedras azules*, as well as a complete skull with its teeth, jawbones, and hair that appeared to belong to an adult man or woman, and many body bones wrapped in a petate, and certain *chalchiuite* beads, and pieces of silver and *esandillas* [?], and eight complete pots. And the said sepulcher was in the form of a rounded vault and measured what appeared to be two *estados*[1] of masonry. And I, the said notary, swear that I saw the aforesaid and that I found present as witnesses Don Gómez de Maraver, Dean

[1] An *estado* is the equivalent of about 1.85 yards.

of Oaxaca, and Fray Francisco Marín of the Order of Santa Domingo, and Alonso de Aldana.

(sgd.) El licenciado Alonso de Aldana
(sgd.) Martín de Campos
Notary

Appendix C–2

The Opening of a Grave in Tiltepec, 1546 (AGN, *Inquisición*, 37, exp. 10).

On April 15, 1546, the said Lord Judge Commissary went to the pueblo of Tiltepec and, being in the presence of myself, the said notary, and the witnesses mentioned below, he asked Domingo, native of Moxcaltepec, to come and indicate the location of the grave and place where were buried the two children that had been killed and sacrificed by order of Don Domingo, as the witness had testified. Domingo stated that truly he had seen them buried but that it had been so long ago that he did not know or remember where it was.

And after the aforesaid on this day, month, and year, the said Lord Judge Commissary left the pueblo of Tiltepec and went one league from the boundaries of the pueblo and in the presence of myself, the said notary, and the said witnesses, in a place that he was shown, ordered the opening of a tomb for investigation of the statement of Alonso Xanu that Don Domingo [cacique-regent of Yanhuitlán] sent a slave, which he purchased from its owners, to the people of Tiltepec so they might sacrifice him [on the occasion of] the death of his [Don Domingo's] brother, and that on this spot they had buried the sacrificial victim. And opening the grave they took from it a complete skull with its teeth, hair, and jawbones, and many bones of the body that were wrapped in a *petate* and the bones appeared to be of an adult man or woman. The grave was located between two fields of maize, one on one side and the other on the other side, and between some magueys and the edge of an arroyo of water and among five hills that circled it, one being very large and the others small. And I, the said notary, swear that I saw the aforesaid as did the witnesses in attendance, the Dean don Gómez Maraver and Fray Francisco Marín and Alonso de Aldana.

Appendix C–3

The Confession of a Native Priest, Yanhuitlán, 1546 (AGN, *Inquisición*, 37, exp. 10).

The said Coquoa, native priest of Yanhuitlán, who in Spanish is called Domingo, sworn witness in the said cause, having been duly sworn by the said Lord Judge Commissary in the language of the said interpreter, was asked the following questions in the presence of the said Dean Gómez de Maraver and Alonso de Aldana who were also under oath:

Asked if he is baptized and for how long, he answered that he had been baptized by a clergyman two years ago.

Asked what his name was prior to baptism, he answered that it was Coquoa. In answer to the general questions he stated that he is more than twenty years of age, and he gave the appearance of being about thirty years old, and he stated that there was nothing else of general importance.[1]

Asked how many years he had been a [native] priest, he answered that he had been a priest for Don Francisco [*principal* of Yanhuitlán] for three years and that by his [Francisco's] order this witness on several occasions sacrificed dogs, quail, pigeons, and other things to the devil in the house of the said Don Francisco.

Asked if he had also sacrificed Indians, he answered that he had not.

Asked what more he used to do, the said witness stated that he cared for the idols in the house of the said Don Francisco.

Asked where the idols are, he answered that they were buried in the house of the said Don Francisco, and that after [Don Francisco] was taken prisoner [by the Inquisition], they were carried to the house of Francisco de las Casas by an Indian named Quynu because the said Francisco de las Casas[2] had asked the Indians and also the present witness for them.

Asked how he knew what the said Francisco de las Casas had said,

[1] In colonial legal proceedings, the "general question" was designed to determine the age of a witness and whether, because of kinship or for other reasons, he might be partial to one of the contending parties.

[2] The encomendero of Yanhuitlán.

he said because Juan, now deceased, interpreter for Francisco de las Casas, had told him of it.

Asked what persons were present, he said that Domingo Estlumeca and Don Juan, *gobernador*, and all the *principales* of the Pueblo were present.

Asked what idols were given to Francisco de las Casas and what they were called, he stated that they were called Cauy and Poco and Quahu and that there were stones and other things used for offering to the devil.

Asked how many priests the said Don Francisco [*principal*] used to have and what they were called, he answered that there were, counting the witness, four priests who were called Xihua, who died, and Numau and Cocoane and this witness who is called Coquoa.

Asked what these priests did, he stated that they sacrificed and called on the devil and burned copal and did everything in the service of the devil.

Asked if they killed people in sacrifice, this witness said that when he was baptized he told and confessed all of his sins and that now he knows nothing.

Asked when he quit being a priest, he said that it was two years ago, more or less.

Appendix C–4

The *Cacicazgo* of Tejupan: Excerpt from Decision Concerning Succession, 1572 (AGN, *Tierras*, 34, exp. 1).

. . . Although it was true that Don Felipe de Austria had been married to the daughter of *Doña* María de Zárate, she had died without children, and this being the case neither law, reason, nor custom could be said to favor his succession, for he was in effect a man foreign to the line and descent of the caciques of that pueblo; and although he had governed [as cacique] for one year, it had not been properly legitimate but by reason of his nomination as governor; and in saying that the said pueblo of Texupa went with the *cacicazgo* of Tepozcolula, or of Tilantongo, it must be understood that when succession is lacking in the house of Texupa, it is separate and distinct from the others and that the cacique will be taken from wherever the natives of the pueblo wish . . . .

Appendix C–5

Personal Service for the Cacique of Yanhuitlán, 1573 and 1581 (AGN, *Tierras*, 400, exp. 1).

Don Martín Enríquez, viceroy, governor, and captain general for his Majesty in this New Spain, and president of the *Royal Audiencia* residing there, etc. Inasmuch as Don Gabriel de Guzmán, cacique and governor of the pueblo of Yanhuitlán, has informed me that as cacique he must, in conformance with ancient custom, bring together in his house many *principales* who attend him and whom he very often feeds, and that because of this, as well as for assistance in serving them, it is necessary that he be given twelve ordinary Indians with their wives in addition to the [usual] assessment, and that they be paid for their work from the *sobras de tributos*. Therefore, mindful of the aforesaid, I order that for the present and that from this time forward there be given to the said Don Gabriel de Guzmán, cacique of the said pueblo of Yanhuitlán, for the service in his house as such cacique six Indians, who are to assist in bringing water and wood, with their wives who are to make bread. These are to be rotated every fifteen days or every month, whichever is customary in the said pueblo, and each person, man and woman alike, is to be paid twenty cacaos each day and is to be fed from the proceeds of the *sobras de tributos* and community funds. Done in Mexico on April 17, 1573. Don Martín Enríquez.

(The above order was reconfirmed by Viceroy Lorenzo Suárez de Mendoza on December 9, 1581).

Appendix C–6

Viceregal Appointment of an Alcalde in the Pueblo of Chiautla, May 26, 1542 (AGN, *Mercedes*, 1, exp. 109).

I, Don Antonio de Mendoza, etc. Inasmuch as Ximón, *indio*, who was alcalde of Chiuatla has passed from this present life, it is appropriate and necessary to name another alcalde [in his place] to see to the welfare of [that] republic. Therefore, for the present, in the name of his Majesty and for the time that it is his will or mine in his royal name, I name as alcalde of the said pueblo of Chiautla you, Melchor, *indio principal* and native of the said pueblo, since it is for the good of the natives [of said pueblo]. And I order you to take charge of the administration of justice among its native residents; that you shall be recognized and obeyed as such alcalde; that you shall give attention to the things that you may feel to be for the good of the republic; that you shall see to it that the natives of the said pueblo and its subject settlements come to know Christian doctrine and hear divine offices, and that they do not perform drunken orgies, sacrifices, or other evil practices in the said pueblo, and that the *macehuales* are not obliged to pay excessive tributes in excess of what they can give in terms of the status and ability of each one of them. And so that you may have cognizance of affairs among the natives of the said pueblo and its *sujetos*, in both civil and criminal matters, in accordance with ordinances that have been issued, and so that you may hear cases and dispense justice according to law, I give you complete authority to possess and have the *vara de justicia*[1] for the said pueblo and its jurisdiction, believing you to be a person who will perform well and faithfully the said office of alcalde and maintain justice in the stated area.

Done in México, May 26, 1542. Don Antonio de Mendoza. By order of his lordship, Antonio de Turcios.

Appendix C–7

Viceregal Appointment of an *Alguacil* in the Pueblo of Quaquechula, June 3, 1550 (AGN, *Mercedes*, 3, f. 84*v*).

I, Don Antonio, etc. I have been informed that it is fitting and necessary to name an *alguacil* in the pueblo of Quaquechula and its *sujetos* to have responsibility for the assemblage of the natives of said pueblo, its *sujetos*, and other pueblos that are visited by the religious of the friary of said pueblo, so that they may come to hear and learn Christian doctrine and understand other things deemed necessary by the said religious, relating to the service of Our Lord and the well-being of said pueblo. Therefore, having been informed that you, Juan Gómez, *indio principal* and native of the said pueblo, are a person who can perform well and faithfully what may be entrusted to you, for the present, in the name of his Majesty and for the time that is my will, I name and appoint you as such *alguacil* in the said pueblo and in the other pueblos visited by the said religious, and as such *alguacil* you may have *vara de justicia* without any impediment;

[1] The *vara de justicia* was the wand, or emblem, of the alcalde's office.

and you shall take special care for assembling the natives of said pueblo to come and learn Christian doctrine, to do and perform other duties pertaining to the service of God Our Lord that may be assigned to you by the said religious; and you shall prevent, by whatever means that may be appropriate, drunken orgies, concubinage, and other public sins,[1] and to insure punishment of wrongdoers in accordance with justice and ordinances that have been promulgated.

Done in México, June 3, 1550. Don Antonio. By order of his lordship, Antonio de Turcios.

[1] "Public sins" (*pecados públicos*) included flagrant violations of established norms of moral conduct, such as theft, perjury, adultery, sodomy, etc.

APPENDIX D
Miscellaneous Information on the Mixtecs

Appendix D–1

Mate Selection in Modern Mixtec Marriage.

Information on marriage patterns among the common classes of the Mixteca is extremely limited. My conclusion that the mode of marriage in the sixteenth century was community endogamy is based upon the following findings:

1. Marriage patterns have been similar in the towns of Yanhuitlán, Tlaxiaco, Tilantongo, Jaltepec, Nochixtlán, Tejupan, Teposcolula, Yucuita, Soyaltepec, and Chachoapan in recent times (1963). In each of these towns I asked about marriage patterns. I inquired of an individual as to the place of his birth, his wife's birth, the birthplace of his father and his mother, his grandparents, and, if known, his parents-in-law. These questions were asked of thirty persons. All answered that in each case the individuals in each generation were born in the community in which I found the informant to reside. Despite important acceleration in the rate of intercourse with the outside world, improved transportation and communication, there remains a firm pattern of community endogamy. There *are* individuals who marry outside the community, and probably there have always been some who cross the boundaries of the community to obtain their mate. For example, one Tilantongo man was married to a woman from Puebla, but all of his ancestors were from the *municipio* of Tilantongo. Butterworth (1962) has indicated that migrants and children of migrants living in Mexico City return to Tilantongo to obtain spouses. The overwhelming impression, even today, is that the universe from which one claims his mate is normally limited by the

confines of his community. The persistence of this trait despite vast external influence offers my strongest proof that this is an ancient and persisting trait.

2. In the available documentation there is an absence of any reference to extended marriage patterns among the common classes comparable to that among the ruling castes.

3. There is mention in the documents that the wives of certain witnesses came from the same pueblo as their husbands.

4. Traditionally there has been a strong identification with the community throughout the Mixteca and Oaxaca.

5. There is a lack of social prescription that would promote or dictate marriage outside the community (or even outside the kin group) or proscribe it within. It is my opinion that in the absence of specific rules against it, marriage in the Mixtec community with limited outside contact will normally take place among those in daily or at least frequent association.

Appendix D–2

Modern Kin Terms from San Juan Numi, District of Tlaxiaco (male speaker).

ñani	brother; first cousin; second cousin
cua'a	sister; first cousin (female); second cousin (female)
nana	mother
x'ito	uncle
xīxì	aunt
ta'ta h'at'no	grandfather
nana h'at'no	grandmother
ta'ta hat^{n}oza	great grandfather
nana h'atnoza	great grandmother
se'e^{t} ciyizan	son or daughter
seyani	grandson; granddaughter; great grandson; great granddaughter
ñani	cousin (male or female)
tataxis^{z}o	father-in-law
nanaxis^{z}o	mother-in-law
xiso	brother-in-law; sister-in-law

nanasa	my mother
tatasa	my father
ñanisa	my brother
cua'asa	my sister
nanatežron	your mother

Appendix D–3

Sixteenth-Century Kin Terms from the Reyes Grammar (1890, pp. 86–88)

De los nombros [*sic*] de parentesco, de affinindad y consanguinidad.

Padre: *dzutu, taa, ñani, yuvua*; segun los diferentes pueblos.

Madre: *dzehe.*

Abuelo: *sij, taatnanu*; Abuela, *sitna, dzehe tnanu*; Bisabuelo, *sijtaandi, sijdzutundi, sijdzucuandi*; Bisabuela, *sitnataandi, sitna dzutundi, sitna dzehendi*; y quando es de madre, *sitnadzucuandi.*

Tatarabuelo: *saqmidzini siindi, saqmitotosijndi*; Tatarabuela, *saqmidzini sitnandi.*

Hijo: *dzayayeendi*; Hija, *dzaya dzehendi.*

Nieto o nieta: *dzaya ñanindi*; Bisnieto, o bisnieta, *dzaya dzucuandi.*

Hermano, los hombres dizen: *ñani*; las mugeres, *cuhua*; Hermano, dizen ellos, *cuhua*; las mugeres, *cuhui*; Primo hermano, dizen los hombres, *ñanitucuchisindi, ñanisanda cundodzo*; Primo hermano, dizen las mugeres, *cuhuatucuchisi*; Prima hermana, dizen ellos, *cuhuatucuchisindi, cuhuasan dacundodzo*; Prima hermana, dizen ellas, *cuhuitucuchisi*; Primo segundo, dizen ellos, *sacuvui vuisichiña nitucuchisi, sacuvui vuitoto ñanitucuchisi*; Primo segundo, dizen ellas, *sacuvui vuisichi cuhua tucuchisindi, sacuvui vuitoto cuhua tucuchisindi*; Prima segunda, dizen ellos, *sacuvui vuisichi cuhua tucuchisindi, sacuvui vuitoto cahua tucuchisindi*; Prima segunda, dizen ellas, *sacuvui vuisichi cuhui tucuchisindi, sacuvui vuitoto cuhui tucuchisindi.*

Pocas vecez usan los naturales destos terminos de primos o primas segundas, su mas comun modo es llamarse todos hermanos, aunque sean primos.

Tio dizen ellos y ellas: *dziso*; tia, *dzidzi.*

Sobrino: *dzasi*; sobrina, *dzicu.*

Suegro: *dzutudzidzo, ñanidzidzo, taadzidzo, yuvuadzidzo.*

Suegra: *dzehedzidzo*; consuegro, a, *tnahadzidondi.*

Cuñado: *dzidzondi.*

Cucuños, que estan casados con dos hermanas: *tnahacadzandi*; quando estan ellas casadas con dos hermanos, *tnaha sanondi.*

Padrastro: *dzutu nindendozondi, yuvuacaindi, dzutu yuvuahuindandi, yuvua yaha ñeendi, dzutu nataa yaha ñeendi.*

Madrastra: *dzehe nindendodzo, dzehe yuvua huindandi*; con los demas, bolvendo el *dzutu* en *dzehe.*

Entenado: *dzayacaindi, dzayayahañeendi*; Entenada, *dzayadzehe yuvua-huinda, dzayadzehe yaha ñeendi, dzayadzehe ninataayahañeendi.*

Hijos avidos en segunda o tercera muger: *dzaya nindento dzondi.* Hermanos melliços de un vientre: *ñanitetnehendi*; si es hermana, *cuhua tetnehendi.*

Hermanas melliças, entre si se llaman: *cuhuitetnehendi*; Hijos desta manera, *dzayatetnehendi, dzayanicacutetnehendi*; Hijo legitimo, *dzaya maindi, dzaya neñeinindi*; Hijo primogenito, *dzaya dzehe-nundi, dzaya dzehe nicanunuu, dzaya dzehe nicacudzina.*

Hijo o hija segunda: *dzaya cuvuivui, dzayatacu, dzayacuvuivui*; Hijo o hija postreros, *dzayanduvui, dzayadzatnu, dzayadzayu.* Hijos de adulterio: *dzayadzaca, dzayayuhu.*

Hijo unico: *dzàyadzo eeni, dzàya dzomââ, dzaya ñatuvui tayu.*

Hijo prohijado: *tay nicuvui dzayandi, tay ninaquacandi, tay nichidzo chiyondi.*

Pariente por sangre: *tnahandi, cuicondi, tnahacuicondi, tnahayaatnu-hundi.*

Pariente por affinidad: *tnahadzidzondi, tnahasanondi*; si es muger, *tnuhutnahandi, dzidzo, sanondi*; Pariente entre señores, *yyanica-cusihi*; Parentesco, contraer ansi, *yonduvuitnuhutnahandi, sasinan-dodzo tnuhu tnahandi quaha, yotnuhundi sihita*; Proximo, *ñani-tnahandi*; Vezino, *tnaha ñuundi, tnaha sañundi*; Amigo, *tnaha quachindi, tnaniquachindi.*

Appendix D–4

Sixteenth-Century Mixtec Place Names from the Reyes Grammar (1890, pp. 188–90).

Yanguitlán	Yodzocahi
Chachuapa	Yuta nani
Cuyotepec	Yucu nana
Tliltepec	Yucutnoo
Tepuzculula	Yucundaa
Tlachiaco	Disinuu
Chicahuaztla	Tnutnono
Cuiquila	Nuu cuine
Ocotepec	Yucuite
Cuixtlahuac	Yodzocoo
Tequitziztepec de Chuchones	Yucuyu
Ychcatlán	Sidzaa
Achiutla	Nuundecu
Malinaltepec	Yucuane
Tlatlaltepec	Yucuquesi
Atayac	Teyta
Tlatzultepec	Yucucuihi
Chalcatongo	Nuundaya
Amoltepec	Yucunama
Yolotepec	Yucuneni
Atlatlauca S. Estevan	Nuuquaha
Apuala	Yutatnoho
Quautla	Dzandaya
Chicahuaztepec	Yucucadza
Nuchiztlán	Atoco
Quautlilla	Yucundeq
Etlantongo	Yucunduchi
Xaltepec	Anute
Tilantongo	Nuutnoo
Mictlantongo	Dzandaya
Patlaixtlahuac	Yodzocono
Texupa	Nuundaa
Tzoyaltepec	Anuu
Tonaltepec	Yucundiz
Tamatzulapa	Tequevui
Tuctla	Yucuyaa, nuuhuiya

Teotzaqualco	Chiyocanu
Tzentzontepec	Yucueetuvui
Penoles, y Elotepec	Yucundedzi
Mixtepec	Yodzonuu huico

Appendix D–5

Population in Certain Communities in the Mixteca Alta: 1565–70 (García Pimentel, 1904, pp. 64–65).

community	*tributarios*
Yanhuitlán	6,000
Teposcolula	4,500
Tlaxiaco	4,500
Coixtlahuaca	3,200
Tamazulapa	1,500
Tejupa	900
Jaltepec	1,500
Tilantongo	1,000
Achiutla	1,200
Zozola	400
Huatla	200
Jaltepetongo	200
Nochixtlán	1,000
Etlantongo	300
Chachuapa	400
Tliltepec	300
Atoyaquillo	300
Malinaltepec	300
Chalcatongo	600
Atoyaque	25
Yolotepec	350
Teozocoalco	600
Tamazola	300
Cuicuila	120
Ocotepec	150
Patlaastlaguaca	360
Zoyaltepec	300

Appendix D–6

Movable Property of Don Gabriel de Guzmán, Cacique of Yanhuitlán, 1591 (AGN, *Tierras*, 400, exp. 1).

The last will and testament of Don Gabriel de Guzmán, executed in 1591, lists the following:

SILVER:

1. An embossed gilded-silver goblet.
2. A plain silver pot (*jarro*).
3. A small silver pot with cover.
4. Another small silver pot (*ollita*) with handle.
5. A plain gilded silver mug (*cubilete*) with decorated border.
6. Another gilded silver mug with an inscription.
7. Six, fluted, silver spoons.
8. Another spoon with tortoise-shell handle.
9. An antique gold cup.
10. A mug with decorated cover.
11. A tall, plain-silver mug *con su romano* (?).
12. A silver cup of Indian manufacture.
13. Four vessels of coconut shell, with silver mountings.

JEWELRY (*joyas*):

1. A large gold piece with the figure of an eagle and twelve cascabels.
2. Another piece with Santiago printed on it, and with six cascabels.
3. Another piece, with the royal arms and seven cascabels.
4. Another gold piece in the form of a pelican.
5. Another gold piece in the image of Our Lady.
6. An alligator, with ten gold cascabels and some *chalchihuites*.
7. A gold piece containing the figure of Christ.
8. Eleven cascabels and a cherubim.
9. Another gold image of the Boy Jesus.
10. An old piece with the royal arms and eight cascabels.
11. A piece of low-grade gold, with the image of Our Lady and five cascabels.
12. Two pieces with figures of Our Lady and seven cascabels.
13. A large Spanish piece with a half-moon and rays in the middle, and with twelve cascabels hanging from gold fish.

LIVESTOCK:

1. Located in named *estancias* are 1,340 goats and 200 kids. Of these, 20 head were the property of Don Gabriel's wife, *Doña* María de Chávez, "which she bought with her own money."
2. A gray horse.
3. A stallion.
4. A colt.
5. A sorrel horse, property of *Doña* María de Chávez.

OTHER GOODS:

1. A quantity of maize in the house of the cacique.
2. Some maize in the possession of Gómez de la Torre of San Francisco Atecomatlan.
3. A book, *Flor Sanctorum*; another book, *Contemptus Mundi.*

After the death of Don Gabriel in 1591, an inventory of his goods was made, which lists additional items as follows:

1. A gold rosary with eighty beads.
2. A gold rosary with seventy-nine beads.
3. Eight brass buttons.
4. Seven crystal *uñas.*
5. A small pearl mirror.
6. A white work-desk with seven drawers.
7. A silver-plated reliquary of the *Agnus Dei.*
8. Some pieces of old iron.
9. A gold jewel with the face of a woman.
10. Some scissors.
11. A black writing box, decorated.
12. White saddle, bridle, and stirrups.
13. A mule bridle and two high stirrups.
14. Another saddle and black bridle.
15. A currycomb.
16. Another bridle.
17. Three spurs.
18. A white box with key.
19. Some leg irons.
20. A metal chain.

21. Three blowguns.
22. A net for catching rabbits.
23. A small box containing a skein of silk, a white sheepskin, a shirt and plaited breeches, and a China nightshirt.
24. Another box containing four old shirts, two cotton manta jackets, four white plaited breeches, three white mantas, and two shawls.
25. A large white box with lock, and a "tiger" skin inside.
26. Another white box with key; inside, a small leather box containing a gold rosary of eighty-five beads.
27. A gold cherub, with eleven cascabels.
28. A gold jewel, with a medal.
29. A small gold box with key.
30. A box containing three black felt hats.
31. Another white box with key.
32. Three pairs of old boots.
33. Five metates.
34. A white box with key, containing two decorated *tilmas*, four white mantas and a huipil, three needlework patterns, and four feathers.
35. A white maguey-fiber pouch.
36. A medal with a coat of arms and five cascabels.
37. Another gold medal, with an image of Our Lady and seven cascabels.
38. Another medal, with a figure of Samson and six cascabels.
39. A gold cord for headdress.
40. One large and two small painted gourds.
41. An old needlework pattern.
42. A wine flask.
43. A pouch with thirty nails.
44. A small box, containing three gourd cups, sixteen tortoise-shell lids, an old leather box, and eight, old, needlework patterns.
45. Three more tortoise-shell lids.
46. Twenty-two gourd cups, large and small.
47. A small Michoacan box.
48. A *chicovite*, containing three needlework patterns, a small leather box, and six skeins of cotton thread.

49. Fifteen needlework patterns and a picture (*pintura*).
50. A gourd vessel, painted and gilded.
51. An empty reed travel case.
52. Two pack saddles, with pads, riatas, and lassos.
53. Nine cakes of soap.
54. Sixteen sheep fleeces.

BIBLIOGRAPHY

An extensive corpus of unpublished manuscript sources has been utilized in the preparation of this book. Most of these materials are preserved in two repositories: the Archivo General de Indias, Sevilla, and the Archivo General de la Nación, Mexico City. Also consulted were unpublished reports and microfilmed materials of anthropological interest on the Mixteca Alta on deposit in the Instituto Nacional de Antropología e Historia, Mexico City.

Archivo General de Indias (AGI)

Three sections of this archive were used: *Patronato*, *Justicia*, and *Escribanía de Cámara*. For our immediate purpose the most valuable single document in this archive comes from *legajo* 162 of *Escribanía de Cámara*, the lengthy record (several hundred pages) of sixteenth-century litigation prompted by efforts of the pueblo of Tecomatlán to achieve independence from the *cabecera* of Yanhuitlán (cited as AGI, *Escrib.*, 162). This document, which deserves a separate study, records significant data for other parts of the Mixteca Alta in pre- and post-Conquest times.

Archivo General de la Nación (AGN)

This is the most important repository of manuscript materials relating to the Mixteca Alta in the sixteenth century. Its holdings are divided into *ramos*, of which the most significant for purposes of this book are:

Ramo de Civil: records of civil litigation before the *Audiencia* of Mexico. Volume 516 contains record of legal proceedings of 1580 to substantiate the legitimacy of title of Don Gabriel de Guzmán to the *cacicazgo* of Yanhuitlán (cited as AGN, *Civil*, 516).

Ramo de General de Parte: miscellaneous decrees of the viceregal government of New Spain.

Ramo de Indiferente General: a recently established *ramo*, being utilized as a classification for previously unclassified materials housed in a storeroom (*bodega*) of the archive.

Ramo de Indios: viceregal decrees relating to various aspects of Indian affairs and government.

Ramo de Inquisición: records of the activities of the Mexican Inquisition in cases of heresy and other deviations from Roman Catholic orthodoxy. *Expedientes* 5–11, Vol. 37, contain the proceedings (1544–46) in the cases of three members of the Indian nobility of Yanhuitlán charged with apostasy and the continuing practice of native religion (cited as AGN, *Inquisición*, 37).

Ramo de Mercedes: viceregal favors (*mercedes*) in the form of land grants, appointments to office, confirmation of the status of caciques and other officials of Indian communities, etc.

Ramo de Tierras: records of litigation over ownership and use of lands. This *ramo* contains extensive documentation dealing with conflicting claims of Indian communities to lands in the Mixteca Alta and with disputes over cacique succession which frequently involved lands said to be part of a cacique's royal patrimony. Many of these documents have been cited in the text (AGN, *Tierras*—with appropriate volume and *expediente* numbers). Volumes 400 and 985–86 contain materials of special value for the *cacicazgo* of Yanhuitlán.

Ramo de Vínculos: documents pertaining, for the most part, to the history of *mayorazgos* (entailed estates). Indian *cacicazgos* were characterized by certain features of an entailed estate, and consequently we find in this *ramo*, as well as in *Tierras*, cases relating to cacique lands and succession. Volume 272, for example, contains valuable material pertaining to the *cacicazgo* of Tututepec in the Mixteca de la Costa and its connections with the *cacicazgo* of Yanhuitlán.

The author has also cited an AGN volume entitled *Libro de Congregaciones*, which contains documentation pertaining to efforts made at the end of the sixteenth century to concentrate Indian villages in New Spain into larger units for administrative and missionary purposes.

Published Materials

Acosta, Jorge R. "*Exploraciones arqueológicas en Monte Albán. XVIII temporada, 1958*," *Revista mexicana de estudios antropológicos*, Vol. XV (1959), 7–49.

———. "Preclassic and Classic Architecture of Oaxaca," in Wauchope and Willey, eds., *Handbook of Middle American Indians, q.v.*

Adams, Robert M. *Land Behind Baghdad*. Chicago, 1965.

Aguirre Beltrán, Gonzalo. *Formas de gobierno indígena*. México, 1953.

Alegria, R. E. "Origin and Diffusion of the term 'cacique,' " in Sol Tax, ed., *Acculturation in the Americas*. Chicago, 1952.

Americanists, International Congresses of. *8 Congrès International des Americanistes*. Paris, 1892.

———. *Actas y Memorias 27° congreso internacional de americanistas*. 2 vols. México, 1947.

———. *Actas y Memorias 35° congreso internacional de americanistas*. 2 vols. Mexico, 1962.

Arana Osnaya, Evangelina. "*Relaciones internas del Mixteco Trique*," *Anales del Instituto Nacional de Antropología e Historia*, Vol. XII (1960), 219–73.

———. "*El idioma de los señores de Tepozcolula*," *Anales del Instituto de Antropología e Historia*, Vol. XIII (1961), 217–30.

Atlas arqueológico de la República Mexicana. Instituto Pan Americana de Geografía e Historia Publicación, No. 41. México, 1939.

Barlow, Robert H. "The Extent of the Empire of the Culhua-Mexica," *Ibero-Americana*, No. 28 (1949).

Bennett, W. C. "The Andean Highlands: An Introduction," in J. H. Steward, ed., *Handbook of South American Indians*, BAE Bulletin No. 143, Vol. II. Washington, 1946.

———. "The Archeology of the Central Andes," in Steward, ed., *Handbook of South American Indians, BAE Bulletin, No. 143*. Vol. II. Washington, 1946.

Berlin, Heinrich. *Fragmentos desconocidos del Códice de Yanhuitlán.* México, 1947.

———. and Robert H. Barlow. *Anales de Tlatelolco, y Códice de Tlatelolco.* México, 1948.

Bernal, Ignacio. "Archaeological Synthesis of Oaxaca," in Wauchope and Willey, eds., *Handbook of Middle American Indians, q.v.*

———. "Archeology of the Mixteca," *Boletín de estudios oaxaqueños,* No. 7 (1958).

———. "Architecture in Oaxaca After the End of Monte Albán," in Wauchope and Willey, eds., *Handbook of Middle American Indians, q.v.*

———. "*Distribución geográfica de las culturas de Monte Albán,*" *El México Antiguo,* Vol. VII (1949), 209–16.

———. "*Exploraciones en Coixtlahuaca, Oaxaca,*" *Revista Mexicana de estudios antropológicos,* Vol. X (1948), 5–76.

———. "Monte Albán and the Zapotecs," *Boletín de estudios oaxaqueños,* No. 1 (1958).

Berreman, Gerald D. *Hindus of the Himalayas.* Berkeley, 1963.

Borah, Woodrow. "Silk Raising in Colonial Mexico." *Ibero-Americana,* No. 20 (1943).

———, and S. F. Cook. "The Population of Central Mexico in 1548," *Ibero-Americana,* No. 43 (1960).

———. "Price Trends of Some Basic Commodities in Central Mexico, 1531–1570," *Ibero-Americana,* No. 40 (1958).

Borhegyi, S. F. "Settlement Patterns in the Guatemala Highlands: Past and Present," in Willey, ed., *Prehistoric Settlement Patterns in the New World, q.v.*

Brandomín, J. M. *Toponimia de Oaxaca, crítica etimológica.* México, 1955.

Bullard, W. R. "The Maya Settlement Pattern in Northeastern Peten, Guatemala," *American Antiquity,* Vol. XXV (1960), 355–72.

Burgoa, Fray Francisco de. *Geográfica descripción.* 2 Vols. México, 1934.

Butterworth, Douglas S. "A Study of the Urbanization Process Among Mixtec Migrants from Tilantongo in Mexico City," *América indígena,* Vol. XXII (1962), 257–74.

Carrasco, Pedro. "*Las Culturas idígenas de Oaxaca*," *América Indígena*, Vol. XI (1951), 99–114.

Cartas de Indios. Madrid, 1877.

Caso, Alfonso. *The Aztecs: People of the Sun*. Norman, 1958.

———. "*Los barrios antiguos de Tenochtitlan y Tlatelolco*," *Memorias de la Academia Mexicana de la Historia*, Vol. XV (1956), 7–63.

———. "*Base para la sincronología mixteca y cristiana*," *Memoria de el Colegio Nacional*, Vol. VI (1951), 49–66.

———. "*El calendorio mexicano*," *Memorias de la Academia Mexicana de la Historia*, Vol. XVII (1958), 41–96.

———. *Calendario y escritura de las antiguas culturas de Monte Albán*. México, 1947.

———. "*La correlación de los años azteca y cristiano*," *Revista mexicana de estudios antropológicos*, Vol. III (1939), 11–45.

———. "*Los dioses zapotecas y mixtecas*," in J. Vivo, ed., *México prehispánico*. México, 1946.

———. "*Explicación del reverso del Codex Vindobonensis*," *Memoria de el Colegio Nacional*, Vol. V (1952), 9–46.

———. "*Exploraciones en Monte Albán, temporada 1931–32*," *Instituto Panamericana de Geografía e Historia Publicación*, No. 7 (1932).

———. "*Exploraciones en Monte Albán, temporada 1934–1935*," *Instituto Panamericana de Geografía e Historia Publicación*, No. 18 (1935).

———. "*Exploraciones en Oaxaca: quinta y sexta temporadas 1936–1937*," *Instituto Panamericana de Geografía e Historia Publicación*, No. 34 (1938).

———. "The Historical Value of the Mixtec Codices," *Boletín de estudios oaxaqueños*, No. 16 (1960).

———. *Interpretación del Códice Gómez de Orozco*. México, 1954.

———. *Interpretation of the Codex Bodley 2858*. México, 1960.

———. "Land Tenure Among the Ancient Mexicans" (translated by Charles Wicke), *American Anthropologist*, Vol. LXV (1963), 861–78.

———. "Lapidary Work, Goldwork, and Copperwork from Oaxaca," in Wauchope and Willey, eds., *Handbook of Middle American Indians*, *q.v.*

———. "*Lienzo de Yolotepec*," *Memoria de el Colegio Nacional,* Vol. III (1957), 41–55.

———. "*Los Señores de Yanhuitlán*," in *Actas 35° congreso internacional de americanistas, q.v.*

———. "*El mapa de Teozacoalco*," *Cuadernos americanos*, Vol. VIII (1949), 145–81.

———. "The Mixtec and Zapotec Cultures: The Mixtecs," *Boletín de estudios oaxaqueños*, No. 22 (1962).

———. "Mixtec Writing and Calendar," in Wauchope and Willey, eds., *Handbook of Middle American Indians, q.v.*

———. "Monte Albán, Richest Archeological Find in America," *The National Geographic Magazine*, Vol. LXII (1932), 487–512.

———. "*Nuevos datos para la correlación de los años Azteca y cristiano*," *Estudios de cultura nahuatl*, Vol. I (1959), 9–25.

———. "Reading the Riddle of the Ancient Jewels," *Natural History*, Vol. XXXII (1932), 464–80.

———. "*Resumen del informe de las exploraciones en Oaxaca, durante la 7a y 8a temporadas, 1937–1938 y 1938–1939*," in *Actas del 27° congreso internacional de americanistas, q.v.*

———. "Sculpture and Mural Painting of Oaxaca," in Wauchope and Willey, eds., *Handbook of Middle American Indians, q.v.*

———. "*Las tumbas de Monte Albán*," *Anales del Museo Nacional de Arqueología, Historia, y Etnografía*, Vol. VIII (1933), 641–47.

———. "Zapotec Writing and Calendar," in Wauchope and Willey, eds., *Handbook of Middle American Indians, q.v.*

———, and Ignacio Bernal. "Ceramics of Oaxaca," in Wauchope and Willey, eds., *Handbook of Middle American Indians, q.v.*

Chamberlain, Robert S. "The Concept of Señor Natural as Revealed by Castilian Law and Administrative Documents," *The Hispanic American Historical Review*, Vol. XIX (1939), 130–37.

Chávez Orozco, Luis. *Manifestations of Democracy Among Mexican Indians During the Colonial Period*. Washington, 1944.

Clark, J. C. *The Story of "Eight Deer" in Codex Colombino*. London, 1912.

Clavijero, Fray Francisco J. *Historia antigua de México*. 4 vols. México, 1958.

Codex Mendoza. Ed. and trans. by J. C. Clark. 3 vols. London, 1938.

Códice Chimalpopoca: Anales de Cuauhtitlan y Leyenda de los soles. México, 1945.

Coe, M. D. *Mexico.* New York, 1962.

———. "Social Typology and the Tropical Forest Civilizations," *Contemporary Studies in Society and History,* Vol. IV (1961), 65–85.

Colección de documentos inéditos, relativos al descubrimiento, conquista y organización de las antiguas posesiones españolas de América y oceanía. 42 vols. Madrid, 1864–84.

Congrès International des Sciences Anthropologiques et Ethnologiques. Compte-Rendu V. Paris, 1960.

Cook, S. F. "Dwelling Construction in the Mixteca," *México antiguo,* Vol. IV (1939), 375–86.

———, and Woodrow Borah. "The Aboriginal Population of Central Mexico on the Eve of the Spanish Conquest," *Ibero-Americana,* No. 45 (1963).

———, and Woodrow Borah. "The Indian Population of Central Mexico, 1531–1610," *Ibero-Americana,* No. 44 (1960).

———, and Woodrow Borah. "*Quelle fut la stratification sociale au Centre du Mexique durant la première moitié de XVI e siècle?,*" *Annales Economies Societés Civilisations,* Vol. II (1963), 226–58.

———, and L. B. Simpson. "The Population of Central Mexico in the Sixteenth Century," *Ibero-Americana,* No. 31 (1948).

Covarrubias, Miguel. *Indian Art of Mexico and Central America.* New York, 1957.

Dahlgren, Barbro. *La Mixteca: su cultura e historia prehispánicas.* México, 1954.

Dark, Philip. *Mixtec Ethnohistory.* London, 1958.

———. "Speculations on the Course of Mixtec History Prior to the Conquest," *Boletín de estudios oaxaqueños,* No. 10 (1958).

Dávila Padilla, Fray Agustín. *Historia de la fundación y discurso de la Provincia de Santiago de México.* México, 1955.

———. *Epistolario de Nueva España.* 16 vols. México, 1940.

Díaz del Castillo, Bernal. *Historia verdadera de la conquista de la Nueva España.* 2 vols. México, 1955.

Durán, Fray Diego. *Historia de las Indias de Nueva España y Islas de Tierra Firme*. 2 vols. México, 1951.

Dyk, Anne. *Mixteco Texts*. Norman, 1959.

Faron, Louis C. "Effects of the Conquest on the Araucanian Picunche During the Spanish Colonization of Chile: 1536–1635," *Ethnohistory*, Vol. VII (1960), 239–307.

Fernández de Miranda, María T., Mauricio Swadesh, and R. W. Weitlaner. "*El panorama etno-lingüístico de Oaxaca y del Istmo*," *Revista mexicana de estudios antropológicos*, Vol. XVI (1960), 135–57.

———. "Some Findings on Oaxaca Language Classification and Culture terms," *International Journal of American Linguistics*, Vol. XXV (1959), 54–58.

García Granados, Rafael. "*Contribución para la geografía, etnografía, y lingüística de Oaxaca*," *Boletín, Sociedad Mexicana de Geografía y Estadística*, Vol. XLIV (1935), 401–10.

García Pimentel, Luis, ed. *Relación de los Obispados de Tlaxcala, Michoacán, Oaxaca y otros lugares en el siglo XVI*. México, 1904.

Gay, J. A. *Historia de Oaxaca*. México, 1881.

Gayangos, Pascual de, ed. *Cartas y relaciones de Hernán Cortés al Emperador Cárlos V*. Paris, 1866.

Gibson, Charles. "The Aztec Aristocracy in Colonial Mexico," *Comparative Studies in Society and History*, Vol. II (1960), 169–96.

———. *The Aztecs Under Spanish Rule*. Stanford, 1964.

———. "Rotation of Alcaldes in the Indian Cabildo of Mexico City," *The Hispanic American Historical Review*, Vol. XXXIII (1953), 212–23.

———. "*El sistema de gobierno indígena de Tlaxcala, Mexico, en el siglo XVI*," *América indígena*, Vol. X (1959), 86–90.

———. *Tlaxcala in the Sixteenth Century*. New Haven, 1952.

———. "The Transformation of the Indian community in New Spain: 1500–1810," *Journal of World History*, Vol. II (1955), 581–607.

Gómez de Cervantes, Gonzalo. *La vida económica y social de Nueva España al finalizar el siglo XVI*. México, 1944.

González de Cossio, F., ed. *El libro de las tasaciones de los pueblos de la Nueva España*. México, 1952.

Greenleaf, Richard. *Zumárraga and the Mexican Inquisition, 1536–1543.* Washington, 1961.

Gudschinsky, Sarah C. "Proto-popotecan: A Comparative Study of Popolocan and Mixtecan," *International Journal of American Linguistics Memoir*, No. 15 (1959).

Guzmán, Eulalia. "*Exploración arqueológica en la Mixteca Alta,*" *Anales del Museo Nacional de Arqueología, Historia, y Etnografía, época V*, Vol. I (1934), 17–42.

Haring, Clarence H. *The Spanish Empire in America.* New York, 1947.

Harvey, Herbert R. *Términos de parentesco en el otomangue.* México, 1963.

Herrera y Tordesillas, Antonio de. *Historia general de los hechos de los castellanos en las Islas y Tierrafirme del Mar Océano.* 15 vols. Madrid, 1947.

Iturribarría, J. F. *Oaxaca en la historia.* México, 1955.

———. *Las viejas culturas de Oaxaca.* México, 1952.

Jiménez Moreno, Wigberto. "*Síntesis de la historia pretolteca de Mesoamérica,*" *Esplendor del México antiguo*, Vol. II (1959).

Jiménez Moreno, Wigberto, ed. *Vocabulario en lengua mixteca, por Fray Francisco de Alvarado.* México, 1962.

———, and Salvador Mateos Higuera. *Códice de Yanhuitlán.* México, 1940.

Kroeber, A. L. "The Chibcha," in Steward, ed. *Handbook of South American Indians*, BAE *Bulletin No. 143.* Vol. III. Washington, 1948.

Kubler, George. *Mexican Architecture of the Sixteenth Century.* 2 vols. New Haven, 1948.

———. "Population Movements in Mexico, 1520–1600," *The Hispanic American Historical Review*, Vol. XXII (1942), 606–43.

———. "The Quechua in the Colonial World," in Steward, ed., *Handbook of South American Indians.* BAE *Bulletin No. 143.* Vol. II. Washington, 1946.

———. Review of "The Population of Central Mexico in the Sixteenth Century" (by S. F. Cook and L. B. Simpson), in *The Hispanic American Historical Review*, Vol. XXVIII (1948), 556–59.

Larco Hoyle, Rafael. "A Culture Sequence for the North Coast of Peru," in Steward, ed., *Handbook of South American Indians*, BAE *Bulletin, No. 143*. Vol. II. Washington, 1946.

Lee, Raymond. "Cochineal Production and Trade in New Spain to 1600," *The Americas*, Vol. IV (1948), 449–73.

Lehmann, W. and O. Smital, eds. *Codex Vindobonensis Mexikanus I, Faksimileausgabe de Mexikanischen Bilderhandschrift der Nationalbibliotek in Wien*. Vienna, 1929.

León, Nicolás. *Códice Sierra*. México, 1933.

Libby, William F. *Radiocarbon Dating*. Chicago, 1955.

Longacre, R. E. "Amplification of Gudschinsky's Proto-Popolocan-Mixtecan," *International Journal of American Linguistics*, Vol. XXVIII (1962), 227–42.

———. "Proto-Mixtecan," Indiana University Research Center in Anthropology, Folklore, and Linguistics, *Pub.* No. 5. (Bloomington, 1957).

———. Review of "*Mapas de classification lingüística de México y las Américas*" (by Mauricio Swadesh), *Language*, Vol. XXXVI (1960), 397–410.

———. "Swadesh's Macro-Mixtecan Hypothesis," *International Journal of American Linguistics*, Vol. XXVII (1961), 9–29.

———, and Rene Millon. "Proto-Mixtecan and Proto-Amuzgo-Mixtecan Vocabularies," *Anthropological Linguistics*, Vol. III, No. 4 (1961), 1–44.

López de Gómara, Francisco. *Historia de la conquista de México*. 2 vols. México, 1943.

Mak, Cornelia. "A Comparison of Two Mixtec Tonemic Systems," *International Journal of American Linguistics*, Vol. XXVII (1953), 85–100.

———. "Mixtec Medical Beliefs and Practices," *América indígena*, Vol. XIX (1959), 125–50.

———. "The Tonal System of a Third Mixtec Dialect," *International Journal of American Linguistics*, Vol. XXIV (1958), 61–70.

———, and R. E. Longacre. "Proto-Mixtec Phonology," *International Journal of American Linguistics*, Vol. XXVI (1960), 23–40.

Marroquín, Alejandro. *La ciudad mercado*. México, 1957.

Martínez Gracida, Manuel. *Catálogo etimológico de los nombres de los pueblos, haciendas y ranchos del estado de Oaxaca*. Oaxaca, 1883.

———. *Colección de "Cuadros sinópticos" de los pueblos, haciendas y ranchos del estado libre y soberano de Oaxaca*. Oaxaca, 1883.

———. "*Los indios oaxaqueños y sus monumentos arqueológicos*," *Boletín, Sociedad Mexicana de Geografía y Estadística, época* 5, Vol. IV (1910), 49–64.

———. *Ita audehui, una leyenda mixteca*. Oaxaca, 1906.

Miles, Suzanne W. *The Sixteenth-Century Pokom-Maya: A Documentary Analysis of Social Structure and Archaeological Setting. Transactions of the American Philosophical Society*, Vol. XLVII, Part 4. Philadelphia, 1957.

Miranda, José. "*Orígenes de la ganadería en la Mixteca*," in *Miscellanea, Paul Rivet octogenario dictata*, Vol. 2 (1958).

Moore, Sally F. *Power and Property in Inca Peru*. New York, 1958.

Nicholson, Henry B. "The Mixteca-Puebla Concept in Mesoamerican Archaeology: A Re-examination," in *Congrès International des Sciences Anthropologiques et Ethnologiques, Compte-Rendu V*, *q.v.*

———. "The Use of the term 'Mixtec' in Mesoamerican Archaeology," *American Antiquity*, Vol. XXVI (1961), 431–33.

Noguera, Eduardo. "*Cultura mixteca*," in J. Vivo, ed., *Mexico Prehispanico*. México, 1946.

Nowotny, Karl. *Codices Becker I/II*. Graz, Austria, 1961.

Oviedo y Valdés, Gonzalo F. de. *Historia general y natural de las Indias*. 4 vols. Madrid, 1851–55.

Paddock, John. "Comments on Some Problems of Oaxaca Archeology," *Boletín de estudios oaxaqueños*, No. 4 (1958).

———. "Exploraciones en Yagul, Oaxaca, "*Revista mexicana de estudios antropológicos*, Vol. XVI (1960), 91–96.

Paddock, John, ed. "Excavations in the Mixteca Alta," *Mesoamerican Notes*, No. 3 (1953).

Paso y Troncoso, Francisco del, ed. *Papeles de Nueva España. Segunda serie*: Vols. I, III–VII. Madrid, 1905–1906.

Peña, Moisés T. de la. "*Problemas sociales y económicas de las Mixtecas*," *Memorias del Instituto Nacional Indigenista*, Vol. 2, No. 1 (1950).

Peñafiel, Antonio. *Lienzo de Zacatepec.* México, 1900.

Pike, Kenneth. "Analysis of a Mixteco Text," *International Journal of American Linguistics,* Vol. XI (1945), 129–39.

———. "Another Mixteco Tone Pun," *International Journal of American Linguistics,* Vol. XII (1946), 22–24.

———. "The Flea: Melody Types and Perturbations in a Mixteco Song," *Tlalocan,* Vol. II (1946), 128–33.

———. "*Una leyenda mixteca,*" *Investigaciones lingüísticas,* Vol. IV (1937), 262–70.

———. "Mock Spanish of a Mixteco Indian," *International Journal of American Linguistics,* Vol. XI (1945), 219–24.

———. "Tone Languages," *University of Michigan Publications in Linguistics,* No. 4. (Ann Arbor, 1948).

———. "Tone Puns in Mixteco," *International Journal of American Linguistics,* Vol. XI (1945), 129–39.

Puga, Vasco de. *Provisiones cédulas instrucciones . . . para el gobierno de la Nueva España.* Madrid, 1945.

Ramírez, J. F. *Códice Ramírez.* México, 1944.

Recopilación de leyes de los Reynos de las Indias. 3 vols. Madrid, 1943.

Revista mexicana de estudios históricos. Vols. 1–2 (1927–28). (Publications suspended 1929; resumed as *Revista mexicana de estudios antropológicos,* 1939).

Reyes, Fray Antonio de los. *Arte en lengua mixteca.* Paris, 1890.

Rickards, C. G. *The Ruins of Mexico.* London, 1910.

Robertson, Donald. *Mexican Manuscript Painting of the Early Colonial Period.* New Haven, 1959.

Romero, Javier. "*Monte Negro, centro de interés antropológico,*" in *Homenaje a Alfonso Caso.* México, 1951.

Rowe, John H. "Inca Culture at the Time of the Spanish Conquest," in Steward, ed., *Handbook of South American Indians.* BAE *Bulletin No. 143.* Vol. II. Washington, 1946.

Roys, Ralph L. *The Indian Background of Colonial Yucatán.* Washington, 1943.

Sanders, W. T. "The Central Mexican Symbiotic Region," in Willey, ed., *Prehistoric Settlement Patterns in the New World, q.v.*

———. *Prehistoric Ceramics and Settlement Patterns in Quintana Roo, Mexico.* Carnegie Institution of Washington *Contributions to American Anthropology and History, No. 60.*

Schmieder, O. *The Settlements of the Tzapotec and Mije Indians, State of Oaxaca, Mexico. University of California Publications in Geography,* Vol. 4. Berkeley, 1930.

Scholes, France V. "Franciscan Missionary Scholars in Colonial Central America," *The Americas,* Vol. VIII (1952), 391–416.

———, and Eleanor Adams. *Cartas del Licenciado Jerónimo Valderrama y otros documentos sobre su visita al gobierno de Nueva España, 1563–1565.* México, 1961.

———, and Ralph L. Roys. *The Maya Chontal Indians of Acalan-Tixchel: A Contribution to the History and Ethnography of the Yucatán Peninsula.* Washington, 1948.

Seler, Eduard. "*Notice sur les langues Zapotèque et Mixtèque,*" *in 8 Congrès International des Americanistes, q.v.*

Shook, E. M., and T. Proskouriakoff. "Settlement Patterns in Mesoamerica and the Sequence in the Guatemalan Highlands," in Willey, ed., *Prehistoric Settlement Patterns in the New World, q.v.*

Simpson, L. B. *The Encomienda in New Spain.* Berkeley, 1950.

———. "Studies in the Administration of the Indians in New Spain, III." *Ibero-Americana,* No. 13 (1938).

Smith, Mary E. "The Codex Colombino: A Document of the South Coast of Oaxaca," *Tlalocan,* Vol. IV (1963), 276–88.

Soustelle, Jacques. *La vida cotidiana de los aztecas en vísperas de la conquista.* Trans. by Carlos Villegas. México, 1956.

Spinden, H. J. "Indian Manuscripts of Southern Mexico," in Smithsonian Institution *Report* for 1933. Washington, 1935.

Spores, Ronald M. "The Genealogy of Tlazultepec: A Sixteenth Century Mixtec Manuscript," *Southwestern Journal of Anthropology,* Vol. XX (1964), 15–31.

———. "The Zapotec and Mixtec at Spanish Contact," in Wauchope and Willey, eds., *Handbook of Middle American Indians, q.v.*

Steward, Julian H., ed. *Handbook of South American Indians,* BAE *Bulletin No. 143.* Multivolume. Washington, 1946——.

Swadesh, Mauricio. "The Oto-Manguean Hypothesis and Macro-Mixtecan," *International Journal of American Linguistics*, Vol. XXVI (1960), 79–111.

Tezozomoc, H. A. *Crónica mexicana*. México, 1944.

Torquemada, Fray Juan de. *Los veinte i un libros rituales y monarchía indiana*. 3 vols. México, 1944.

Veytia, Mariano. *Historia antigua de México*. México, 1944.

Wauchope, Robert, and Gordon R. Willey, eds. *Handbook of Middle American Indians*. Multivolume. Austin, 1965——.

Willey, Gordon R. *Prehistoric Settlement Patterns in the Virú Valley, Perú*. BAE *Bulletin No. 155*. Washington, 1953.

———. "Problems Concerning Prehistoric Settlement Patterns in the Maya Lowlands," in Willey, ed., *Prehistoric Settlement Patterns in the New World, q.v.*

Willey, Gordon R., ed. *Prehistoric Settlement Patterns in the New World*. Viking Fund *Publications in Anthropology*, No. 23. New York, 1956.

Willey, Gordon R., W. R. Bullard, J. B. Glass, and J. C. Gifford. *Prehistoric Maya Settlements in the Belize Valley*. *Papers* of the Peabody Museum, Vol. LIV. Cambridge, 1965.

Zavala, Silvio A. *La encomienda indiana*. Madrid, 1935.

———. *Estudios indianos*. México, 1948.

———, and M. Castelo. *Fuentes para la historia del trabajo en Nueva España*. 8 vols. México, 1939–46.

Zavala, Silvio A., and José Miranda. "*Instituciones indígenas en la colonia*," in *Métodos y resultados de la política indigenista en México*. México, 1954.

Zorita, Alonso de. *Breve relación de los señores de la Nueva España*. México, 1941.

INDEX

THE CIVILIZATION OF THE AMERICAN INDIAN SERIES

of which *The Mixtec Kings and Their People* is the eighty-fifth volume, was inaugurated in 1932 by the University of Oklahoma Press, and has as its purpose the reconstruction of American Indian civilization by presenting aboriginal, historical, and contemporary Indian life. The following list is complete as of the date of publication of this volume.

1. Alfred Barnaby Thomas (tr. and ed.). *Forgotten Frontiers:* A Study of the Spanish Indian Policy of Don Juan Bautista de Anza, Governor of New Mexico, 1777–1787. Out of print.
2. Grant Foreman. *Indian Removal:* The Emigration of the Five Civilized Tribes of Indians.
3. John Joseph Mathews. *Wah'Kon-Tah:* The Osage and the White Man's Road. Out of print.
4. Grant Foreman. *Advancing the Frontier, 1830–1860.* Out of print.
5. John H. Seger. *Early Days Among the Cheyenne and Arapahoe Indians.* Edited by Stanley Vestal.
6. Angie Debo. *The Rise and Fall of the Choctaw Republic.*
7. Stanley Vestal. *New Sources of Indian History, 1850–1891:* A Miscellany. Out of print.
8. Grant Foreman. *The Five Civilized Tribes.*
9. Alfred Barnaby Thomas (tr. and ed.). *After Coronado:* Spanish Exploration Northeast of New Mexico, 1696–1727.
10. Frank G. Speck, *Naskapi:* The Savage Hunters of the Labrador Peninsula. Out of print.
11. Elaine Goodale Eastman. *Pratt:* The Red Man's Moses. Out of print.
12. Althea Bass. *Cherokee Messenger:* A Life of Samuel Austin Worcester. Out of print.
13. Thomas Wildcat Alford. *Civilization.* As told to Florence Drake. Out of print.
14. Grant Foreman. *Indians and Pioneers:* The Story of the American Southwest Before 1830. Out of print.
15. George E. Hyde. *Red Cloud's Folk:* A History of the Oglala Sioux Indians.
16. Grant Foreman. *Sequoyah.*
17. Morris L. Wardell. *A Political History of the Cherokee Nation, 1838–1907.* Out of print.

18. John Walton Caughey. *McGillivray of the Creeks.*
19. Edward Everett Dale and Gaston Litton. *Cherokee Cavaliers:* Forty Years of Cherokee History as Told in the Correspondence of the Ridge-Watie-Boudinot Family. Out of print.
20. Ralph Henry Gabriel. *Elias Boudinot, Cherokee, and His America.* Out of print.
21. Karl N. Llewellyn and E. Adamson Hoebel. *The Cheyenne Way:* Conflict and Case Law in Primitive Jurisprudence.
22. Angie Debo. *The Road to Disappearance.* Out of print.
23. Oliver La Farge and others. *The Changing Indian.* Out of print.
24. Carolyn Thomas Foreman. *Indians Abroad.* Out of print.
25. John Adair. *The Navajo and Pueblo Silversmiths.*
26. Alice Marriott. *The Ten Grandmothers.*
27. Alice Marriott. *María:* The Potter of San Ildefonso.
28. Edward Everett Dale. *The Indians of the Southwest:* A Century of Development Under the United States. Out of print.
29. *Popol Vuh:* The Sacred Book of the Ancient Quiché Maya. English version by Delia Goetz and Sylvanus G. Morley from the translation of Adrián Recinos.
30. Walter Collins O'Kane. *Sun in the Sky.*
31. Stanley A. Stubbs. *Bird's-Eye View of the Pueblos.* Out of print.
32. Katharine C. Turner. *Red Men Calling on the Great White Father.*
33. Muriel H. Wright. *A Guide to the Indian Tribes of Oklahoma.*
34. Ernest Wallace and E. Adamson Hoebel. *The Comanches:* Lords of the South Plains.
35. Walter Collins O'Kane. *The Hopis:* Portrait of a Desert People. Out of print.
36. Joseph Epes Brown (ed.) *The Sacred Pipe:* Black Elk's Account of the Seven Rites of the Oglala Sioux. Out of print.
37. *The Annals of the Cakchiquels,* translated from the Cakchiquel Maya by Adrián Recinos and Delia Goetz, with *Title of the Lords of Totonicapán,* translated from the Quiché text into Spanish by Dionisio José Chonay, English version by Delia Goetz.
38. R. S. Cotterill. *The Southern Indians:* The Story of the Civilized Tribes Before Removal.

39. J. Eric S. Thompson. *The Rise and Fall of Maya Civilization.* (Revised Edition).
40. Robert Emmitt. *The Last War Trail:* The Utes and the Settlement of Colorado.
41. Frank Gilbert Roe. *The Indian and the Horse.*
42. Francis Haines. *The Nez Percés:* Tribesmen of the Columbia Plateau. Out of print.
43. Ruth M. Underhill. *The Navajos.*
44. George Bird Grinnell. *The Fighting Cheyennes.*
45. George E. Hyde. *A Sioux Chronicle.*
46. Stanley Vestal. *Sitting Bull, Champion of the Sioux:* A Biography.
47. Edwin C. McReynolds. *The Seminoles.*
48. William T. Hagan. *The Sac and Fox Indians.*
49. John C. Ewers. *The Blackfeet:* Raiders on the Northwestern Plains.
50. Alfonso Caso. *The Aztecs:* People of the Sun. Translated by Lowell Dunham.
51. C. L. Sonnichsen. *The Mescalero Apaches.*
52. Keith A. Murray. *The Modocs and Their War.*
53. Victor Wolfgang von Hagen (ed.). *The Incas of Pedro de Cieza de León.* Translated by Harriet de Onis.
54. George E. Hyde. *Indians of the High Plains:* From the Prehistoric Period to the Coming of Europeans.
55. *George Catlin:* Episodes from "Life Among the Indians" and "Last Rambles." Edited by Marvin C. Ross.
56. J. Eric S. Thompson. *Maya Hieroglyphic Writing:* An Introduction.
57. George E. Hyde. *Spotted Tail's Folk:* A History of the Brulé Sioux.
58. James Larpenteur Long. *The Assiniboines:* From the Accounts of the Old Ones Told to First Boy (James Larpenteur Long). Edited and with an introduction by Michael Stephen Kennedy.
59. Edwin Thompson Denig. *Five Indian Tribes of the Upper Missouri:* Sioux, Arickaras, Assiniboines, Crees, Crows. Edited and with an introduction by John C. Ewers.
60. John Joseph Mathews. *The Osages:* Children of the Middle Waters.
61. Mary Elizabeth Young. *Redskins, Ruffleshirts, and Rednecks:* Indian Allotments in Alabama and Mississippi, 1830–1860.

62. J. Eric S. Thompson. *A Catalog of Maya Hieroglyphs.*
63. Mildred P. Mayhall. *The Kiowas.*
64. George E. Hyde. *Indians of the Woodlands:* From Prehistoric Times to 1725.
65. Grace Steele Woodward. *The Cherokees.*
66. Donald J. Berthrong. *The Southern Cheyennes.*
67. Miguel León-Portilla. *Aztec Thought and Culture:* A Study of the Ancient Nahuatl Mind. Translated by Jack Emory Davis.
68. T. D. Allen. *Navahos Have Five Fingers.*
69. Burr Cartwright Brundage. *Empire of the Inca.*
70. A. M. Gibson. *The Kickapoos:* Lords of the Middle Border.
71. Hamilton A. Tyler. *Pueblo Gods and Myths.*
72. Royal B. Hassrick. *The Sioux:* Life and Customs of a Warrior Society.
73. Franc Johnson Newcomb. *Hosteen Klah:* Navaho Medicine Man and Sand Painter.
74. Virginia Cole Trenholm and Maurine Carley. *The Shoshonis:* Sentinels of the Rockies.
75. Cohoe. *A Cheyenne Sketchbook.* Commentary by E. Adamson Hoebel and Karen Daniels Petersen.
76. Jack D. Forbes. *Warriors of the Colorado:* The Yumas of the Quechan Nation and Their Neighbors.
77. Ralph L. Roys (tr. and ed.). *Ritual of the Bacabs.*
78. Lillian Estelle Fisher. *The Last Inca Revolt, 1780–1783.*
79. Lilly de Jongh Osborne. *Indian Crafts of Guatemala and El Salvador.*
80. Robert H. Ruby and John A. Brown. *Half-Sun on the Columbia:* A Biography of Chief Moses.
81. Jack Frederick and Anna Gritts Kilpatrick (trs. and eds.). *The Shadow of Sequoyah:* Social Documents of the Cherokees.
82. Ella E. Clark. *Indian Legends from the Northern Rockies.*
83. William A. Brophy and Sophie D. Aberle, M.D. (compilers). *The Indian:* America's Unfinished Business.
84. M. Inez Hilger, with Margaret A. Mondloch. *Huenun Ñamku:* An Araucanian Indian of the Andes Remembers the Past.
85. Ronald Spores. *The Mixtec Kings and Their People.*

The text for *The Mixtec Kings and Their People* has been set on the Linotype in eleven-point Granjon with two points of leading between lines for added legibility. The paper on which the book is printed bears the watermark of the University of Oklahoma Press and has an effective life of at least three hundred years.